# SOCIOLOGY
## of SPORT
## AND
## SOCIAL
## THEORY

**Earl Smith, PhD**

Wake Forest University
Winston-Salem, North Carolina

**Editor**

**Human Kinetics**

**Library of Congress Cataloging-in-Publication Data**

Sociology of sport and social theory / Earl Smith, editor.
    p. cm.
 Includes bibliographical references and index.
 ISBN-13: 978-0-7360-7572-5 (hard cover)
 ISBN-10: 0-7360-7572-0 (hard cover)
 1. Sports--Social aspects. I. Smith, Earl, 1946-
 GV706.5.S6455 2010
 306.4'83--dc22

                                   2009015767

ISBN-10: 0-7360-7572-0 (print)          ISBN-10: 0-7360-8556-4 (Adobe PDF)
ISBN-13: 978-0-7360-7572-5 (print)      ISBN-13: 978-0-7360-8556-4 (Adobe PDF)

The Web addresses cited in this text were current as of April 2009, unless otherwise noted.

**Acquisitions Editor:** Myles Schrag; **Developmental Editor:** Amanda S. Ewing; **Assistant Editors:** Lee Alexander, Casey A. Gentis, and Christine Bryant Cohen; **Copyeditor:** Tom Tiller; **Indexer:** Craig Brown; **Graphic Designer:** Joe Buck; **Graphic Artist:** Dawn Sills; **Cover Designer:** Bob Reuther; **Photo Asset Manager:** Laura Fitch; **Photo Production Manager:** Jason Allen; **Art Manager:** Kelly Hendren; **Associate Art Manager:** Alan L. Wilborn; **Illustrator:** Alan L. Wilborn; **Printer:** Sheridan Books

Printed in the United States of America   10   9   8   7   6   5   4   3   2   1

The paper in this book is certified under a sustainable forestry program.

**Human Kinetics**
Web site: www.HumanKinetics.com

*United States:* Human Kinetics
P.O. Box 5076
Champaign, IL 61825-5076
800-747-4457
e-mail: humank@hkusa.com

*Canada:* Human Kinetics
475 Devonshire Road Unit 100
Windsor, ON N8Y 2L5
800-465-7301 (in Canada only)
e-mail: info@hkcanada.com

*Europe:* Human Kinetics
107 Bradford Road
Stanningley
Leeds LS28 6AT, United Kingdom
+44 (0) 113 255 5665
e-mail: hk@hkeurope.com

*Australia:* Human Kinetics
57A Price Avenue
Lower Mitcham, South Australia 5062
08 8372 0999
e-mail: info@hkaustralia.com

*New Zealand:* Human Kinetics
Division of Sports Distributors NZ Ltd.
P.O. Box 300 226 Albany
North Shore City
Auckland
0064 9 448 1207
e-mail: info@humankinetics.co.nz

# Contents

## PART III   THEORIES OF INEQUALITY. . . . . . . . . . 95

# Contributors

**Robert Beamish, PhD**
Associate Professor
Department of Sociology
Queen's University

**Bonnie Berry, PhD**
Director
Social Problems Research Group

**Teresa Blake, BA**
2008 Graduate
Wake Forest University

**Cheryl Cooky, PhD**
Assistant Professor
Department of Kinesiology
California State University, Fullerton

**Benny Cooper, BA**
2008 Graduate
Wake Forest University

**Bryan E. Denham, PhD**
Charles Campbell Professor of Sports
    Communication
Department of Communication Studies
Clemson University

**Eric Dunning, PhD**
Emeritus Professor of Sociology
University of Leicester

**Angela J. Hattery, PhD**
Professor
Department of Sociology, and Women's
    and Gender Studies
Wake Forest University

**Rhonda F. Levine, PhD**
Professor
Department of Sociology and
    Anthropology
Colgate University

**Roy D. McCree, PhD**
Fellow
Sir Arthur Lewis Institute of Social and
    Economic Studies (SALISES)
The University of the West Indies, St.
    Augustine, Trinidad and Tobago, WI

**Charles E. Mellies, BA**
2008 Graduate
Wake Forest University

**Mark S. Nagel, EdD**
Associate Professor
Department of Sport and Entertainment
    Management
University of South Carolina

**Ian Ritchie, PhD**
Associate Professor
Department of Physical Education and
    Kinesiology
Brock University

**Kimberly S. Schimmel, PhD**
Associate Professor
School of Exercise, Leisure and Sport
Kent State University

**Richard M. Southall, EdD**
Assistant Professor
Department of Exercise and Sport
    Sciences
University of North Carolina at Chapel
    Hill

**Nancy E. Spencer, PhD**
Associate Professor
Sport Management, Recreation, and
    Tourism Division
Bowling Green State University

**David Yamane, PhD**
Associate Professor
Department of Sociology
Wake Forest University

# Preface

*S**ociology of Sport and Social Theory* provides a new look at the core theories, theories of the middle range, and microlevel theories in the discipline of sociology with applications to various issues in the study of sport.

Sociology is the study of how human beings behave in their social interaction with other individuals, in groups, in relationship with institutions, and in interactions within social networks. Sociology of sport involves the study of sport institutions that regulate sports (e.g., the National Collegiate Athletic Association, the International Olympic Committee, the National Basketball Association). It also involves the application of sociology to the study of teams, individuals who participate in sports, coaches, and the relationships between these individuals and institutions, as well as their relationships with institutions outside of sport, including government bodies, health systems, and the economy.

The goal for this book, then, is to address a wide range of theories, topics, and issues at the forefront of both scholarly and public discourse as they relate to the study of sport. The focus is twofold: to provide committed scholars and their students with (1) a new and different way of thinking about traditional and contemporary sociological theory and (2) a new and different lens for examining issues typically studied by sport scholars.

In order to accomplish this goal, the book pulls together material from some of the leading scholars who have researched issues related to sociological theory and sport. For example, the book offers a Weberian analysis of sport, a demonstration of how C. Wright Mills' theory of the sociological imagination can provide a lens for an athlete-author to use in analyzing athletic events, and my own chapter explaining the dominance of golf phenomenon Tiger Woods and his incredible mastery of the field of the world's greatest golfers—something that begs for analysis yet to be provided—by using reversal theory as a systematic way to explain Woods' career. Each essay explores a traditional or contemporary social theory and examines its utility for understanding some aspect of the institution of sport. This text provides scholarly research focused on contemporary issues (e.g., violence in sport, Title IX, coaching, religion, the commercialization of sport) that often receive treatment in popular media outlets such as the *New York Times, Sports Illustrated,* and *USA Today.*

For the sociologist of sport, these scholarly essays examine topics typically covered in the subdiscipline but addressed here through a theoretical treatment that is broader and, indeed, unique. The subdiscipline of sport sociology has a well-developed literature that *describes* various issues related to sport and society, but it has not been as successful in analyzing these phenomena through the critical lenses provided by various traditional and contemporary sociological theories. Since this volume includes essays framed by the core theories in sociology, as well as contemporary theories in the discipline, it exposes readers to a theoretical treatment of key issues in the study of sport.

For the general sociologist or social theorist, this text provides applications of theory—both traditional and contemporary—that are often not seen in other theoretical texts. The subfield of the sociology of sport has held marginal status in the larger discipline of sociology. Yet many of the issues that sport sociologists study are the same as those studied by other subdisciplines in the field, including work, violence, gender, race, age, and commercialization. Furthermore, many sociologists are sport enthusiasts, and perhaps physically active people, who have never considered studying this topic. Thus, the opportunity that this text provides to consider how mainstream and contemporary social theories can be applied to an understudied set of issues will necessarily broaden any reader's understanding of theory.

We sometimes forget, especially some 40 years after the fact, that the subdiscipline known as the sociology of sport, often derided for its atheoretical underpinnings, did indeed have a loftier beginning, even though it was not well sustained. In 1969, John W. Loy Jr. and Gerald S. Kenyon published an edited volume titled *Sport, Culture and Society*. It was well received as the first attempt to bring some organization to a disorganized amazement of journalistic accounts, book chapters, and articles describing the growing importance of the institution of sport in American society. Loy and Kenyon's book was highly credited by Harry Edwards, who four years later published his doctoral dissertation as *Sociology of Sport*, one of the first single-author monographs on the subject of sport by a social scientist. While Edwards' book cannot be said to be the first or the only theoretically framed examination of sport and society, the dissertation[1] which led to the book publication represented one of the first systematic efforts to utilize social theory to empirically examine the world of sport and identify sport as a microcosm of society.

The 15 chapters of this book attempt to build on the careful work of Edwards and others who birthed the subdiscipline and to expand the discussion far beyond the narrow group of theoretical paradigms that have typically been used by sport sociologists. These essays build on the traditional theories that any first- or second-year sociology student is familiar with (conflict theory and structural functionalism), as well as on the theories of race and inequality that, beginning with Edwards, form the theoretical toolbox most widely drawn upon by scholars of sport, and as such the chapters in this book expand our repertoire by considering the utility of feminist theory, social capital theory, relational theory, and theories of religion—just to name a few.

This book is organized in three parts. Part I looks at three of the greatest sociologists of the 20th century. Part II includes chapters that focus on what Merton (1965) refers to as theories of the middle range, including urban sociological theory and secularization theory. Part III covers theories of inequities and examines issues such as Title IX, race, masculinity, and at-risk girls. Finally, part IV explores micro-level theories including symbolic interactions or dramaturgy and reversal theory.

---

[1] Note that Professor Harry Edwards, the newly minted PhD from Cornell University, wrote his doctoral dissertation under preeminent theoretical sociologist Robin M. Williams Jr.

Useful features of the text include the following:

- Each chapter begins with a quick overview of the relevant theory. The overview covers leading proponents of the theory and quickly describes its basic tenets.
- At the end of each chapter, suggested research ideas are provided. These ideas can help future sport sociologists use the theory described in a given chapter to examine other sociological issues.
- Each chapter is also accompanied by an annotated list of additional resources that will be of particular value to students as they learn more about sociological theories and the sport topics discussed.

My intent for this book is to take what is best from the past and add to it in order to show progress made as we move into the future of sport sociology and theory.

# Acknowledgments

This book resulted from a special type of teamwork—teamwork from afar, as the late Robert K. Merton, doyen of sociological theorists, might have put it—on the part of scholars not only from across the United States but also from Canada, Great Britain, and the Caribbean.

Whatever measure of success this book finds, I am very appreciative of the *yes* that I received from everyone, and I want especially to thank the authors here: Robert Beamish, Bonnie Berry, Teresa Blake, Cheryl Cooky, Benny Cooper, Bryan Denham, Eric Dunning, Angela Hattery, Rhonda F. Levine, Roy McCree, Charles Mellies, Mark Nagel, Ian Ritchie, Kimberly Schimmel, Richard Southall, Nancy Spencer, and David Yamane. Their pioneering work makes a sound contribution not only to this volume but also to the project of elevating the subdiscipline of the sociology of sport to a new level of excitement and scholarly contribution.

I am also grateful to Myles Schrag at Human Kinetics, whose willingness to think critically helped in the development of this volume, and to Amanda Ewing, also at Human Kinetics, for her careful shepherding of this book through the maze of the production process.

Finally, this book is dedicated to all of the sport scholars who came before, on whose shoulders this book stands.[1]

---

[1] This is, of course, a paraphrase of the famous statement, "If I have seen farther it is by standing on the shoulders of giants." The phrase is most famously attributed to Sir Isaac Newton, writing in a letter to Robert Hooke (February 15, 1676), but sociologist Robert K. Merton found that the aphorism originated with Bernard of Chartres in the 12th century. See, especially, Merton's *On the Shoulders of Giants* (1965).

# Introduction

It is rare to find an entire book devoted to the sociology of sport and social theory. Several sport scholars have written books about sport, globalization, violence against women in sport, and other important topics by utilizing, where necessary, some aspect of theory that has been a part of the sociology of sport since its inception as a field of inquiry in the 1970s (Dunning 1999; Edwards 1973; Loy 1992; Loy and Kenyon 1969; Maguire and Young 2002; Smith 2007). Few of these books, however, include a variety of theoretical perspectives in their analyses of sport. In order to address this neglect on both sides of the equation, this book constitutes an attempt both to bring theory into discussions of sport and to bring empirical examples from sport into discussions of theory.

The purpose of the volume is to clarify for students, sociologists, psychologists, kinesiologists, and others who study sport how social theory can provide a suitable framework for understanding patterns that exist in the social world. It provides social theorists with examples and illustrations from the world of sport. One aim of the book, then, is to show American students how exciting the study of sport and theory can be when they are wedded together.

Eric Dunning has noted, in discussing (in chapter 2 of this text) the work of his mentor, Norbert Elias, that Elias stressed

> [t]he need in sociology for a constant two-way traffic between theory and research. Elias argued that theory without research is liable to be abstract and meaningless, and research without theory to be arid and descriptive.

In a practical sense, the mission of the book is to present theory first and have authors apply the theoretical perspectives they utilize in their respective chapters to important empirical examples from the world of sport. I chose to approach this project in the form of an edited collection rather than a single-author work because a collected volume allowed me to draw upon some of the very best scholars of sport as well as top scholars of sociology who typically do not examine sport. Thus the goal of the book was achieved by presenting the same challenge—how to bring social theory to the study of sport—to the authors. I think readers will agree that they have risen to the occasion and provided a sound understanding of various sociological theories and of how these theories provide a framework for examining various phenomena in sports.

I have previously used the term *SportsWorld* (Smith 2007) to refer to the institutionalization of everything having to do with sport—for example, the ratcheting up of player and coach contracts; coast-to-coast travel for Little League and Pop Warner teams; multibillion-dollar contracts to televise contests and tournaments; and the outright ownership of athletes and their skills, as well as the insuring of their body parts. This process moves sport—contests, participants, fans, leagues—from the realm of the individual to the realm of the institutional, and in so doing it connects SportsWorld to other social institutions, including the economy, the system of higher education, and the criminal justice system. It is now driven by partnerships involving hypercommercialism and exploitative mass media that dictates the scheduling of college contests regardless of colleges' academic calendars and is bankrolled by the ever-expanding corporate world.[1] Indeed, SportsWorld is driven at all levels by the values associated with unrational capitalism.[2]

---

[1] Just recently, at the height of the worst economic downturn since the Great Depression, the U.S. government bailed out several megabanks to the tune of billions of dollars, only to see several of them spend taxpayer money on naming rights for sports stadiums. Citibank has paid the New York Mets US$400 million to name the team's new stadium Citi Field (I saw this for myself during a taxi ride from LaGuardia Airport on December 22, 2008). Additionally, the struggling American International Group (AIG) paid British soccer team Manchester United US$125 million for the privilege of having its logo appear on Man U's uniforms (Rood 2008).

[2] Unrational capitalism is a systemic problem with the capitalist mode of production. Decision makers are now making decisions that are no longer in their best interest. The best treatment of this phenomenon is given by economist Fareed Zakaria (2008).

| Theory | Summary |
|---|---|
| Feminist theory | Aims to understand the nature of inequality; focuses on gender politics, power relations, sexuality. While generally providing a critique of social relations, feminist theory focuses largely on analyzing gender inequality and on promoting women's rights, interests, and issues. Themes explored include art history, contemporary art, aesthetics, discrimination, stereotyping, objectification (especially sexual), and oppression. Patriarchy is conceptualized as a system of power and oppression valuing men and male activities and qualities over women and their activities and qualities. Feminists argue that gender is a core organizing principle of social life, existing across time and geography, and that it both creates and requires gender difference and thus essentializes masculinity and femininity. |
| Figurational theory | Figurational theory, or process sociology, focuses on relationships between power, behavior, emotion, and knowledge over time. Elias traced how postmedieval European standards applied to violence, sexual behavior, bodily functions, table manners, and forms of speech were transformed by increasing thresholds of shame and repugnance, working outward from a nucleus in court etiquette. The internalized "self-restraint" imposed by increasingly complex networks of social connections developed the psychological self-perceptions that Freud recognized as the superego. |
| Hegemonic masculinity | Consistent with traditional gender ideals, the hegemonically masculine male is independent, powerful, emotionally unexpressive, strictly heterosexual, unflinching in the face of adversity, indifferent to pain, and unwilling to compromise his core values. |
| Institutional logics | Determine what practices and symbolic constructions—which both constitute organizing principles available to organizations and individuals to guide the evaluation and implementation of strategies, establish routines, and create precedence for further innovation—are acceptable or unacceptable. |
| Interpretive social action theory | Sociology is a comprehensive science of social action that pursues universal truths about an infinitely complex world even though that objective is ultimately unattainable. Sociologists develop "pure type" concepts that focus attention on key aspects of social action. Science, as a form of social action, can itself be examined as a pure type. This analysis shows that science is limited in what it can prescribe as an ultimate ethical basis for social action, leaving the determination of social values to the political realm of social action. The key to moral conduct is the creation of a fully open debate within the political realm of societies. |
| Race, class, and gender theory | Focuses on ways in which power, privilege, and oppression are organized by race, class, gender, and other systems of domination (e.g., sexuality, religion, age, ability status). |

Yet, as important as intellectual inquiry into the commercialization of SportsWorld is, there are also many other avenues for inquiry driven by a diverse range of theories—not simply those associated with capitalism or traditional social theory. This wider paradigm of exploration—into institutions such as religion, the criminal justice system, and urban development—is unique and sets this book apart from the mainstream examination of sport and social institutions.

The table in this introduction provides easy-to-follow information about the theories used in this book. It is my intention that readers, regardless of their background, will find something new and intriguing in this approach that weds theory to empirical examples from the world of sport. Though the authors of each chapter seek to use theoretical paradigms to answer empirical questions, in many cases they raise more questions than they answer, and this approach leaves readers with starting points from which to embark on their own examinations of the intersections of sociological theory and sport.

| Proponents | Seminal work in sociology of sport |
| --- | --- |
| Claudia Card, Susan Bordo, Joan Acker, Cynthia Fuchs Epstein, Judith Lorber, Susan Griffin, Susan Brownmiller, Emily Kane, Mary K. "Mimi" Schippers, Patricia Hill Collins, Rebecca Walker, Jennifer Baumgardner, Patricia Yancey Martin, Charlotte Perkins Gilman | Messner, M. 2002. *Taking the field: Women, men, and sports.* Minneapolis: University of Minnesota Press. |
| Norbert Elias, Eric Dunning, Joseph Maguire | Elias, N., and E. Dunning. 1986. *Quest for excitement.* New York: Blackwell. |
| R.W. Connell | Kimmel, M. 2003. *The invisible sex: Masculinity in contemporary America.* Berkeley: University of California Press. |
| Peter L. Berger, Thomas Luckmann, Margaret C. Duncan, Barry Brummett, Roger Friedland, Robert R. Alford, Richard R. Nelson, Sidney G. Winter, Richard M. Southall, Mark S. Nagel, John Amis, Crystal Southall, Marvin Washington, Marc J. Ventresca | Washington, M., and M. Ventresca 2004. How organizations change: The role of institutional support mechanisms in the incorporation of higher education visibility strategies, 1874–1995. *Organization Science* 15:82-97. |
| Max Weber, Anthony Giddens, Jürgen Habermas | Giddens, A. 2006. *Sociology.* New York: Wiley. |
| Bonnie Thornton Dill, Michael Messner, Patricia Hill Collins | Edwards, H. 1969. *The revolt of the Black athlete.* New York: Free Press. |

*(continued)*

*(continued)*

| Theory | Summary |
|---|---|
| Reversal theory | This psychological theory addresses the flexibility and changeability of individuals. It focuses specifically on individuals' motivation and capacity to change, depending on circumstances. |
| Secularization theory | Achieved paradigmatic status in the sociology of religion in the 20th century. Scholars built on the ideas of sociology's founding theorists to understand how religion is transformed in the modern world. Yamane stresses the *double movement of secularization*: the broad movement in the history of the West toward a decline in the scope of religious authority vis-à-vis secular authorities, and the persistence or reemergence of religious organizations under the secularized conditions established in the first movement. We can see how sport as a social institution has been largely secularized, so that religious groups seeking to be involved in sport are constrained to work in ways that articulate with and are accommodative of the reality of a secular society. At the individual level, we may find some people who integrate their religious beliefs and athletic practices but will find that for most people religion and sport offer separate, even competing, roles. |
| Social reproduction theory with emphasis on social and cultural capital | Seeks to explain how inequality and the class structure are generationally reproduced. *Social capital* refers to how social networks can provide resources that help in attainment of upward mobility. *Cultural capital* refers to the general knowledge, experience, style, and self-presentation one has acquired through the course of life that enables him or her to succeed in certain social settings to a greater extent than do those with less experienced backgrounds. |
| Sociological imagination | Requires a capacity of mind that enables users to perceive connections between their personal biographies and historical conditions in which they live. Mills believed that the sociological imagination was our most-needed quality of mind, felt that one's intellectual journey was incomplete without coming to grasp the articulation between biography and history, and advocated keeping a file or journal to organize and document one's intellectual journey. |
| Sociology of science | This body of theories, which study the social context within which science is produced, hold in common the contention that what is considered scientific "fact," as well as what is considered worthy of scientific study in the first place, are reflections of the social environment. |
| Structuration theory | Argues that social structure is always both constraining and enabling. *Structure* refers to the "rules and resources, or sets of transformative relations, that are organized as properties of social systems" (Giddens 1984, 25), as well as the "institutionalized features of social systems, stretching across time and space" (185). Structure shapes the production and reproduction of social interactions, and through social interactions social structure is reproduced. This is what Giddens refers to as the "duality of social structure." |
| Symbolic interactionism and dramaturgy | Through the use of outward and visible social symbols, we influence our society in hopes of being viewed in a favorable light. These symbols (e.g., clothing, body size) hold symbolic meaning (e.g., power, success). Through our interaction with other societal members, we create an image, if not a reality, of ourselves and our place in society in a process often thought of as impression management. We can think of this process as playing a part in a play (hence, *dramaturgy*). |
| Urban political economy and urban regime theory | Urban development is fraught with conflict concerning the use of space. The burdens and benefits of urban development are unequally distributed, and politics and human agency matter in the economic and development outcomes of cities. |

It is no longer necessary to argue that sport is an important institution in modern society (Smith 2007). That fact has been well established, if only by the heavy multimedia support for all types of sports, from beach volleyball to motocross racing to the annual Iditarod Trail Sled Dog Race. In North America, we are blessed each year with a growing number of intercollegiate football bowl games, professional football's Super Bowl, and March Madness, also known as the National Collegiate

| Proponents | Seminal work in sociology of sport |
|---|---|
| Michael Apter (psychologist) | Apter, M. 2006. *Reversal theory: Motivation, emotion and personality*, 2nd ed. Oxford, UK: Oneworld. |
| Robert Bellah, Peter Berger, José Casanova, Mark Chaves | Mathisen, J. 1992. From civil religion to folk religion: The case of American sport. In *Sport and religion*, ed. S. Hoffman, 17–34. Champaign, IL: Human Kinetics. |
| James Coleman, Pierre Bourdieu | Bourdieu, P. 1978. Sport and social class. *Social Science Information* 17:819–40. |
| C. Wright Mills, Hans Gerth, Steven P. Dandaneau, Todd Gitlin, Norman Denzin, Laurel Richardson, Zygmunt Bauman, Carolyn Ellis, Robert Coles, Studs Terkel, Arlie Hochschild | Coakley, J., and P. Donnelly. 1999. *Inside sports: Using sociology to understand athletes and sport experiences.* New York: Routledge. |
| Robert Merton, Thomas Kuhn, Bruno Latour | Beamish, R., and I. Ritchie. 2006. *Fastest, highest, strongest: A critique of high-performance sport.* New York: Routledge. |
| Anthony Giddens, Alan Ingham, John Sugden, Alan Tomlinson | Giddens, A. 1984. *The constitution of society: Outline of the theory of structuration.* Berkeley: University of California Press. |
| George Herbert Mead, Harold Garfinkel, Erving Goffman | Fine, G.A. 1987. *With the boys: Little league baseball and preadolescent culture.* Chicago: University of Chicago Press. |
| Harvey Molotch, John Logan, Clarence N. Stone | Reiss, S. 1989. *City games: The evolution of American urban culture and the rise of sport.* Champaign: University of Illinois Press. |

Athletic Association (NCAA) women's and men's basketball championships. Media network CBS paid the NCAA the whopping sum of US$6.3 billion across 11 years for exclusive television rights to the championship games between 2003 and 2013. This figure more than doubles the original deal CBS made with the NCAA in 1983 to exclusive broadcast rights between 1983 and 2002. CBS paid similarly for the rights to broadcast NFL games not only in the United States but also abroad as part of the expansion of NFL audiences to Europe. Simultaneously, the NBA is having games broadcast throughout eastern Europe and Asia. Hence it is clear that sport is an important institution deeply embedded within our global culture, and it is critically important to analyze this growing institution and its relationship to other institutions.

With such data in hand, it is necessary to develop a way to explain all of the events that take place under the rubric I have labeled SportsWorld. This is a task for sociological theory charged with providing a framework for analyzing these real world events, and part I of this book, "Great Theorists," begins this process.

While all of this might seem "irrational" in the current economic climate, Robert Beamish uses chapter 1, "Toward a Sport Ethic: Science, Politics, and Weber's Sociology," to help us analyze such phenomena through the lens provided by one of the fathers of sociological theory, Max Weber. According to Beamish, Weber worried that material goods would eventually gain too much power over the individual lives of men and women, and, for Beamish, the hypercommercialization of sport is a clear confirmation of Weber's fears.

Social theories are important not only because they exemplify critical thinking attached to important events but also because when we reflect on a theorist such as the late Robert K. Merton (1957, 1968)—who, with incredible range, could assess so many critical situations, making complex, life-changing events accessible—we begin to understand the incredible power of "theorizing." Theorists of the middle range, as Merton was, are noted for their ability to apply theory in practical ways that are accessible to wider audiences. Thus, several chapters of this book examine the ways in which these middle range theories can be applied to the institution of sport.

Part II, "Research Guided by Mid-Level Sociological Theories," treats theories that get at specific events affecting human lives. For example, Kimberly Schimmel argues in chapter 5, "Political Economy: Sport and Urban Development," that unless we empirically examine the economic impact of stadium building on cities, we might be duped, as so many are, into believing that stadiums bring economic development to American cities.

Part III, "Theories of Inequality," addresses gender, race, and social class and offers a range of perspectives allowing readers to examine both individual and group life chances. For example, a good deal of research has informed us of changes in the life chances for women in sport and has critically called out, when necessary, institutional malfeasance that short-shrifts girls and women in their quest for parity (Messner 2002). Yet so much of this work has been descriptive and atheoretical (e.g., Carpenter and Acosta 2008). In this book, Angela Hattery, a new voice in sport sociology and research on gender—trained as a sociologist, not in sport management or kinesiology—brings the theoretical tools of sociology to the study of gender and sport.

Whereas the chapters in part III use theories of inequality to examine patterns in differential access, the chapters in part IV, "Microlevel Theories," demonstrate the ways in which microlevel interactions can be examined so that patterns in these processes become visible, taking us, for example, into the issues addressed in chapter 14, Bonnie Berry's "Making It Big: Visible Symbols of Success, Physical Appearance, and Sport Figures." Berry's analysis uses the theory of symbolic interactionism to illustrate how everyday things like clothes and hairstyles become imbued not only with symbolic meaning but—when the meaning attached is used to signify success—with power as well.

Another example appears in chapter 13, where I explore the world of golf and Tiger Woods' position as the most dominant player in a highly competitive field. I use relational theory, which provides a clearer lens than is offered by journalistic assessments, and a framework that allows us to see why, Sunday after Sunday, Woods dominates in a manner that is otherwise as unexplainable as it is unbelievable.

Readers looking for an explicit discussion of race and sport will likely notice that there is no chapter dedicated specifically to a discussion of race. Yet let me reassure readers that several chapters included here analyze race—along with social class and gender—and I would point interested readers specifically to the following three chapters: (1) Rhonda F. Levine's essay on the role of socialization on the athletic experiences of African American high school men, (2) my chapter on the relationship between race and the likelihood of arrest among high-profile athletes who commit acts of violence against women, and, for an international perspective, (3) Roy McCree's chapter, "Sport and Multiple Identities in Postwar Trinidad: The Case of McDonald Bailey." Finally, in one of my other books, *Race, Sport, and the American Dream*, I explicitly address the relationship between race and the institution of sport in the United States.

Though I could point out each and every chapter in *Sociology of Sport and Social Theory* and the contribution its author makes to the intersection of sport and social theory, the table presented earlier in this chapter does so exhaustively, and for me to reconsider each chapter in depth would be redundant. Thus it is my intention that after reading this introduction, readers—be they scholars of sport, scholars of theory, students, or sport enthusiasts—will be thirsty for more and will dive into the book looking for answers and questions that are seldom explored in this manner.

# PART

# I

# Great Theorists

Part I of *Sociology of Sport and Social Theory* is titled Great Theorists for the simple reason that the chapters in this part treat three of the greatest sociological minds of the 20th century: Max Weber, Norbert Elias, and C. Wright Mills.

## Weberian Analysis

In chapter 1, "Toward a Sport Ethic: Science, Politics, and Weber's Sociology," Robert Beamish provides a precise introduction to the grand wizard of sociology, Herr Max Weber, about whom every graduate student has nightmares when assigned to read his work. Beamish takes as his point of departure Weber's most complex theories of society and makes them accessible by examining Weber's understanding of the world in which he lived and how the extension of that understanding can be molded to the world in which we live and particularly to the institution of sport. Beamish is adept at translating key pieces of Weber's original German, and this makes the chapter all the more accessible to students.

Beamish argues that "in the case of high-performance and professional sport, Weber's fear that the systematic, cold calculation of means–ends efficiency would dominate people's lives was well founded." He goes on to show that "Weber did more than identify the growing impact of goal-rational action in the modern world; he recognized that once reason had 'disenchanted' the world, then neither tradition nor religion could guide ethical conduct." Consider the case of Roger Clemens, who strove not only to stay in the game longer (longer than his age of 40 years would seem to allow), but chose to do so amidst a ménage rife with unethical doings and surroundings. We are not sure if Clemens used performance-enhancing drugs, but we do know that he moved in circles that are now suspect.

How do we interpret Clemens' actions beyond the individual choices he made? Beamish suggests that we turn to Weber: "sociological analysis can offer a greater precision of concepts" by "striving for the highest possible degree of adequacy on the level of meaning." Thus, a close reading of "Toward a Sport Ethic" helps us make sense of Clemens' actions by allowing us to better understand what Weber has come to identify as "concepts."

## Figurational Theory

In 1969, Norbert Elias' magnum opus *The Civilizing Process* was translated into English, giving a larger audience open access to his theoretical perspective, "figurational sociology." In 1986, the important *Quest for Excitement: Sport and Leisure in the Civilizing Process*, jointly authored with Eric Dunning, was published. In the current volume, Dunning uses chapter 2, "Civilizing Sports: Figurational Sociology and the Sociology of Sport," to introduce readers to figurational theory by providing an accessible overview of Elias' contributions to theoretical sociology via figuration.

Dunning points out that there are five parts of Elias' theory (this volume, p. 21): "Summing up, and at the risk of some oversimplification, one could express Elias' theory by saying that he held 'civilizing processes' basically to be a consequence of five interdependent and interacting part-processes or sub-processes:

- State formation
- Pacification under state control
- Growing social differentiation and the lengthening of interdependency claims
- Growing equality of power chances between social classes, between men and women, and between the older and younger generations
- Growing wealth"

Dunning concludes by examining the ways in which figurational theory can explain hooliganism in soccer (or, as it is called in much of the world, football). This chapter provides readers not only with a glimpse of the utility of figurational theory in analyzing sport but also a view into the world of European football, about which many readers, in the United States at least, know very little.

## C. Wright Mills

In chapter 3, "Beyond the Sociological Imagination: Doing Autoethnography to Explore Intersections of Biography and History," Nancy Spencer explicates the major work of C. Wright Mills. According to Spencer, "Mills articulated his vision of the sociological imagination as providing a means to enable its users 'to understand the larger historical scene in terms of its meaning for the inner life and the external career of a variety of individuals' (5). The lives of individual scholars were particularly important to Mills, who indicated that the best scholars 'do not split their work from their lives' (195)." Spencer places herself inside the "sociological imagination" to better understand and explain how our own biographies connect to social history.

TORU YAMANAKA/AFP/Getty Images

# 1 | **Toward a Sport Ethic**

## Science, Politics, and Weber's Sociology

*Robert Beamish, PhD*

---

**Social theory:** Interpretive social action theory

**Proponents of the theory:** Max Weber, Anthony Giddens, and Jürgen Habermas

**What the theory says:** Sociology is a comprehensive science of social action that pursues universal truths about an infinitely complex world even though that objective is ultimately unattainable. In that quest, sociologists develop "pure type" concepts that focus attention on the key aspects of social action. Science, as a form of social action, can itself be examined as a pure type. This analysis shows that science is limited in what it can prescribe as an ultimate ethical basis for social action, leaving the determination of social values to the political realm of social action. The key to moral conduct is the creation of a fully open debate within the political realm of societies.

---

At the end of *The Protestant Ethic and the Spirit of Capitalism*, Max Weber (1958a, 181–182) maintained that when Puritan asceticism "was carried out of the monastic cells into everyday life, and began to dominate worldly morality, it did its part in building the tremendous cosmos of the modern economic order." The result was a world dominated by "the technical and economic conditions of machine production"—a world that determined, with "an irresistible force," "the lives of all individuals who are born into this mechanism," not simply those "directly concerned with economic acquisition."

Citing Richard Baxter's view that concerns regarding the external world "should only lie on the shoulders of the 'saint like a light cloak which can be thrown aside at any moment,'" Weber (1958a, 181) noted that as "material goods . . . [had] gained an increasing and finally an inexorable power over the lives of men [and women] as at no previous period in history," rather than resting lightly on humanity's shoulders, the external world had become a "shell as hard as steel." No one knew, Weber (1958a, 182) continued, who would live in the prison of materialism in the future, "or whether at the end of this tremendous development entirely new prophets might arise" or "a rebirth of old ideas and ideals" would take place. If neither happened, however, a "mechanized petrification" would occur, leaving a world of "specialists without spirit [and] sensualists without heart"—an existence that T.S. Eliot would describe a few years later in "The Waste Land" and "The Hollow Men."

Now, when multimillion-dollar contracts are routine in professional sport and high-performance athletes clamor for cash as single-mindedly as they pursue Olympic gold, it is apparent that Weber's fears have become reality. Every aspect of sport is imprisoned within the cash nexus. But Weber's focus extended beyond the economic; he was more concerned with how "the lives of all individuals who are born into this mechanism" would be shaped by the domination of "goal rationality" (*Zweckrationalität*) in social life as a belief in reason and rational calculation became the secular faith of modernity. In the case of high-performance and professional sport, Weber's fear that the systematic, cold calculation of means–ends efficiency would dominate people's lives was well founded (see Beamish and

Ritchie 2006; Fainaru-Wada and Williams 2006; Hoberman 1992). Sport, as Jean Marie Brohm (1978) aptly noted, has become "a prison of measured time."

Weber did more than identify the growing impact of goal-rational action in the modern world; he recognized that once reason had "disenchanted" the world, then neither tradition nor religion could guide ethical conduct. In a world dominated by goal rationality, Weber was deeply concerned with how humankind would find a moral compass to guide its behavior. In modern sport, issues such as the steroid controversy, substance use on the Tour de France, and U.S. Presidents George W. Bush's and Barack Obama's concerns about role models in professional sport all highlight the problem that Weber identified—one that extends from the professional level right down to children's sport. Can there be ethical guideposts for sport in an era dominated by instrumental reason? Fortunately, Weber's sociology provides some answers—although they are not simple.

Two key essays demonstrate the importance that Weber placed upon questions of ethical behavior, and they document the high standards he set for scholars and policy makers. In "Wissenschaft als Beruf [Scholarship as a Calling]" and "Politik als Beruf [Politics as a Calling]," Weber (1968, 1958b) explicitly addressed the legitimate spheres of activity and social responsibilities of scholars and policy makers.[1] Viewed within the context of his sociology as a whole, the essays also differentiate the roles that each can play in providing a moral direction to human life in modernity. This chapter explores the roles that scholarship and politics must play in providing a moral compass to sport.

## FOUR PURE TYPES OF ACTION

Weber's sociology was fundamentally empirical, and though he rejected the notion that sociologists could ever develop universal social laws of human behavior, for Weber its mandate was not confined to the description of unique events. Weber (1956, 4) noted that sociologists interpretively grasp the meaning of social action in one of three contexts: "the actually intended meaning for the specific action (as in the historical approach)," "the average of, or an approximation to, the actually intended meaning (as in cases of sociological mass observation)," or "the meaning appropriate to a *pure* type [*reinen Typus*] (an ideal type) of a common phenomenon."

Weber (1956, 9) emphasized that "sociology constitutes—as we have frequently assumed as self-evident—*type*-concepts and seeks *general* rules of events." "This is in contradistinction to history" he continued, "which seeks causal analyses and explanation of *individual, culturally* significant actions, structures, and personalities."

---

[1] These essays were first translated into English by Hans Gerth and C. Wright Mills (Weber 1946a, 1946b) as "Science as a Vocation" and "Politics as a Vocation." The choice of "Science" for *Wissenschaft* and "Vocation" for *Beruf* is not incorrect, but there are sound reasons for using "scholarship" and "calling" instead. Translating *Wissenschaft* as scholarship emphasizes how Weber's approach to knowledge differed from the one generally associated with "science." Weber rejected the idea that the methods of the natural sciences (*Naturwissenschaften*) were appropriate to sociology; his approach was heavily influenced by the humanities (*Geisteswissenschaften*) and the importance of interpretive meaning (see Weber 1956, 1–9). Similarly, though "vocation" suggests more than an "occupation," Weber used *Beruf* with precise intention, as the essays indicate—scholarship and politics were "callings" that placed extraordinary demands on those called to those particular communities—a point developed in this chapter.

Sociologists seek to develop explanations that move from the specific to the general and ultimately to broadly inclusive explanations of social behavior. In terms of meaningful social action—the fundamental basis of Weber's sociology—there were four pure types of social action: goal-rational, value-rational, affective, and traditional.

- Goal-rational action is characterized by the calculated pursuit of a specific goal—for example, the use of long-term resistance training to build an athlete's physical work capacity.
- Value-rational action is guided by a particular value. Setting aside years of one's life and training intensively to win gold for one's nation is a common form of value-rational action in high-performance sport.
- In affective or emotional action, one's actions are guided by desires or emotions (e.g., fear, anger, hate, vengeance, lust, love); the emotional and affective dimensions of sport are evident at every level. The predominant emotions shift from pleasure, freedom, and joy to controlled fury and icy determination as one proceeds from youth and recreational to professional and high-performance sport.
- Traditional action is rooted in the dictates of the past, and while science has largely taken the place of tradition in professional and high-performance sport, athletes can still be observed doing things "old-school" or "because it's always been that way," even at sport's highest levels.

The creation of pure (or ideal) types of social action involved the process of conceptualization or abstraction from the immediately observable types of action found in everyday life. Weber (1956, 9) acknowledged that, as with every generalizing science, abstract sociological concepts—when compared with the actual complexity of reality—are simplifications, but he saw this as a strength rather than a limitation. "To compensate for this disadvantage," he wrote, "sociological analysis can offer a greater precision of concepts," which is obtained by "striving for the highest possible degree of adequacy on the level of meaning." Through the use of concepts, the sociologist can focus on the most significant aspects of human action in order to produce a rich, "thick description" of an action, event, or social trend. Rather than dealing with the complete phantasmagoria of a professional wrestling match in infinite detail, for example, the sociologist can employ specific concepts, such as masculinity or compulsory heterosexuality to focus on the most significant symbolic meanings associated with the event.

As a result, Weber viewed an ideal type (or pure type) as a deliberate conceptualization that sociologists produce on the basis of their comprehensive understanding of the social action in people's everyday lives. The sociologist constructs the pure type so that it sharply and precisely identifies key characteristics pertinent to the action under study (e.g., goal-rational action). The ideal type brings to conscious awareness aspects of action that are often only partially conscious or even subconscious, thereby enriching the analysis that the sociologist can undertake.

While Weber and other sociologists have used pure or ideal types to explore a vast array of human activities, it is the use of pure type analysis as it applies to scholarly analysis—to *Wissenschaft*—that is of greatest significance to this chapter.

Properly and fully conceptualized, can science—particularly social science—serve as the ethical guide to human action in an era dominated by reason? Put in different terms—are there limits to scientific (or scholarly) knowledge?

## SCIENCE AND ETHICS: THE LIMITS OF GOAL-RATIONAL ACTION

Weber lived through the turmoil in Europe that led up to the First World War; he lived through the war and he lived long enough to experience all of the political tensions and personal anxieties that Germans, in particular, and others in Western Europe experienced at the end of the war. Western Europe was an extremely divided region of the world with no consensus on any of the fundamental questions that societies and people must address.

At the end of the 19th century, the iconoclastic philosopher Friedrich Nietzsche (1882/1974, 181–182) announced in "The Parable of the Madman" that God was dead: "God is dead. God remains dead. And we have killed Him." "What are these churches now," the madman asked as he was led out of one, "if they are not the tombs and sepulchers of God?"

Although the philosophy behind the parable is complex, Nietzsche did not mourn the death of God, because he felt that humankind had to take charge of its own affairs rather than passively accept the dictates of the church. Whether people agreed with him or not, Nietzsche struck a chord with people's lives at the turn of the 20th century, and many asked: Where is the moral compass that should guide human behavior? What is the basis for ethical conduct? If it is not to be found in traditional religion, can it be located in the new "religion" of science?

As a committed scholar, and one who believed that social science should inform people's lives at every level—from the mundanity of daily life to the formation of national policies—Weber wrestled with that question: Can science be the ultimate source of ethical conduct? Weber's answer was no. In reaching that conclusion, he made important contributions concerning how one should understand scientific inquiry as meaningful human action, as well as how one must understand ethical decision making as a type of social action.

Weber's answer to the question of whether science can serve as the moral compass for humanity stems directly from his fourfold typology of social action. Looking at science as meaningful social action—action that has meaning to the agent and takes into account the behavior of others—Weber noted that the goal of science is to produce propositions of fact and statements of causality or, in the case of the social sciences, comprehensive interpretations of social action. The social action that characterizes scientific or scholarly action is goal-rational action. Scientists and scholars, working within the modernist conception of science, use rational means (the specific techniques of their fields of science or scholarship) to pursue a specific goal—universally valid truth.[2]

---

[2] The phrase "universally valid truth" can cause confusion because even though natural scientists and social scientists differ in their interest in "universal laws" (in the natural sciences) versus generalized understandings (in the social sciences), all scientists working within the modernist conception of science want to produce knowledge that has truthful validity that anyone, anywhere, at any time can examine and test.

As the pursuit of universally valid truth, it might seem that science could serve as the moral compass for the modern world. But scientific action involves not only goal-rational action. The actions of scholars and scientists are also value-rational because they are committed to a specific value.[3] Scientific action is fundamentally committed to the value of truths demonstrated by universally valid facts or arguments. In fact, before a scholar can engage in scientific activity as a goal-rational action, she or he has already made a commitment to the value of truths demonstrated by universally valid facts or arguments. Any scholar who manipulates data, fails to examine alternative hypotheses (no matter how uncomfortable or unpopular), or in any other way fails to subject his or her findings, arguments, and conclusions to rigorous analysis and critique does not place a high enough value upon the pursuit of truth to be a genuine scholar or scientist. Without this unyielding commitment to the value of scientific truths, scientific action could never serve as the means to the discovery of universally valid truths.

Scientific action, it turns out, is goal-rational and value-rational, and it is in the value-rational dimension of scholarship that the real problem lies for anyone's aspirations that science could serve as the ultimate moral compass for society or as the basis for a system of absolute ethics. The value-rational dimension of scholarly action poses three limitations to science as the definitive moral compass for a society or the possibility that it could determine a universal ethics.

First, scientific activity is in and of itself a value-rational activity. As such, it represents one specific commitment to a particular value—the importance of the pursuit and discovery of universally valid truth. But as one specific value commitment, it cannot also serve as an unbiased, independent judge of all other values.

On what basis could anyone, even a scientist, argue that the pursuit of the universally valid truths of science is a higher value than the pursuit of truth through, say, the Bible, the Talmud, the Qur'an, or Plato's Theory of Forms? Commitment to a particular value or value system, Weber maintained, was a judgment of value (*Werturteil*, a commitment to a value—a value judgment) that cannot be assessed, supported, or undermined by any transcendental position of supreme wisdom. A judgment of value, a commitment to a value, is precisely that—the placing of a high value on a key notion or set of notions (*Wert- ur- teil*). That judgment may be based on reasoned calculation, faith, emotional attachment, fear, pragmatism, false consciousness, repressed desire, or charismatic attraction to certain values, but it is not—and cannot be—based on any absolute measure. This is the first way in which science is limited and thus cannot stand as the definitive moral compass for contemporary society.

The second reason is quite simple. The world (natural and social) is infinitely complex. It can never, ever be fully known.

Science generates abstract theories that give meaning to the world and allow humankind to meaningfully interact with and, to a certain extent, control it; but even the most advanced scientific insights remain incomplete. Science makes the world intelligible—but not fully known and comprehended. Scientists commit

---

[3] Scientific action also has elements of affective and traditional action, but these aspects are not central to the analysis here. They are not considered because they would not change the conclusions that ensue.

themselves to an impossible task. They commit themselves to a fundamental value judgment that is ultimately unrealizable (though the commitment to that value ensures that their work unerringly *strives* towards the realization of that value). Scientists seek to discover universally accepted truths that can advance scientific knowledge, but the abstract laws it generates will never achieve an absolute form of knowledge, because an infinite world can never be fully known. This does not mean that scientific activity is useless. It has produced countless accomplishments in the process of trying to achieve its ultimate goal, and countless performance advancements in the world of sport confirm how powerful an instrument science is, but attaining universal truths for an infinitely complex and continually changing world is simply not possible.

Finally, the ways in which science has developed and advanced would not and cannot lead to the development of absolute knowledge. Weber argued that scholars assess the world in which they live and work and that certain questions, problems, or issues become important to them. Through a process of relevance—what Weber termed value-relevant (*Wertbeziehung*) action—scholars choose the issues they will research. Part of the reason a question or issue becomes relevant is internal to a scholar's discipline at a particular point in time; part of it may involve personal interest.

For example, prior to the 1968 Olympics in Mexico City, exercise physiologists became intensely interested in the effect that high altitude would have on endurance events such as the marathon. Would athletes' health be at risk? In the process of testing athletes under various oxygen concentrations found at various altitudes, researchers discovered that if athletes trained at high altitude prior to competition, they could significantly elevate their concentration of red blood cells and then safely compete in a demanding endurance event at high altitude.

This research had two spillover effects. First, it led to the discovery that training at high altitude not only raised one's hematocrit value and made it safe to compete at high altitude but also enhanced performances in sea-level competition. Second, learning that high-altitude training increased hematocrit value and knowing that it would enhance endurance performance, researchers wondered what would happen if one extracted blood with a high hematocrit value following high-altitude training, stored it for a while, and then returned it to the athlete's blood supply at a later date. Thus, in conducting research into the potential dangers of endurance events at high altitude, researchers not only discovered "blood boosting," as it was then called, but also perfected the optimal techniques for a performance-enhancing practice that endurance athletes legitimately used until it was banned following the 1984 Olympics (see Beamish and Ritchie 2006, 109–110).

In a similar manner, prior to the Mexico Games, sport sociologists were drawn into the study of racial inequality in sport as black athletes began to organize a boycott in support of the ongoing struggle for civil rights in the United States. Simply by investigating whether or not there was any basis for black athletes' concerns over racial inequality in what many assumed was the meritocracy of sport, sport sociologists opened up a rich area of social analysis that demonstrated the effect that racism had upon not just black athletes but blacks in the American population as a whole. Racism in sport, they found, had a tremendous effect throughout the American social structure—an effect that went well beyond the world of sport (see Edwards 1969).

Weber acknowledged that the questions scholars address are related to issues that hold value relevance to them. The value relevance that motivates a scholar to pursue a particular question may be strictly scholarly, but it may also involve broader, extrascientific concerns, and in either case a chosen value shapes the selection of a research problem.[4]

The issue can be made more complex, though the outcome will be the same. If scientific action is a form of value-relevant action, one might think that a scientist would engage only with questions directly related to the pursuit of universally valid truths. This might mean that she or he would never be interested in a question because of its political importance or personal relevance. This claim is problematic, but even if one assumes that all scientists pursue questions only because of the contribution such pursuit will make to universally valid truth, would this approach result in the inevitable advancement of science toward its value-relevant goal (universally valid truth)? The answer is no.

During the quest for absolute, universal knowledge, the selection of topics and issues would be tied to value-relevant interests and questions that stemmed from less than perfect knowledge. There would be no guarantee that the scientific community would necessarily pursue the absolutely necessary value-relevant questions that would lead to absolute universal truth. From an imperfect comprehension of the world, one might ask and pursue the right questions, but it is more likely that only by chance could scientists choose the "correct" issues to lead to absolute knowledge. And in a world of infinite complexity, the odds of posing the correct questions are astronomically stacked against science. For example, even given everything that is known about exercise physiology, anatomy, genetics, and the mapping of the genome, do sport scientists know for sure what questions must be asked and answered to be able someday to predict who will and who will not become a world-class athlete (let alone who will be the fastest distance runner in the world)? The way in which research problems are and must be determined is a serious hindrance to the prospect of the scientific community's ever posing all the right questions that would lead to absolute knowledge—despite the fact that once a problem is chosen, scientists would follow the value-rational commitment to the pursuit of universal truths.

On the basis of all these arguments, Weber drew the conclusion that the goals or ends that an individual, a group, a society, or even all of humankind chooses to pursue can never be determined by an infallible ethical system based upon science. Scientific knowledge is limited; it is just one form of knowledge among many and, as a result, could never be an infallible guide to human action. The goals that individuals, groups, or societies pursue, Weber argued, are and must be determined

---

[4] Once a scientist or scholar chooses a value-relevant question or issue, she or he is then committed, as a scientific scholar, to suspending her or his personal interest in the question and pursuing that question on the basis of commitment to the value of scholarship (i.e., the value judgment or value commitment to the pursuit of universal truth). Scholars are committed to the pursuit of universally valid truths because that is both the goal of science and the value that distinguishes acceptable from unacceptable behavior and action as a scientist.

within the realm of political discussion, debate, and decision making. Once those goals are chosen, then science can serve as an important guide to reaching them. Science can serve as one of the most effective means of goal-rational action, but it cannot determine any system of absolute ends.

## THE POLITICS OF ETHICAL CONDUCT IN SPORT

The standards for scholarship that Weber placed upon natural and social scientists were extremely high—setting aside one's interests and biases in the pursuit of universally valid truth (even though such knowledge is unachievable). Weber's standards for policy makers were even higher because policy makers are engaged in an area of human life filled with particular interests; politics, in essence, is a system of competing ideas and policy claims.

In the reality of everyday life, political decision making is intimately tied to the advancement of specific, vested interests; however, the pursuit of narrow, individual interests can never bring a society together collectively. Those policies would ultimately divide rather than integrate. Power, in various guises, might create an apparent agreement, but the underlying reality would be otherwise—it would be one of dynamic tension.

As goal-rational action, politics and policy making are, fundamentally, the use of human reason to reach goals that meet a society's or community's needs and interests. The true goal rationality of political action is the use of reason to meet universally valid interests. The true standard for political action as genuinely meaningful goal-rational action is exceptionally high.

Like scholarship, which is both goal-rational and value-rational action, political action is also a form of value-rational action. If the fundamental objective of policy making is universally valid interests, then the value commitment of policy makers has to be a commitment to uphold the collective interest of the society or community as the highest goal and thus, a commitment to policies that meet a universal—rather than partial—interest. In the same way that it is impossible for scientists to ever achieve universally valid truth, it is impossible for policy makers to ever ultimately determine a community's universally valid interest(s), but the pursuit of such a goal must guide all debates of policy and political decision making.

The standard for ethical conduct in sport in the age of reason is not based on some transcendental truth; it rests on the highest standards of political action as both goal-rational and value-rational action. The discussion over the ends of sport—an essential policy outcome before the best means to those ends can be determined—has to reach higher than mere particular vested interests. It must strive to attain a universally valid interest despite the impossibility of attaining that goal. The difficulty this poses is that a genuinely ethical sport system demands exceptionally high standards of policy making; the comforting aspect is that those standards are within the grasp of genuinely committed, thoughtful people acting in the real world of sport.

At present, specific vested interests control the ends to which sport is directed; the partial interests of individuals or groups dominate. The key to moving forward is to open the discussion far more widely than is currently the case and to aspire to policy goals that are far loftier than the immediate interests of powerful people in positions of influence. Whether it is the debate on steroid use (in particular, performance-enhancing substances), more general practices such as racism, sexism, violence in sport, or the safety of professional and high-performance sport forms themselves, the sport system will exclude the interests and needs of disempowered groups and individuals until policy makers commit themselves to seeking out the universal interests in sport and determine the political decisions that are needed to bring such a sport form into existence. The key to a moral compass for sport in the modern world lies in the standards for scholarship and policy making that Weber detailed in "Scholarship as a Calling" and "Politics as a Calling."

## CONCLUSION

The world of modern sport is dominated by science, technology, and instrumental reason. Athletes increasingly rely on cutting-edge science to push their performances closer and closer to the absolute limits of human athletic achievement. Science is the foundation of sport's performance ethic, but can it also serve as the fundamental basis for a universal ethic of conduct?

Weber's interpretive social action theory establishes very high standards for both science and politics as forms of social action. Upon close examination, it is apparent that neither science—natural or social—nor politics can serve as the basis for a universal ethic of conduct, though it is in the political realm, under social conditions where people strive for universality, that decisions of ethical conduct must be made.

Science is a form of social action like all others. It has a goal-rational dimension which commits it to the pursuit of universally valid truth. It also has a value-rational element that values, above all else, the pursuit of universal truths, but science is also only one value commitment among others in society. As such, scientific knowledge is limited in any claims it can make about ethical conduct.

Political action also has a goal-rational dimension that centers on the integration and harmonization of the social whole—the use of human understanding to create the best conditions for social existence. This is also its value-rational commitment—the pursuit of a community's universally valid, collective interests. Although this objective is also impossible to fully attain, the conditions for its pursuit can be established; those conditions rest on the fully open exchange of ideas, knowledge, and lived experience so that the best alternatives can be understood, debated, selected, and followed. For sport, this means that the movement toward a universal ethic of conduct must come from considering the best scientific knowledge possible within an environment that is as free as possible from inequality and domination, where collective decisions, in the interests of all, can be made and continually reviewed and perhaps revised.

### Suggested Research

1. Contemporary high-performance sport relies heavily on a number of performance-enhancing practices and substances (e.g. "sharkskin" suits; aerodynamic carbon-fiber bikes; erythropoietin, or EPO; anabolic ste-

roids). Some of those practices and substances are banned, while others are accepted. To what extent does the use of any performance-enhancing practice or substance violate the ethical bases for contemporary world-class sport? Or is the banning of selected substances contrary to the ethics of modern sport?

2. Olympic athletes in many sports make an increasingly early commitment to the all-out pursuit of their sport to the exclusion of other activities, interests, and opportunities for more rounded personal development. On the basis of what arguments might a child advocate argue that the pursuit of world-class, high-performance sport is a deviant form of activity that society as whole should neither fund financially nor support morally and socially?

# Additional Resources

### Theory

Giddens, A. 1984. *The constitution of society*. Berkeley: University of California Press.

Drawing heavily upon Weber's interpretive perspective, Giddens presents a fully developed argument about how societies are constituted and reconstituted through the actions of skilled, knowledgeable social agents within an existing context of rules and resources.

Habermas, J. 1984, 1987. *The theory of communicative action*. 2 vols. Trans. T. McCarthy. Boston: Beacon Press.

These two volumes draw heavily upon Weber's work, but the emphasis on the creation of social conditions that would establish a "domination free discourse," Habermas's critical theory of social action, differs from Weber even though Habermas remains heavily indebted to Weber's work. This development of Weber's ideas has been very influential among sociologists in Europe and North America.

Kalberd, S., ed. 2005. *Max Weber: Readings and commentary on modernity*. Oxford, UK: Blackwell.

This collection provides an excellent introduction to Weber's work, with particular reference to modernity. The book contains key excerpts from Weber's work, including material related to the limits of ethical action and his analyses of power, political action, and social policy.

### Sport Topic

Cantelon, H., and A. Ingham. 2002. Max Weber and the sociology of sport. In *Theory, sport and society*, ed. J. Maguire and K. Young, 63–83. Oxford: Elsevier Science.

This is one of the best introductions to Weber's work as it applies to the study of sport. The essay examines Weber's theory of interpretive social action, pure types, rationalization, and the role of instrumental rationality in modern life.

Dimeo, P., and M. McNamee, eds. 2009. *Doping and public health*. Odense: University of Southern Denmark Press.

This collection of essays addresses the use of performance-enhancing substances from philosophical, sociological, political, and policy-making perspectives. The collection addresses the role of instrumental rationality and its dominance in the world of sport, as well as the policy implications that its widespread use has for the health of athletes and for larger issues in the arena of public health.

Guttmann, A. 2004. *From ritual to record: The nature of modern sports*. 2nd ed. New York: Columbia University Press.

One of the first book-length treatments of Weber's relevance to the study of sport, this volume presents a good overview of the key elements of Weber's sociology, then links it to key issues within modern sport. The updated version takes into account the growing use of performance-enhancing substances in sport.

ANDREW YATES/AFP/Getty Images

# 2 | Civilizing Sports

## Figurational Sociology and the Sociology of Sport

*Eric Dunning, PhD*

---

**Social theory:** Figurational theory

**Proponents of the theory:** Norbert Elias, Eric Dunning, Joseph Maguire

**What the theory says:** Figurational theory, or social process theory, acknowledges that individuals and institutions are engaged in processes, that these processes have been unstructured and are primarily the *unintended* consequences of *intended* individual actions, and that individuals are interdependent; their very existence is a result not of their own individual actions but rather of their interactions with others. For example, parents create children; children don't create themselves. And, finally, power is a universal condition of all relationships.

---

The figurational tradition of sociological research and theory was pioneered by Norbert Elias (1897–1990), a German of Jewish descent who became a naturalized Englishman in 1952. His work is best seen as an attempt to synthesize the central ideas of Auguste Comte, Karl Marx, Max Weber, and Sigmund Freud. Other influences included Georg Simmel, Kurt Lewin, Wolfgang Köhler, J.B. Watson, and W.B. Cannon. Elias studied philosophy and medicine to the doctoral level in Breslau (now Wroclaw in Poland) before switching to sociology in Heidelberg in 1925. There he came under the influence of Karl Mannheim, a key figure in the early development of the sociology of knowledge, and Alfred Weber, a leading cultural sociologist and brother of the more famous Max. Elias' sociology cannot be properly understood without taking his immersion in the sociology of knowledge centrally into account.

The following aspects of Elias' life help explain some of the characteristic features of his sociological approach.

1. His experience of the First World War sensitized Elias to the part played by violence and war in human life. He served in the Kaiser's army on the Eastern and Western fronts, and during the 1920s and 1930s he directly witnessed the rise of the Nazis and their street battles with the Communists. Such experiences intensified his awareness of "decivilizing" as well as "civilizing" processes—he described the rise of the Nazis as a "breakdown of civilization"—and reinforced his view that "civilizing controls" rarely, if ever, amount to more than a relatively thin veneer or shell. He was not, as is sometimes alleged, an "evolutionary" or "progress" theorist. His work, that is, was not moralistic; it was hardheaded, realistic, and scientific in the strictest sense of the term.

2. The repeated interruption of his career by wider events—the First World War, the German hyperinflation of 1923, the Nazi takeover 10 years later, his exile to France and then to Britain, and his internment in Britain as an "enemy alien" at the start of the Second World War in camps at Huyton, Lancashire, and on the Isle of Man—all helped sensitize Elias to the interplay of "the individual" and "the social," "the private" and "the public," and "the micro" and "the macro."

3. Elias' study of medicine and philosophy up to the doctoral level helped problematize for him key aspects of Western philosophy, which in turn contributed to his switching to sociology and making original contributions to what have come

to be known as the sociology of the body and the sociology of emotions. That Elias was a pioneer of the sociology of sport is perhaps best understood in the context of his background in medicine and philosophy, but also relevant is the fact that he was an amateur boxer in his youth. Above all, he was opposed to the "mind–body" dichotomy; he held that our "minds" are material, bodily functions of our complex brains. Nor did he share the common prejudice, perhaps particularly pronounced in academic or "intellectual" circles, that sport is a "physical" phenomenon of lower value than phenomena connected with the realm of "mind." The theory of "civilizing processes" is generally regarded as having been Elias' major sociological contribution, but he made other contributions, too, perhaps particularly the theory of "established–outsider" group relations (1965, 1994).

The core features of the figurational approach to sociology pioneered by Elias are as follows:

1. The shared conviction that, like the universe at large, human individuals and the societies they form are processes.

2. The idea that the processes undergone by societies have tended, up to now, especially in the longer term, to be "blind," in the sense of being the largely unintended consequences of aggregates of intended individual acts. To illustrate this point, Elias sometimes used the metaphor of history as a runaway express train. It was his hope that sociological knowledge will help us bring the "train" of history under greater conscious control. He was fully aware, of course, that his stress on the relative lack of control runs counter to the self-love of people who like to believe that they are always on top of things, always in control.

3. The idea that human societies consist of individuals who are radically interdependent with others. That is, we are born, as a result of an act by our interdependent parents, into a structured collectivity or social world—a world of interdependencies or figurations—that we ourselves played no part in forming and that occupies a particular historical-geographical position or particular position in time and space.

4. The idea that power is a universal property of human relations at all levels of social integration, ranging from two-person groups to humanity as a whole. Power, according to Elias, is (a) a function of interdependency ties (your power over me is a consequence of the degree of my dependency on you); (b) a question of labile, shifting balances or ratios; and (c) not explainable solely by reference to single factors such as ownership of the means of production or control of the means of violence.[1] Elias also took account of such bodily power resources of individuals as physical and intellectual strength and such structural power resources of collectivities as degrees of group unity and cohesion. Bodily power resources such as speed and strength are, of course, centrally relevant to the sociology of sport.

---

[1] It is, of course, mainly Marxists who explain social structure and social change reductively by reference to ownership of the means of production or "economic forces." Max Weber added control of the means of violence to the equation. Elias, however, rejected both "factor theorizing" and the idea that lawlike explanations are adequate in relation to the human-social level of reality. He favored what he accurately but rather clumsily called "structure and process explanations."

5. The need in sociology for a "constant two-way traffic" between theory and research. Elias argued that theory without research is liable to be abstract and meaningless, and research without theory to be arid and descriptive.

6. The position that sociologists should see as their primary concern the activities of building up, and adding to, bodies of reliable knowledge. He stood firmly against the intrusion of political, religious, and other ideologies into sociological research and suggested that research into, for example, football hooliganism, we should aim, first of all by means of what he called "a detour via detachment," to build up a "reality-congruent" picture of what football hooliganism involves and of how and why it is socially and psychologically generated. Then, through a process of what he called "secondary involvement," we should use our more reality-congruent knowledge to devise more realistic and effective policies for dealing with the problem than were previously applied.

7. The view that the theory of "civilizing processes" constitutes what Elias called a "central theory" through which a variety of apparently diverse and separate phenomena can be related.[2] Let me briefly provide a flavor of what the theory of "civilizing processes" entails.

Contrary to a fairly widespread misconception, Elias did not use the concept of "civilizing processes" in a moral or evaluative way. He signaled this fact by tending to enclose the term "civilization" and its derivatives in quotation marks. "Civilizing process" was, for him, a technical term. He did not intend to suggest by it that people who can be shown to stand at a more advanced level in a "civilizing process" than some others—for example, ourselves relative to the people of feudal Britain—are in any meaningful sense "better than" or "morally superior to" those medieval people. That, of course, is almost invariably how the people who call themselves "civilized" view themselves. But how, Elias used to ask, can people congratulate themselves when they are the chance beneficiaries of a blind or unintended process to the course of which they have not personally contributed? To say this, of course, is not to deny that, just as tends to be the case with social processes more generally, there are victims as well as beneficiaries of "civilizing processes." For example, the abolition of the death penalty in Britain in the 1950s for all crimes except treason is generally regarded as having been a "civilizing" development, but executioners were deprived of their jobs, and the families and friends of murder victims were deprived of what many people in that situation feel is the only appropriate way of dealing with their understandable feelings of anger and desire for revenge.

The theory of "civilizing processes" is in equal measure theoretical and empirical. Empirically, it is based on a substantial body of evidence or data, principally on the changing manners of the secular upper classes—the knights, kings, queens, court aristocrats, politicians, and business leaders, but not, for the most part, the higher clergy—between the Middle Ages and modern times up to the Second

---

[2] Whereas Elias and Dunning used the theory of civilizing processes in relation to the sociological study of sport, Johan Goudsblom (1992) did so in relation to the study of fire, Stephen Mennell (1987) in relation to the study of food, and Jason Hughes (2003) in relation to smoking.

World War. These data indicate that, in the major societies of Western Europe—Elias' principal focus was on France, Germany, and England—a long-term social process that was "blind," unplanned, and unintended took place involving four main interrelated and interacting components:

1. An elaboration and refinement of social standards
2. An increase in the social pressure on people to exercise stricter, more continuous, and even more self-control over their feelings, behavior, and bodily functions
3. A shift in the balance between external constraints and self-constraints in favor of self-constraints
4. An increase at the levels of personality and habitus in the importance of "conscience" or "superego" as a regulator of behavior. That is, social standards came to be internalized more deeply and to operate not simply consciously and with an element of choice but also beneath the levels of rationality and conscious control.

## THE FIGURATIONAL SOCIOLOGY OF SPORT AND ITS CRITICS

Beginning with Elias, a school of scholars, crossing multiple generations, has developed in the United Kingdom and Western Europe:

- Norbert Elias
- Eric Dunning
- Patrick Murphy (Murphy and Dunning 1990), Kenneth Sheard (2004), and Ivan Waddington (Waddington, Malcolm, and Jones 2000; Waddington, Roderick, and Parker 2000)
- Grant Jarvie and Joseph Maguire (Jarvie and Maguire 1994; Maguire 1999, 2000)
- Sharon Colwell (2004), Graham Curry (2001), Dominic Malcolm (1997), and Stuart Smith (2004)
- Ken Green (2004), Daniel Bloyce (2004), Katie Liston (2005), and Andrew Smith (Smith and Waddington 2008)
- Maarten Van Bottenburg (Van Bottenburg 2001) (the Netherlands)
- Michael Krüger (1977) and Bero Rigauer (2000) (Germany)

Let me turn now to the issue of critique and testing.

## CRITICIZING AND TESTING ELIAS

Elias insisted on the testability of his concepts and theories and called for what he described as a "constant two-way traffic" between research and theory. As a consequence, Elias' concepts and theories are, like those in the natural sciences, permeated more by factual observation and hence less abstract than has often been the case in sociology.

Elias' insistence on the testability of his concepts and theories is contradicted by a frequently touted judgment to the contrary. For example, Dennis Smith, a lecturer in the Leicester Department of Sociology in the 1960s and 1970s, argued in 1984 that the theory of "civilizing processes" is "irrefutable." Such an argument was echoed two years later by the anthropologist Edmund Leach, who suggested in a review of Elias and Dunning's *Quest for Excitement* (1986, 2009) that the "theory is impervious to testing" (Leach 1986). An example from the sociology of sport can be found in Gary Armstrong's 1998 statement that Elias' theory "is a fusion of untestable and descriptive generalisations" (317). Richard Giulianotti went so far in 1999 as to claim that Elias introduced the concept of "decivilizing spurts" in order "to rebut . . . counter evidence" (45). Such arguments are wrong because they involve false projection onto Elias' work of evaluative notions such as "progress." Elias' work was about "decivilizing" as well as "civilizing processes" from the beginning. One of many examples is furnished by his discussion of feudalization (Elias 2000, 195–236). Another is provided in the following passage:

> *If the whole many-layered fabric of historical development is considered, . . . the movement is seen to be infinitely complex. In each phase there are numerous fluctuations, frequent advances or recessions of the internal and external restraints (Elias 2000, 157).*

Aspects of the theory have also been tested by scholars other than Elias and Dunning, for example Benn and Benn (2004), Bloyce (2004), Cooper (2004), Curry (2001), Kiku (2004), Maguire (1999, 2000), Malcolm (1999, 2002, 2004), Sheard (2004), S. Smith (2004), Twitchen (2004), and Waddington and colleagues (2000). The sports on which these tests were carried out include baseball, boxing, cricket, gymnastics, motor racing, rugby, and shooting. The figurational studies by Maguire and Waddington deal with sport in general—in Maguire's case with sport and "globalization" and in Waddington's with sport, health, and drugs. The figurational tradition in the sociology of sport is clearly healthy and growing.

An aspect of this overall "civilizing process" which is of central relevance for understanding the development of modern sport has been the increasing control of violence and aggression *within* societies, though much less so in relations *between* societies. According to Elias, this taming of aggression took place together with a long-term decline in most people's capacity for obtaining pleasure from inflicting pain on others or from directly witnessing seriously violent acts. Elias referred in this connection to a dampening of *Angriffslust*—literally, that is, to a damping down or curbing of the lust for attacking, and a taming of people's conscious desire to obtain pleasure from attacking others and seeing them suffer, together with a reduction at the levels of personality and habitus in their learned capacity for doing so. This dampening was connected, according to Elias, with an increase in mutual identification—that is, in reciprocal sympathy and understanding.

The terms "violence" and "civilization" tend to be popularly understood as antitheses. However, the "civilizing processes" of Western Europe were seen by Elias as the unplanned outcomes of violent struggles for supremacy between monarchs and other feudal lords. These struggles led to the establishment within the emergent European nation-states—at different times and in somewhat differing ways—of relatively stable and effective state monopolies on violence and taxation, which are the major means of ruling in societies above the level of tribes. To a large extent, such modern nation-states were formed for purposes of war, but their violence and tax monopolies helped their central rulers not only in relation to external attack and defense but also with regard to internal pacification. As nation-states became more internally pacified, so the personality and habitus structure of the majority of their people became more peaceful, and, as we shall see, this change was reflected in what they began around the 18th century to call their "sports." The evidence suggests that this development in terminology, habitus, and leisure institutions began to take place first of all in England.

Summing up, and at the risk of some oversimplification, one could express Elias' theory by saying that he held "civilizing processes" basically to be a consequence of five interdependent and interacting part-processes or sub-processes:

- State formation
- Pacification under state control
- Growing social differentiation and the lengthening of interdependency claims
- Growing equality of power chances between social classes, between men and women, and between the older and younger generations
- Growing wealth

Elias also showed how, in the course of a "civilizing process," overtly violent struggles tend to be transformed into relatively peaceful struggles for status, wealth, and power—struggles in which, in the most frequent course of events and for the majority of people, destructive urges come to be kept for the most part beneath the threshold of consciousness and not translated into overt action. Status struggles of this kind appear to have played an important part in the divergent development of the soccer and the rugby forms of football (Dunning and Sheard 2005).

## THE "CIVILIZING" OF MODERN SPORT

An aspect of these overall European "civilizing processes" which is crucial for understanding the development of modern sport has been the increasing control of violence and aggression within societies. According to Elias, in "modern" societies in which the dominant groups consider themselves to be "civilized,"

> . . . belligerence and aggression find socially permitted expression in sporting contests. And they are expressed especially in "spectating" (e.g., at boxing matches), in the imaginary identification with a small number of combatants to whom moderate and precisely regulated scope is granted for the release of such affects. And this living-out of affects in spectating or even in merely listening (e.g., to a radio commentary) is a particularly characteristic feature of "civilized" society. It partly determines the development of books and theatre, and decisively influences the role of the cinema in our world. This transformation of what manifested itself originally as an active, often aggressive expression of pleasure into the passive, more ordered pleasure of spectating (i.e., the mere pleasure of

*the eye) is already initiated in education, in the conditioning precepts for young people. . . . It is highly characteristic of "civilized" people that they are denied by socially instilled self-controls from spontaneously touching what they desire, love or hate (Elias 2000, 170).*

Data also suggest that sport generally underwent "civilizing processes" in conjunction with these wider "civilizing" developments. That this is the case has been shown by

1. studies of the violent antecedents of modern sport in the ancient and medieval European worlds (Elias 1971, Elias 2009);
2. studies of the initial development of modern sport in 18th- and 19th-century England (Elias 1986, Dunning 1999, Dunning and Curry 2004);
3. intensive case studies of the long-term development of rugby and soccer (Dunning and Sheard 2005; Dunning 1999), boxing (Sheard 2004), and cricket (Malcolm 2004); and
4. intensive studies of soccer hooliganism as an English and world problem (Williams, Dunning, and Murphy 1988, 1989; Dunning, Murphy, and Williams 1988; Murphy, Williams, and Dunning 1990; Dunning 1999; and Dunning, Murphy, Waddington, and Astrinakis 2002).

Because figurational sociologists have probably become best known for their work on soccer hooliganism, this subject deserves fairly lengthy treatment in the context of this chapter.

## SOCCER HOOLIGANISM AS AN ENGLISH AND WORLD PROBLEM

The figurational approach to football (soccer) hooliganism does not constitute a "super theory" that explains everything about the phenomenon; it is offered only as a beginning on which to build. Its distinctive features are that it is based on a synthesis of psychology, sociology, and history and that it involves an exploration of the meanings of hooligan behavior to the hooligans themselves. In this last regard, analysis of a range of hooligan statements made over a period of more than 20 years revealed that, for the (mainly) young men involved—females and older males sometimes take part as well—soccer hooligan fighting is basically about masculinity, territorial struggle, and excitement. For them, fighting is a central source of meaning, status or reputation, and pleasurable emotional arousal. They speak of the respect among their peers that they hope their hooligan involvements will bring, and of "battle excitement," "the adrenaline racing," and "aggro" (short for aggression) as almost erotically arousing. Indeed, Jay Allan, a leading member of the Aberdeen Casuals, a Scottish football hooligan "firm" in the 1980s, wrote of fighting at football as even more pleasurable than sex (1989). American author Bill Buford, who traveled with English football hooligans in the 1980s, described it thusly: "Violence is one of the most intensely lived experiences and, for those capable of giving themselves over to it, one of the most intense pleasures. . . . [C]rowd violence was their drug" (Buford 1991, 201).

Research on the social class of football hooligans in Scotland (Harper 1990), Belgium (Van Limbergen, Colaers, and Walgrave 1987), the Netherlands (Van der

Brug 1986), and Italy (Roversi 1994) suggests that hooligans in other countries tend to come from social backgrounds similar to those of their English counterparts.

The fact that violent spectator disorder occurs more frequently in conjunction with soccer than any other sport would thus appear to be partly a function of the social composition of its crowds. Soccer is the world's most popular team sport, and a majority of its spectators worldwide tend to be male and to come from the lower reaches of the social scale—that is, from social backgrounds where norms tend to legitimate a higher incidence of overt aggressiveness and violence in everyday social relations than tends to be the case among the middle and upper classes. More particularly, lower-class males tend to develop a violent and aggressive habitus and mode of presenting themselves to the world more frequently than do males in the classes above them. This habitus involves a complex of learned traits which seem fundamentally to derive *inter alia* from (a) a pattern of early socialization characterized by a readiness to resort to violence by parents and siblings and (b) adolescent socialization on the streets in the company of age peers, for example, in adolescent "gangs" (Dunning, Murphy, and Williams 1988). In these contexts, because ability and willingness to fight are criteria for membership of and prestige within the group (i.e., for the status of these males in their own and others' eyes as "men"), they learn to associate adrenaline arousal in fight situations with warm, rewarding, and hence pleasurable feelings rather than with the guilt and anxiety that have tended to surround the performance and witnessing of "real" (as opposed to mimetic) violence in the wider society. (By "real" I mean violence that has an intent as opposed to violence that is merely an extraneous expression with no intended outcome.)

This kind of violent habitus tends to be reinforced to the extent that such males live and work in contexts characterized by high levels of gender and age-group segregation. That effect occurs because of the relative absence in such contexts of "softening" pressure from females and older men. Furthermore, in most societies, members of groups that are lower on the social scale are less likely to be highly individualized and more likely to readily form intense "we-group" bonds and identifications (Elias 1978, 134–148) that involve an equally intense hostility toward "outsiders" (Elias 1994) than is the case among the more powerful, more self-steering, and usually more inhibited groups who stand above them. At a soccer match, of course, the outsiders are the opposing team, its supporters, and in some cases the match officials. Soccer tends to be chosen by these groups as a context in which to fight because it, too, is about masculinity, territory, and excitement. Given a widespread pattern of travel to away matches, the game also regularly provides a set of ready-made opponents with whom to fight. Moreover, large crowds form a context where it is possible to behave violently and in other deviant ways with a relatively good chance of escaping detection and arrest.

Having said this, it would be wrong to view soccer hooliganism as always and everywhere a function solely or mainly of class. As a basis for further research, it is reasonable to hypothesize that the problem is contoured and fueled, *ceteris paribus*, by what one might call the major fault lines of a particular country. In England, that means class and regional inequalities and differences; in Scotland and Northern Ireland, religious sectarianism; in Spain, the partly language-based subnationalisms of the Catalans, Castilians, and Basques; in Italy, city-based particularism and perhaps the division between North and South as expressed in the formation of the Northern League; and in Germany, relations between the generations (Elias 1996) and those between East and West. Religious, subnational, city-based, regional, and generation-based fault lines may draw into football hooliganism more people from higher on the social scale than tends to be the case in England. Arguably, however, all of these fault lines—and, of course, each can overlap and interact with others in a variety of complex ways—share the characteristic of corresponding to what Elias (1994) called "established–outsider figurations," that is, social formations involving intense we-group bonds ("us") and correspondingly intense antagonisms toward outsiders or they-groups ("them").

The association of hooliganism with soccer is also partly a function of the greater worldwide media exposure that the game receives. Other sports do not get as much media coverage; accordingly, such violence as accompanies them is not so publicly apparent. The media also tend to generate myths, and these, too, contribute to public perceptions. For example, from the late 1920s to the mid-1960s, the occurrence of soccer hooliganism in Central and South America, continental Europe (especially the Latin countries), Scotland, Wales, and Northern Ireland was regularly reported in the English press, together with statements to the effect that such behavior "couldn't happen in England." However, unruly behavior had been rife at English soccer matches before the First World War and had never died out completely (Dunning, Murphy, and Williams 1988, 32–90). The 1960s saw the beginning of the emergence of present-day forms of English football hooliganism and media coverage which sometimes approached the levels of a moral panic. Since the 1990s, the national and local press have tended to underreport the English domestic problem of football hooliganism. Nevertheless, the problem continues to occur, though perhaps with less frequency and visibility than in the 1960s, 1970s, and 1980s.

## CONCLUSION

In this chapter, figurational theory has been used to analyze fan behavior in European football, or what North Americans refer to as *soccer*. The theory demonstrates its superiority to other perspectives and has withstood the scrutiny of scholars such as Leach (1986) and D. Smith (1984); its durability is also demonstrated by the rising popularity of figurational theory being used by globalists such as Maguire (1999, 2000). Inherent in the theory is the idea that power is a product of dependency and is subject to a shifting of ratios and balances, including physical size or intellectual prowess, not simply relationship to the means of production (Marx) or the ability to invoke violence (Weber).

### Suggested Research

1. Future research should move in the direction of reinforcing the utility of figurational theory and its ability to assess group process, explain abnormal British football fan behavior, and predict future occurrences of hooliganism.

2. Figurational theory should be tested on its ability to explain fan behavior among spectators of other sports (e.g., basketball, hockey) and in other countries (e.g., the United States, Italy, Afghanistan).

# Additional Resources

### Theory

Fletcher, J. 1997. *Violence and civilization: An introduction to the work of Norbert Elias.* Cambridge: Polity Press.

Fletcher takes a look at Norbert Elias and the "civilizing process," as well as violence. At the heart of the "civilizing process" is the concept of people's control and perception of violence and bloodshed.

Elias, N., and E. Dunning. 2009. *Quest for excitement: Sport and leisure in the civilizing process.* Oxford: Blackwell.

The founding father of figurational sociology lays out the theory and demonstrates that the emphasis is on human beings forming chains of interdependent relationships. These relationships show that individuals and society cannot be separated and that individuals are bound together on many levels and in many ways.

### Sport Topic

Foer, F. 2004. *How soccer explains the world: An unlikely theory of globalization.* New York: HarperCollins.

Soccer, like basketball, is an inexpensive sport—get a ball and a pair of sneakers, find a field, and anyone can play. Maybe this is why soccer is such a big sport in industrializing nations such as Brazil and Ecuador. Soccer has connected the world.

Allison, L., ed. 2005. *The global politics of sport: The role of global institutions in sport.* London: Routledge.

Allison argues for a reconsideration of a new century where international sport organizations such as the International Olympic Committee (IOC) or United European Football Association (UEFA) have gained power and become just as important as, if not more important than, nation-states. The author approaches organizations such as the International Olympic Committee as movers and brokers on the international sport scene.

Tony Triolo/Sports Illustrated/Getty Images

# 3 | Beyond the Sociological Imagination

## Doing Autoethnography to Explore Intersections of Biography and History

*Nancy E. Spencer, PhD*

---

**Social theory:** Sociological imagination

**Proponents of the theory:** C. Wright Mills, Zygmunt Bauman, Norman Denzin, Carolyn Ellis, Hans Gerth, Laurel Richardson, Robert Coles, Steven P. Dandaneau, Todd Gitlin, Arlie Hochschild, Studs Terkel

**What the theory says:** The sociological imagination requires a capacity of mind that enables its users to perceive connections between their personal biographies and historical conditions in which they live. C. Wright Mills believed that the sociological imagination was our most-needed quality of mind. He felt that one's intellectual journey was incomplete without coming to grasp the articulation between biography and history. Mills advocated keeping a file or journal to organize and document one's intellectual journey.

---

In arguably his best-known work, *The Sociological Imagination*, sociologist C. Wright Mills (1959/2000) admonished scholars to examine the intersection between personal problems (troubles) and social issues (history). Mills advocated using that special capacity of mind that he referred to as the "sociological imagination." In the 50 years since Mills' provocative text first appeared in print, the inspiration of his writing has exerted far-reaching influences that could hardly have been anticipated at the time. Although Mills' writing has subsequently been critiqued by generations of scholars, much of his work has passed the test of time and remains relevant to contemporary sociologists and critical thinkers in the new millennium.

In addition to influencing sociologists (Dandaneau 2000; Denzin 1989, 1990; Richardson, 1997), Mills' work has inspired sport sociologists, some of whom have applied their sociological imaginations to examinations of sport (Loy and Booth 2004; Theberge and Donnelly 1984). Although my initial exposure to Mills' work came when I was an undergraduate sociology major, his greatest influence upon me occurred when I began to read Norman Denzin's writings (1989, 1990) as a graduate student at the University of Illinois. In one particular class, I learned about interpretive interactionism, which Denzin (1989, x) formulated from his readings of the sociological imagination that were "biographical, interactional, and historical."

In his later work, Denzin (1990, 1) would seek "to dismantle and recast" the twin concepts of "the sociological imagination and lived, biographical experience," arguing instead for a "theoretically minimalist interpretive sociology" (p. 6). Denzin's call for minimalist social texts coincided with the emergence of interpretive or performance ethnographies (Denzin 1997, 2003) and autoethnographies (Bochner and Ellis 2002; Ellis 2004; Ellis and Bochner 2003; Richardson 1997, 2003).

Mills articulated his vision of the sociological imagination as providing a means to enable its users "to understand the larger historical scene in terms of its meaning for the inner life and the external career of a variety of individuals" (5). The lives of individual scholars were particularly important to Mills, who indicated that the best scholars "do not split their work from their lives" (195). In interpretive interactionism, Denzin (1989) also emphasized the importance of personal experience by suggesting that scholars should "attempt to make the problematic lived experiences of ordinary people" accessible to readers (xi). As a result, Denzin (1989) concluded that "persons with a sociological imagination self-consciously make their own experience part of their research" (71).

On the basis of the sociological imagination and interpretive interactionism, I perceived that my personal experiences as a former tennis professional were relevant to the questions I asked as a sport sociologist and to the ways in which I framed my research studies. In attempts to utilize the sociological imagination, I have employed several strategies to explore the intersections of biography and history. To explore biography, I have found it most useful to write personal narratives about my experiences in tennis. Denzin (1989, 15) initially referred to such personal narratives as "epiphanies" or "interactional moments that leave marks on people's lives"; he believed that writing epiphanies had "the potential for creating transformational experiences" for people. Denzin (1997) would later refer to such writings as "performance ethnographies."

In order to interrogate the historical conditions in which my personal experiences occurred, I have used textual analysis, or what has more recently been referred to as "reading sport critically" (Birrell and McDonald 2000; McDonald and Birrell 1998, 1999). Writing epiphanies and reading sport critically have enabled me to explore meanings of the personal (biography) and the public (historical), albeit in separate texts. In order to explore their intersections, I have most recently discovered the utility of autoethnography. Richardson (2003, 512) defines autoethnography as involving "highly personalized, revealing texts in which authors tell stories about their own lived experiences, relating the personal to the cultural." By connecting the personal to the cultural, writers are able to explore the intersection between history and biography. I have ultimately concluded that (for me) to utilize the sociological imagination means to do autoethnography.

In this chapter, I begin by briefly outlining C. Wright Mills' (1959/2000) articulation of the "sociological imagination" and providing illustrations of sport sociology scholarship that has been informed by Mills' concepts. Furthermore, I offer several studies in which I have used techniques of reading sport critically to explore specific historical conjunctures in professional women's tennis. In the first study (Spencer 1997), I examined the subculture of professional women's tennis as it progressed through the cycle of subcultural formation, that includes oppression, defusion, resistance, and incorporation (see Hebdige 1979). In the second study (Spencer 2000), I explored how the "Battle of the Sexes" tennis match between Billie Jean King and Bobby Riggs was interpreted differently when it occurred (during second-wave feminism) than when it was celebrated 25 years later amidst a third-wave feminist agenda. In a third study, I examined events that occurred at a tennis tournament in 2001, when the Williams sisters and their father, Richard, faced white racism at Indian Wells (Spencer 2004).

Each of these studies enabled me to probe historical conditions in which the events occurred—but absent personal narratives by the actors themselves. However, as I would subsequently discover, doing autoethnography allowed me to explore the intersections of personal biography and history in a single text, which I did in my presidential address at the annual conference of the North American Society for the Sociology of Sport (Spencer 2007). In that address, I shared stories about my firsthand encounters with Billie Jean King, as well as historical conditions in which those encounters occurred. My ultimate goal was to both consider and reconsider how we might come to a better understanding of the politics of community.

## SOCIOLOGICAL IMAGINATION

In 1959, C. Wright Mills forwarded the notion of the sociological imagination as a way to enable us "to grasp history and biography and the relations between the two within society" (6). Mills argued that unless scholars comprehend the intersection between history and biography, no study will have "completed its intellectual journey" (6). More specifically, the sociological imagination allows its users to see the distinction between "the personal troubles of milieu" and "the public issues of social structure" (8). Troubles are defined as occurring "within the character of the individual," whereas issues have to do with matters that transcend "local environments of the individual" (8). Ultimately, Mills felt that "neither the life of an individual nor the history of a society" could be "understood without understanding both" (3).

Even though Mills articulated his vision of the sociological imagination during that era of modernity known as the Cold War, he was one of the first sociologists to offer the notion of postmodernism (Dandaneau 2000; Denzin 1990). Forty years after Mills wrote of his vision, Dandaneau (2000: xiv) suggested that sociological thinking as advocated by Mills was still "the most needed form of self-consciousness in the emergent postmodern world," especially in light of the escalation of collective and individual problems confronting this era of postmodernity. Todd Gitlin (2000) found it remarkable that writing which appeared over 40 years ago remained as valid as ever. Within contemporary society, Richardson (1997, 15) believed that the promise of the "sociological imagination" provided a way to "give voice to silenced people, to present them as historical actors by telling their collective story."

Thus, in the years since Mills first offered the idea of the sociological imagination, scholars have continued to be informed by his work (Dandaneau 2000; Denzin 1989, 1990; Gitlin 2000; Richardson 1997). While some believe that the sociological imagination has not lost its relevance (Dandaneau 2000; Gitlin 2000), others suggest that it can no longer fulfill the promise it offered in 1959 (Denzin 1990). Recently Denzin (2003, xi) suggested that we employ a "critical sociological imagination" that enables us respond to our "successive crises of democracy and capitalism" in three ways: by critiquing repressive formations; by revealing how people can "bring dignity and meaning to their lives;" and by providing hope "for how things might be different, and better." In effect, Denzin advocated specific ways to apply the sociological imagination to contemporary cultural conditions.

## APPLYING THE SOCIOLOGICAL IMAGINATION TO RESEARCH

Given Mills' admonition to utilize the "sociological imagination," as well as the continuing relevance of its appeal, how then do scholars set about to apply it? How do we come to grasp the intersections between history and biography? Furthermore, how can we achieve this application within the same text? Although I have ultimately concluded that autoethnography provides the ideal way for me to do that, it has taken time for me to see *how* to be able to do it, especially in light of the barriers to doing certain kinds of research within academia. Thus, it has been a gradual process through which I have finally come to embrace this way of knowing and articulating the interface between biography and history—by doing autoethnography.

My first step in becoming open to autoethnography as an expression of the sociological imagination was through Denzin's (1989) articulation of interpretive interactionism. In a popular sociology class at the University of Illinois, Denzin introduced his interpretive framework by suggesting that we write epiphanies. I was among a large cohort of sport sociology students and faculty members who took his classes and became intrigued by this new way of writing. I found it both challenging and stimulating to attempt to write in this way. Previously, I had been discouraged from writing in the first person, and thus, it seemed risky to write myself into the text. Yet how better to explore the meanings of biography than through writing personal narratives? Denzin encouraged us to do so, noting that "we can only really write about ourselves" (personal communication 1993). That was fine for Denzin's class, but would it translate into publications in the "real" world?

It would not take long for me to discover that the "publish or perish" mantra still prevailed in academia. Three years into a tenure-track position, I met with the interim dean at my school and found myself explaining my dilemma about writing personal narratives. After I outlined the resistance I had encountered from certain faculty members, the interim dean suggested that perhaps I could do such writing as a "hobby." I was astonished to think that my efforts, which had been nurtured by colleagues and faculty at the University of Illinois, were not encouraged by faculty members in my new position. Perplexed by this discovery, I knew that I would need to find other ways to do research. Fortunately, the methodology of "reading sport critically" was presented at this time (Birrell and McDonald 2000; McDonald and Birrell 1998, 1999), and it provided a way for me to explore historical conditions through narratives, even though I would not appear explicitly in the texts.

In reading sport critically, McDonald and Birrell (1999, 283) offered a "new form of critical sport analysis" as a way to "conceptualize particular sporting events or celebrities as texts." Although this methodology had already been taken up by sport scholars (Cole and Andrews 1996; Jackson 1994, 1998), McDonald and Birrell (1999, 283) argued for greater "legitimacy" of this "particular way of doing cultural criticism." Informed more by developments in cultural studies than by Mills' articulation of the "sociological imagination," the method of reading sport critically nevertheless drew upon the importance of historical context to understand events that occurred in popular culture. Influenced also by the work of Foucault (1973), McDonald and Birrell (1999, 283) encouraged scholars to utilize this methodology as a means for "interrogating power."

Thus "reading sport critically" provided a way for me to scrutinize my personal investment in tennis by interrogating historical events that had occurred in that sport (Spencer 2000, 2004). Previously, I had explained how professional women's tennis became a site of celebrity as it progressed through what Dick Hebdige referred to as the cycle of subcultural formation, "proceeding from oppression to defusion and resistance to incorporation" (Spencer 1997, 284). I identified key events occurring between 1970 and 1973 that mapped onto Hebdige's notion of subculture. These included *oppression* of women's tennis by the United States Lawn Tennis Association (USLTA); the match between Billie Jean King and Bobby Riggs (*defusion*); emergence of a separate Virginia Slims tour (*resistance*); and the eventual merging of the Virginia Slims tour with the USLTA tour (*incorporation*). This process provided a framework for me to use in analyzing subsequent developments in professional women's tennis. In particular, I examined specific conjunctural moments: the "Battle of the Sexes" between King and Riggs in 1973 (Spencer 2000) and the Williams sisters' encounter with racism at Indian Wells in 2001 (Spencer 2004).

## Reading Between the Lines

The article "Reading Between the Lines" (Spencer 2000) was prompted by my observation of the extensive media coverage afforded to the tennis match between Billie Jean King and Bobby Riggs on the occasion of its 25th anniversary. The match, which was staged on September 20, 1973, occurred during the historical moment characterized by second-wave feminism. The contest, which pitted a 29-year-old woman (King) at the top of her game against a 55-year-old former Wimbledon champion-turned-hustler (Riggs), might not seem as if it would have garnered the ratings that it did; yet overnight Trendex ratings indicated that the match captured 52 percent of the viewing audience, meaning that 48 million Americans had tuned in to watch what turned out to be a media circus (Gallagher 1973). Many historians felt that the match resonated with people largely because it coincided with the zeitgeist of that era. In particular, radical feminism had begun to capture the imagination of mostly middle-class and white women (Echols 1993), many of whom could identify with Betty Friedan's now-classic *The Feminine Mystique*.

Despite the media attention focused on the "Battle of the Sexes" in the 1970s, few would have anticipated the kind of acclaim the match was given 25 years later. Yet in 1998 historians and journalists proclaimed that the match had produced far-reaching consequences for the culture at large. According to Richard Lapchick, King's victory over Riggs had translated into "victories for women in the board room, in higher education and in other areas of life" (qtd. in Hahn 1998, 25). Jennifer Frey, a journalist for the *Washington Post*, indicated that the results of "the King-Riggs match served to instill the belief that a woman could succeed in a man's world just as King did in 1973" (qtd. in Spencer 2000, 387). Feminist leader Gloria Steinem was more measured in her assessment of its effect, saying that the victory was more important for its symbolic impact than for actually changing the lives of women tangibly, as a law would do (Hahn 1998). On the subject of a law, King claims in retrospect that one reason she felt it was critical for her to win the match was that Title IX had just been passed and she saw a link between the two (personal communication, March 30, 2007).

Following McDonald and Birrell (1999), my critical reading of the King–Riggs match enabled me to glean an understanding of the historical context in which the event occurred, in contrast to the conditions in which the event was celebrated 25 years later. Occurring as it did in the midst of second-wave feminism, the match positioned King as the leading character to embody the meanings of the women's liberation movement. In her autobiography, she acknowledged that she was regarded as "the Feminist Athlete Doll" and was mentioned in the same breath as

Betty Friedan and Gloria Steinem (King and Deford 1982, 160–61). Yet the acclaim that appeared 25 years later had to be understood amidst third-wave feminism, an era that was regarded by some as postfeminist (Brooks 1997; Heywood and Drake 1997). In light of gains made during the women's liberation movement (the second wave), some thought that there was no longer a need for a women's movement and thus that feminism was "over." Reading sport critically enabled me to comprehend the proliferation of narratives written about this key conjunctural moment as it reflected the shift from second- to third-wave feminism.

## Sister Act VI: Venus and Serena at Indian Wells

In "Sister Act VI" (Spencer 2004), I explored the racial context of an incident that occurred in the aftermath of a semifinal match at Indian Wells in 2001 that would have been only the sixth time that Venus and Serena Williams were to play one another. Moments before the match that was to be aired live on ESPN, Venus announced that she would not be able to play due to an injury. While her default left tournament organizers scrambling to appease thousands of angry fans, that was nothing compared to the backlash that the Williams sisters and their father, Richard, would face two days later during the final. In this article, I described what occurred when Richard and Venus Williams entered a stadium full of booing fans to watch the singles final between Serena Williams and Kim Clijsters. Using the optic of white racism, I analyzed how this racialized incident made the persistence of racism visible within the space of professional women's tennis.

When Serena Williams was introduced for the women's singles final at Indian Wells, she was roundly booed, and the booing continued throughout the first three games, all of which Serena lost. The booing worsened upon the courtside arrival of Richard and Venus Williams as they entered the stadium to take their seats in the family box. Following the match, Richard reported that racial epithets were hurled at them as he and Venus attempted to take their seats, and that one fan yelled that if it were 1975, he would "skin him alive" (Smith 2001).[1] Indian Wells' tournament director Charlie Pasarell later responded that "if Richard says someone yelled something, maybe they did, but I know that's not Indian Wells people" (Smith, 2001, p. 1C). Some believed that the vitriolic response stemmed from reports suggesting that Richard may have fixed the 2000 Wimbledon semi-final match in which Venus defeated Serena ("Wimbldeon fixed?" 2001). Yet, even if fans felt justified in being

---

[1]There is in fact continuing disagreement about what actually happened at Indian Wells, and whose account ought to be believed. From Richard's, Venus', and Serena's perspectives, there clearly were racist epithets yelled. Some fans have acknowledged them as well. I strongly believe that such comments were said, based on what I observed of the match that was televised. At the time, the tournament director, Charlie Pasarell, stated that if Richard said that he heard such comments, that could have been true, but, they were not Indian Wells people. In my article, I interrogated that response from Charlie Pasarell, wondering why it was so important to distance "Indian Wells people" from racist epithets that may have been hurled. I recently showed footage of this match to one of my graduate classes, and they were appalled at the reception that Venus and Richard faced when entering the stadium to watch Serena play Kim Clijsters in the finals. From watching the clip, they understood fully why the Williams sisters have continued to boycott Indian Wells. Whether fans were motivated by the belief that Richard had fixed matches (which was only an allegation and has never been proved to be true--in fact, the CEO of the WTA has denied that there was any truth to those allegations), nonetheless, even if fans were suspicious, that does not justify such blatantly racist behavior. However, the issue has reached a stalemate that might have come to a head in this year's Indian Wells tournament since it became a required event.

upset, my perception was that there was no justification for the racialized incident that ensued. In "Sister Act VI," I pondered how we could understand the events that occurred at Indian Wells at a time when some scholars had gone so far as to suggest that "race was over."

Although Mills reportedly hated racism, Gitlin (2000) said that Mills "did not sufficiently apply his sociological imagination to the vexing, central problem of race" (239). Nonetheless, through the work of Feagin and Vera (1995), I discovered an explanation for how racism persisted in late-20th-century U.S. culture through "sincere fictions." Even though most whites adhere to the belief that they are not racists, the creation of sincere fictions may belie that belief. The creation of such mythologies occurs as follows:

> *Whites generally use these fictions to define themselves as "not racist," as "good people," even as they think and act in anti-Black ways. It is common for a White person to say, "I am not a racist," often, and ironically, in conjunction with negative comments about people of color. The sincere fictions embedded in White personalities and White society are about both the Black other and [italics in original] the White self (Feagin and Vera 1995, 14).*

Using the framework of white racism to analyze the racialized incident involving the Williams sisters at Indian Wells, I wanted to explore the historical conditions of that conjunctural moment. I was specifically interested in examining the response by Charlie Pasarell who also reported cringing at what he heard from fans during Serena's match. I believed that Pasarell's comment that these were "not Indian Wells people" illustrated an example of a "sincere fiction" based upon Feagin and Vera's description of how white racism operates. Nonetheless, reading sport critically and using the framework of white racism did not allow me to include the voices of the actors themselves.

## 15 Minutes of Fame: Doing Autoethnography

Even though I was able to examine issues (history) by reading sport critically, I had found only limited opportunities to write personal narratives that allowed me to explore my troubles (biography). Moreover, neither writing epiphanies nor reading sport critically had enabled me to analyze the *intersections* of biography and history within the *same* texts. As I learned more about autoethnography, I began to realize that perhaps I could merge the two within one text. For the 2007 North American Society for the Sociology of Sport (NASSS) conference in Pittsburgh, where I prepared to give the presidential address, I contemplated using that moment to present my ideas about doing autoethnography as a way to apply the sociological imagination. I titled my address "Fifteen Minutes of Fame: Billie Jean King, the 'Battle of the Sexes,' and the Politics of Community." In my presentation, I wove together my personal encounters with Billie Jean King with observations about the specific historical moments in which they occurred.

Given that NASSS was meeting near the Andy Warhol Museum, I drew upon Warhol's theorem about "15 minutes of fame," since calling the lines for the "Battle of the Sexes" had seemingly become *my* 15 minutes. Calling lines for the King vs. Riggs match required me to sit on the center service line where I judged whether the players' serves were in or out. At the time, I had no inkling that this match would become one of the most celebrated matches in sporting history. Yet I wanted to reach beyond that celebrated moment, and beyond understanding the historical conditions in which that match occurred. I wanted to reflect on the personal meanings it had for me. In reading the "Battle of the Sexes" critically, I had focused primarily on meanings of that match for Billie Jean King and for the culture at large. And yet, my voice was missing.

As I examined how to include my voice, Pirkko Markula emphasized to me that "it is necessary to have a voice and bring it to one's research writing to illustrate political, social, historical and cultural issues" (personal communication, August 10, 2007). I definitely wanted to be able to illustrate various issues, but I feared that *my* personal stories might seem irrelevant. Yet again, Pirkko encouraged me by explaining the efficacy of using autoethnography: "Autoethnographers use their personal experiences to understand larger social issues (about femininity, sport, politics, injustice, need for change). Therefore, the personal experience in itself is not the focus, but what it says about society, sport" (personal communication, October 27, 2007). Ultimately, is this not what Mills advocated when he suggested that we utilize the sociological imagination?

## APPLYING CRITICAL SOCIOLOGICAL IMAGINATION TO MY STUDIES

Following Denzin's admonition (2003, xvi) to utilize a "critical sociological imagination," I will report on how my research fits his three criteria. The first way in which a critical sociological imagination can respond to crises that shape our daily lives is by criticizing those formations that "repressively enter into and shape the stories and performances persons share with one another" (Denzin 2003, xvi). Therefore, in exploring the subcultural formation of women's tennis (Spencer 1997), I critiqued the incorporation of professional women's tennis that occurred between 1970 and 1974, as it became a repressive site that shaped the lives of those involved in it. Using a critical sociological imagination, coupled with Hebdige's (1979) theory of subcultural formation, I was able to see that women's tennis is no longer the site of resistance it once was.

The second reason for using a critical sociological imagination is to see "how people bring dignity and meaning to their lives" (Denzin 2003, xi). In my 2007 presidential address at NASSS, I employed autoethnography to explore one of the events that occurred in the process of subcultural formation—i.e., the "Battle of the Sexes." In "Reading Between the Lines" (Spencer 2000), I had acknowledged my participation in that historical moment only as a footnote. Yet my personal encounters with Billie Jean King were less memorable. In April 2007 I met the legendary King after she spoke at the City Club of Cleveland. In that unique moment when I wanted to say so many things, King appeared to be eager to complete her commitment and leave. In retrospect, I realize that because I was one of the last persons who stood in the way of finishing her obligation, I interpreted her interaction with me as abrupt. By writing and performing my presidential address as autoethnography, I was able to go beyond my "15 minutes of fame" to uncover personal meanings of multiple encounters with Billie Jean King within the larger scope of my life.

Finally, Denzin (2003, xi) suggests that using a critical sociological imagination might offer "kernels of utopian hope . . . for how things might be different, and better." That is what I hoped to demonstrate in writing "Sister Act VI" about the Williams sisters' encounter with white racism at Indian Wells. Although I was not present at the site when it happened, I watched in horror as the events unfolded on television. Angered by the vulgar actions of that crowd at Indian Wells, I felt certain that the tournament director would do something to address the behavior of the crowd. At the least, I thought, the Women's Tennis Association (WTA) would acknowledge the evidence of racist behavior at Indian Wells and confront what I perceived to be a problem of racism in tennis.

I felt that I must somehow voice my outrage and, I hoped, become part of the solution. I wanted to insert myself into that scenario but was unsure how to do so. Since I was halfway through the tenure-track process at the time, I used the only avenue available to me, which was to write "Sister Act VI". Through that article, I examined how white racism works historically and in contemporary circumstances through the operation of sincere fictions. In the future, I know that I can do more than document the historical conditions that exist within culture. Since I now believe that for me to utilize the sociological imagination is to do autoethnography, I know that I must become personally invested in what I critique. In that sense, I must find a way to confront racism such as occurred at Indian Wells.

## CONCLUSION

The sociological imagination has clearly informed my scholarship by pointing me toward autoethnography. Instead of doing scholarship as disparate ventures without overlap, I am able to explore intersections of biography and history within the same text. But I believe that Mills requires more of those who would employ the sociological imagination. More specifically, Mills (1959/2000) suggested that "the most admirable thinkers within the scholarly community . . . do not split their work from their lives" (195). This suggests to me that it is imperative to explore how I use the sociological imagination to understand my life. One of the ways in which I have attempted to do that most recently is by considering how to encourage students to employ the sociological imagination, so that they can explore the intersections between their personal biographies and historical conditions as well. Toward that end, I offer the following ideas for suggested research that may be useful for professionals as well as undergraduate and graduate students.

## Suggested Research

1. Doing autoethnography allows scholars to integrate studies that employ seemingly disparate techniques. By "reading sport critically," cultural critics of sport may use textual analysis as a way to analyze how power operates within our cultural milieu. Writing epiphanies, or doing performance ethnography, offers a means for writing personal (biographical) narratives. Doing autoethnography enables scholars to use the sociological imagination in one text, as Mills advocated.

2. Following Mills' admonition to keep a file or write a personal journal, scholars as well as students may find it useful to keep a journal (with personal

reflections) or a blog (making their personal reflections public). Such tools enable users to reflect upon ideas that occur to them while exploring connections between their personal biographies and historical conditions in which they live.

3. Writing epiphanies or personal narratives may be useful ways to encourage undergraduate or graduate students to begin to explore their biographies. Such an assignment in a history class may be followed by asking students to explore the historical circumstances of their lived biographies. In other words, they may consider how history helps them to write their biographies, while their personal biographies enable them to better comprehend history.

## Additional Resources

### Theory

Denzin, N.K. 1989. *Interpretive interactionism.* 2nd ed. Thousand Oaks, CA: Sage.

Denzin articulates his view of interpretive perspectives by advocating, among other things, the practice of writing epiphanies, a notion that he draws from Dostoyevsky. An epiphanic moment involves a moment of clarity that illuminates crisis; afterward, a person is never the same.

Denzin, N.K. 2003. *Performance ethnography: Critical pedagogy and the politics of culture.* Thousand Oaks, CA: Sage.

More recently, Denzin has sought to infuse traditional ethnography with an emphasis on performance that stems from the arts and humanities. Unlike traditional ethnography which seeks to inscribe culture as a way to increase awareness, performance ethnography utilizes performance of everyday rituals as a method of understanding.

Fuller, S. 2006. *The new sociological imagination.* London: Sage.

Fuller revisits key social theories and theorists, including Mills, in an attempt to formulate a vision of what a contemporary sociological imagination might look like. Fuller is ultimately motivated to identify social theories that create a utopian vision of heaven on earth.

Mills, C.W. 1959/2000. *The sociological imagination.* 40th anniversary ed. London: Oxford University Press.

In his classic text, Mills sought to inject humanist sensibilities into the social sciences by encouraging scholars to examine the intersections between the personal (biography) and the public (history).

Richardson, L. 1997. *Fields of play: Constructing an academic life.* New Brunswick, NJ: Rutgers University Press.

In this compelling work, Richardson writes about negotiating the often treacherous terrain of academia in order to nurture her voice and writing. She shares her academic struggles in the hope of encouraging others who face comparably challenging situations.

**Sport Topic**

Carrington, B. 2008. "What's the footballer doing here?" Racialized performativity, reflexivity, and identity. *Cultural Studies/Critical Methodologies* 8:423–52.

> Carrington revisits his earlier ethnographic work to explore complexities of "racial identity formation." He critiques autoethnography by articulating the limits to autobiographical texts absent consideration of historically grounded foundations that contribute to identity formation.

Rail, G., ed. 1998. *Sport and postmodern times.* Albany: SUNY Press.

> This anthology offers new ways of writing about sport that are informed by postmodern sensibilities. Such writings are informed more by cultural studies and postmodernist theories than by traditional social theories.

Giulianotti, R., ed. 2004. *Sport and modern social theorists.* New York: Palgrave MacMillan.

> This collection of articles includes accounts of key social theories and theorists, written by scholars in the sociology of sport who apply specific social theories to sport. In particular, Loy and Booth consider C. Wright Mills' writing pertaining to the craft of scholarship.

Jarvie, G. 2006. *Sport, culture, and society: An introduction.* New York: Routledge.

> Jarvie acknowledges the centrality of sport within contemporary society and examines how sport is interwoven with the fabric of local and global cultures. Jarvie ultimately uses sport as a way to understand the dynamics of social change.

Theberge, N., and P. Donnelly, eds. 1984. *Sport and the sociological imagination.* Fort Worth: Texas Christian University Press.

> This text contains articles that emerged from the third annual conference of the North American Society for the Sociology of Sport, held in Toronto in 1982. Specific sections of the text focus on topics including sport and popular literature, feminist analyses of sport, sport and social problems, and sport and social policy.

# PART

# Research Guided by Mid-Level Sociological Theories

Chapter contributions in part II address what Merton described as "theories of the middle range."[1]

## Sociology of Science

In this chapter, titled "The Sociology of Science: Sport, Training, and the Use of Performance-Enhancing Substances," Ian Ritchie argues "that in order to truly understand sport we must have an understanding of the social and historical contexts within which sport is practiced." To elaborate, Ritchie describes transformative changes in the ways in which athletes train for performance: "While one cannot pinpoint an exact date at which changes took place, it is safe to say that the mid-20th century was an important period that witnessed significant changes in the approaches that athletes, coaches, medical scientists, and others took to athletic training. Theories of science provide us with insight into how and why these changes occurred."

## Urban Political Economy and Urban Regime Theory

In her chapter, "Political Economy: Sport and Urban Development," Kimberly Schimmel argues that the conventional wisdom that sporting enterprise brings economic development to cities needs to be carefully scrutinized. In fact, she argues the opposite: "Scholars who study sport-related urban development, how-

---

[1] Sociologist Robert K. Merton developed his perspective of "middle range theories" in response to the "grand theorizing" of his mentor, Talcott Parsons. Merton firmly believed that middle range theory starts its theorizing with delimited aspects of social phenomena rather than with a broad, abstract entity such as society or the social system. He put it thus: "Sociological theory, if it is to advance significantly, must proceed on these interconnected planes: 1. by developing special theories from which to derive hypotheses that can be empirically investigated and 2. by evolving a progressively more general conceptual scheme that is adequate to consolidate groups of special theories." See *Social Theory and Social Structure*, chapter 2 ("Sociological Theories of the Middle Range"), p. 51.

ever, refute the notion that this type of civic investment provides real benefits for a city as a whole. Empirical evidence shows that while some groups in a city may profit, others are burdened." Using theories developed by urban sociologists Harvey Molotch, Joe Feagin, and others, Schimmel makes the case that the city of Indianapolis may not have received all the promised largess for becoming a major sport city in the Midwest.

## Institutional Logics

Using what is probably one of the most unusual theories addressed in this book, Southall and Nagel examine how an organizational theory—institutional logics theory—can be applied to the institution of sport as an organization. In their chapter, "Institutional Logics Theory: Examining Big-Time College Sport," they argue that "[w]ithin an organization or institution, institutional logics determine what practices and symbolic constructions—which constitute organizing principles available to organizations and individuals to guide the evaluation and implementation of strategies, establish routines, and create precedence for further innovation—are acceptable or unacceptable."

## Secularization Theory

In the fourth chapter of part II, "Playing for Whom? Sport, Religion, and the Double Movement of Secularization in America," David Yamane, Charles E. Mellies, and Teresa Blake examine the relationship between the secularizing of the institution of sport and the role of religion at both the institutional and individual levels inside sport. They argue that "we can see how sport as a social institution has been largely secularized, so that religious groups which seek to be effectively involved in sport are constrained to work in ways that articulate with and are accommodative of the reality of a secular society."

Keystone Pictures Agency/Zuma Press/Icon SMI

# 4 | The Sociology of Science

## Sport, Training, and the Use of Performance-Enhancing Substances

*Ian Ritchie, PhD*

---

**Social theory:** Sociology of science

**Proponents of the theory:** Robert Merton, Thomas Kuhn, Bruno Latour

**What the theory says:** The sociology of science is not just one theory but a body of theories that study the social context within which science is produced. The theories hold in common the contention that what is considered scientific "fact," as well as what is considered worthy of scientific study in the first place, are reflections of the social environment.

---

August 16, 1954, is an important date in the history of modern sport. On that date, the first issue of *Sports Illustrated* was published. The magazine would become the most recognized, widely read sports periodical in the English language, and it would have a dramatic influence on public perceptions of what was important in the world of high-performance professional and amateur sport in the latter half of the 20th century—and now into the early part of the 21st. Two articles stand out in that first issue.

In the magazine's first full-length feature article, Paul O'Neil described the recently run "Mile of the Century" race at the British Empire & Commonwealth Games between England's Roger Bannister and Australia's John Landy as "the most widely heralded and universally contemplated match foot-race of all time" (1954, 21). His description was likely not an exaggeration. The race's status was so high in part because Bannister had been the first to break the 4-minute-mile barrier at Oxford's Iffley Road Track in May of that year, only to have Landy break the record in a race in Finland in June. In addition, the world of sport in the 1950s was fixated on who would be the first man to break the 4-minute barrier (Bascomb 2004). The fascination with high-performance running, world records, and pushing the limits of human endurance was so great that *Sports Illustrated* made the Bannister–Landy confrontation the topic of its first ever full-length feature article.

A second article in the publication's first issue, this one authored by Gerald Holland and including information compiled by the magazine's editors, provides another revealing glimpse into the world of sport in the early 1950s. Titled "The Golden Age is Now" (1954, 46–52, 83–86, 91–94), this piece touts the 1950s as the second golden age of sport, following in the footsteps of an initial golden age in the 1920s. The article cites fan interest, media attention, financial payoffs, world-record-breaking performances, participation rates, and general popular fascination (and, no doubt, the magazine's self-validation was pertinent as well) as justification for its claim that the world was entering the next golden age. However, despite the article's generally positive tone, Holland does not let concerns regarding the extreme nature of Cold War competition—especially in the Olympic Games—escape readers' attention: "The Iron Curtain itself was forced to collaborate in a dramatic demonstration of what the human spirit could do," Holland ominously warns, then continues:

*Russia and her satellites had sent a new breed of athlete out into the free world. He was a superbly trained, coldly efficient, intensely suspicious fellow. He worked full time at sports, although he competed as an amateur, and he swiftly built up a legend of invincibility (48).*

Although Holland's description of the Russian überathlete resorts to hyperbole, he was prescient in his warning of the coming tensions of "Cold War sport," in which nations would compete for political supremacy and push the human body to increasingly rarified heights of strength and endurance. Thus *Sports Illustrated* was reiterating George Orwell's 1945 warning that sport had become "war minus the shooting" (Orwell 2003, 198), wherein athletes acted as the central combatants in the emerging conflict.

These two articles in the first edition of *Sports Illustrated* highlight three points. First, sport in the 1950s was in a dramatic state of transition, one reflected particularly in Holland's comments. However, no one could fully anticipate the full extent of the changes that would occur in the ensuing Cold War years, when human performance would be pushed beyond anything imaginable in those early days. Second, the manner in which athletes trained their bodies to perform was also changing dramatically—not only in terms of hours spent, training intensity, usage of scientific discoveries and technological advances to perform, and the like, but also in terms of a new, emerging approach to how the human body functioned under training and performance stress. In short, a new ontology of performance was emerging (Beamish and Ritchie 2005). Contrary to Holland's suggestion, however, this new ontology was not limited to the "coldly efficient" Russian athletes. Ironically, as we will see later in this chapter, none other than Roger Bannister, who considered himself one of the last few bastions of pure amateurism and who lamented creeping professionalism in sport, represented the coldly efficient new form of athlete who, as readily as any Russian athlete, would use virtually any means possible to break physical barriers (Bascomb, 2004; Beamish and Ritchie 2006, 59–60, 136–37; Bale 2004).

Finally, and most relevant to this chapter and to the topic of using social theory to understand sport, the transitions in performance and training to which the first issue of *Sports Illustrated* referred remind us that sport, contrary to common perceptions, does not have any single, static, universal "truth." It is a constantly changing social enterprise that is both shaped by and a shaper of the social and cultural world around it. For sociologists, this point is taken for granted, but in popular culture there remains a commonly accepted axiom that sport has essential, universal elements that remain unchanged over time and between cultures. Contrary to this axiom—this myth—sport, and modern sport specifically, as historian Bruce Kidd summarizes, should be "understood best as distinct creations of modernity, fashioned and continually refashioned in the revolutionizing conditions of industrial capitalist societies" (Kidd 1996, 12). One of the central purposes of sociological theories is to denaturalize sport—in other words, to bring to light the fact that in order to truly understand sport we must have an understanding of the social and historical contexts within which sport is practiced (Ritchie 2008).

This chapter highlights this point by looking at how one specific body of theory affects our understanding of two important issues in the modern world of high-performance sport: (1) training and how assumptions about the human body have changed over time, and (2) the use of performance-enhancing substances.[1] The body of theory in question is the sociology of science. It is impossible to summarize the huge body of literature in this area. Instead, this chapter presents a brief summary of some important theories and studies which remind us that, while many people think of science as consisting of an accumulation of facts, the making of important discoveries, and the advancement of knowledge based on generally accepted scientific methods, the production of knowledge in real-life scientific settings is a far more complex matter. Careful sociological analyses of science demonstrate that over time science carries with it social and cultural assumptions and that those assumptions influence the practice of science, its findings, and indeed the very choice of what is worthy of study in the first place. Science is a social institution just like any other social institution and is therefore the subject of careful sociological study.

One scientific doctrine is considered here as an example of how the sociology of science allows us to better understand its subject matter; that doctrine is the conservation of energy. The final sections of this chapter discuss how theories in the sociology of science help us understand the conservation of energy and, in turn, how that doctrine influenced sport and the ways in which "training" practices in sport changed in the 20th century. This background also helps us understand the present-day issue of the use of performance-enhancing substances.

## THEORIES IN THE SOCIOLOGY OF SCIENCE

It may be taken for granted by many today that science plays an important role in society and that there is a body of experts rigorously studying various aspects of the natural, the physical, and perhaps even the social world, but the practice of science is a relatively new phenomenon in human history. Moreover, it is only relatively recently that the three main humanities and social science disciplines

---

[1] In this chapter, the common terms *drug*, *drugs*, and *doping* are avoided. Although these are generally accepted popular terms—and ones used by people and organizations fighting the use of performance-enhancing substances—they are in fact ideological terms, and they come loaded with assumptions. For one, not all substances and practices included in the World Anti-Doping Agency's formal banned list are drugs per se. Second, the terms *drugs* and *doping* evoke an image of social or recreational drug users in society in general and therefore demonize or automatically label the users as deviant. Strictly speaking, however, the issues of drug use in society in general and the use of (banned) performance-enhancing substances and practices, while similar in some respects, involve for the most part very different questions. Finally, the historical and sociological literature seriously undermines the legitimacy of the organizations that police substance use in sport—especially the World Anti-Doping Agency—and the assumptions upon which their prohibitions are based. See Beamish and Ritchie (2006) and Dimeo (2007).

[2] Obviously, this chapter concentrates on sociological studies of science. However, there is much overlap between the three disciplines of philosophy, history, and sociology in terms of their approaches to the study of science. If, however, generalizations can be made regarding their respective approaches, they are as follows: history has tended to focus on the genesis and progression over time of the various scientific subdisciplines and important figures, and there has been a specific focus on the scientific revolution itself; philosophy has tended to focus on the underlying principles or "rules" of science and scientific methodology; and sociology has tended to focus on the norms of scientific practice and the structure of scientific institutions. See Bowler and Morus (2005) and Eriksson (2007, 4097).

that study science and have formulated theories about the past and present practice of science—history, philosophy, and sociology[2]—have generated their theories. Indeed, the coordinated body of work in the sociological study of science started only in the 1950s, after which time it experienced a period of limited growth until the 1970s, when new studies in laboratory life and in what became known as the "sociology of scientific knowledge" emerged, leading to a greater state of maturity in the discipline (Eriksson 2007; Storer 1973).

Most studies of science in general begin with at least some reference to the "scientific revolution" itself. The term refers to a 17th-century social movement that included a series of important discoveries and new methods for thinking about and studying the world and the heavens. More generally, it was the beginning of a whole new world view in which people's understanding of the world, the universe around them, and their place in the cosmos was dramatically redefined. Undoubtedly, the discoveries and writings of Galileo Galilei, Tycho Brahe, Johannes Kepler, René Descartes, Robert Boyle, Francis Bacon, Isaac Newton, and many others were immensely important. However, while there is no question that what scientists said and did in the 17th century challenged the existing authority structure and, to some degree, existing assumptions about the world and people's place in it, the assumed importance of the "revolutionary" changes is now widely debated. First, recent historical scholarship has demonstrated that what 17th-century "revolutionaries" thought of their own crafts was likely far different from what we today think of as "science." Second, it is now believed that there was much more in common between medieval ideas and the "new" science than most historians in the past recognized. Finally, there was certainly no agreed-upon scientific method that suddenly emerged in the 17th century; indeed, some claim that agreements regarding the appropriate methods for studying the natural and physical world scientifically did not really emerge until as late as the 20th century (Bowler and Morus 2005, 23–53; Shapin 1996).

Three major figures—Robert Merton, Thomas Kuhn, and Bruno Latour—and their seminal works highlight the historical trajectory of theories in the sociology of science, as well as the general ways in which sociology understands and critically analyzes science. The first—and likely most important—figure is the famous American sociologist Merton. Treated in virtually all standard introductory texts for his work in the theory of functionalism and his introduction of "manifest" and "latent" functions (Merton 1957, 19–84), Merton is less well known by general readers in sociology for his work in the sociology of science. That work, however, is no less important, and Merton spent much of his career studying science.

Writing in the 1930s, during the rise to power of Adolf Hitler and National Socialism in Germany, Merton was part of a growing movement of concerned scientists and other intellectuals who were carefully monitoring the emergence of "Nazi science," or Nazi-inspired scientific practices and findings that publicly deplored "Jewish" or "non-Aryan" science while explicitly supporting science that furthered the cause of National Socialism. Merton voiced these concerns in a paper published in 1938 titled "Science and the Social Order" (1973, 254–266), which both deplored the use of science in totalitarian regimes, specifically under fascism in Germany, and defended the autonomy of science in liberal democratic societies (Storer 1973; Turner 2007). Merton would go on to expand the definition of this autonomy in a famous paper published in 1942 by specifying four "norms" that for him constituted the necessary means by which science must be conducted in order to maintain its independence and objectivity. Merton's four norms are as follows: universalism, or the ideal that scientific claims should be based on general objective criteria and not personal attributes of the claim maker; communism, or the ideal that scientific findings should be considered the "property rights" of the community at large and not of the individual scientist; disinterestedness, or the ideal that scientists should not skew findings to cater to "clients" who might not have impartial motives; and, finally, organized skepticism, or a "suspension of judgment" and a level of detachment in terms of the criteria used in scientific inquiry (Merton 1973, 267–78).

Merton's work was groundbreaking in the discipline of sociology. It ushered in decades of work based, first, on the notion that whether science is meeting its objectives or not depends upon the more general social confines in which science is practiced—the "norms" of scientific inquiry (and certainly race, in particular, was for Merton an important factor that should not influence scientific objectivity, given his and others' criticisms of science under National Socialism in Germany); and, second, on Merton's more general claim that social environment (*social* being an umbrella term within which we should also include political and economic environments), whether it be totalitarian or liberal democratic, or, for that matter, another sociopolitical context, can determine what constitutes "acceptable" science and scientific findings. At the same time, Merton's work was criticized on a number of fronts, most importantly for its idealization of science in liberal democratic societies, a position that became more difficult to defend as time wore on after the War and scientific communities in such societies were clearly influenced by commercial, state, and other interests (Turner 2007, 4111). Nevertheless, Merton's work opened the way for future works in the sociology of science, and thus he should be considered a "father" of the area.

Merton's position was challenged by the second crucial figure in the sociology of science to be considered here—Thomas Kuhn, whose *The Structure of Scientific Revolutions*, published in 1962, is likely the most important single text produced in the sociology (and history) of science. It shifted the focus away from the immediate day-to-day norms of scientific inquiry and the study of "proper" methods that scientists should follow and toward much broader historical trends. Scientists, Kuhn claimed, follow conventions or "paradigms" in which there are a series of assumptions and guidelines—some explicitly stated, some not—that form the basis for scientists' questions and studies within a particular discipline. Scientific world views operate smoothly as long as there is consensus regarding findings and a community of supporters to buttress the paradigm, but inevitably science encounters crisis moments in which enough counterevidence, alongside personal and institutional support, creates conditions conducive to scientific revolution and substantial change. Far from the belief in science as a series of "factual" discoveries in an ongoing effort to achieve greater and greater truth and knowledge, Kuhn claimed that science occurs as a series of discontinuities. At the height of a paradigm's influence, the "normal science" that results involves scientists' "puzzle solving," in which the relatively minute and specific problems within the paradigm are studied but the assumptions underlying the discipline are not questioned (Kuhn 1970; Stanfield and Wrenn 2007).

Kuhn's groundbreaking work was followed by a period of increased scholarship and theoretical sophistication, from the 1970s onward, involving inquiry into the specific social conditions under which science is produced, in particular in the emerging subdisciplinary area of the "sociology of scientific knowledge" (Eriksson 2007). One important branch within that area became known as "laboratory studies" and included the third important study. French philosopher Bruno Latour spent almost 2 years acting as a participant-observer in a neuroendocrinology laboratory in California and, alongside English sociologist Steve Woolgar, produced *Laboratory Life: The Social Construction of Scientific Facts* (Latour and Woolgar 1979). Latour and Woolgar supported, to a great degree, Kuhn's points about the production of "paradigmatic" scientific knowledge while demonstrating that Merton's idealized norms might be little more than a pipe dream because of how science is practiced in its real institutional settings. Latour's 2-year observation demonstrated that scientists produce copious amounts of inconclusive data, which are explained away as the fault of either bad equipment or bad methodologies in order to remain consistent with scientific projects' original theories and premises. Scientists learn how to selectively and subjectively keep some results while discarding others; otherwise, nonsensical data gradually but systematically become accepted scientific "facts." In Latour's and Woolgar's words:

> *Despite [scientists'] well-ordered reconstructions and rationalizations, actual scientific practice entails the confrontation and negotiation of utter confusion. The solution adopted by scientists is the imposition of various frameworks by which the extent of background noise can be reduced and against which an apparently coherent signal can be presented (36–37).*

The theories and studies presented here only scratch the surface of those in the sociology of science,[3] but the most important point to get out of this brief description of the seminal works of Merton, Kuhn, and Latour and Woolgar is that in recent times theories of science have increasingly pointed toward the necessity to consider social and cultural life as an integral part of science. Science does not act alone or in a vacuum, nor does it necessarily produce a series of facts while working its way toward greater truth and knowledge about the world. One very important scientific doctrine—the conservation of energy, and the manner in which it influenced training in sport in the past—provides an important example.

## SPORT AND THE SCIENCE OF TRAINING: THE CONSERVATION OF ENERGY AND BEYOND

Many people today assume that athletes in the past trained to compete in more or less the same way they do today; that is, there is a general assumption that athletes have always used the most efficient training knowledge and methods of the day to enhance performance. History, however, tells us something different. The manner in which athletes train today is a reflection of relatively recent changes in the

---

[3] For a recent discussion of the sociology of science, see Bourdieu's treatment (2004, especially pages 4–31) of Merton, Kuhn, and Latour and Woolgar, as well as others in the classic tradition of sociology of science.

world of sport. While one cannot pinpoint an exact date at which these changes took place, it is safe to say that the mid-20th century was an important period that witnessed significant changes in the approaches that athletes, coaches, medical scientists, and others took to athletic training. Theories of science provide us with insight into how and why these changes occurred.

Sport historian John Hoberman (1992) has provided insight into the world of training in the 19th century and how vastly different it was from training today. Hoberman demonstrates that the origins of performance enhancement as we know it today can be traced to the bonds formed between biomedical scientists and athletes in the last few decades of the 19th century. During most of the 19th century, scientists were not interested in helping athletes perform—they cared little about how well athletes did on the tracks, in the swimming pools, on their bikes, in their rowing shells, and so on. The reason for this, as Hoberman shows, is that scientists were interested in studying athletes to discern the biological and physiological effects on people who put their bodies through physical extremes. They were, in other words, interested in learning the biophysiological "truths" of the human body and in discovering the manner in which the human body as a whole functioned. As Hoberman says, "scientists who turned their attention to athletic physiology during the late 19th and early 20th centuries did so not to produce athletic wonders but to measure and otherwise explore the biological wonders presented by the high-performance athlete of this era" (8).

Another important reason that scientists were not interested in boosting athletes' performances—a reason not discussed by Hoberman—was the influence of the scientific doctrine of the conservation of energy in the 19th century. It is important to carefully consider the conservation of energy because it was a central doctrine in the development of the history of modern, scientific thought. Its central tenets were carried over into assumptions about the nature of social and cultural life—about the nature of people, their actions, and their ways of life—and the doctrine had an important effect on sport and on assumptions about the ways in which athletes should train to become more efficient in their respective events.

Simplified greatly, the law of the conservation of energy states that energy can be transformed from one system to another but cannot be created or destroyed—the total amount of energy must remain static. The original impetus for the discovery of the conservation of energy occurred between the 1820s and 1850s, in what Kuhn refers to as a fairly remarkable case of "simultaneous discovery" by scientists in Germany, France, and England, the most important of whom were James Prescott Joule, William Robert Grove, Michael Faraday, Julius Robert von Mayer, and Hermann von Helmholtz (Kuhn 1962; Bowler and Morus 2005, 79–102). The original experiments in the conservation of energy developed out of concerns with mechanical operations of machines such as the steam engine, but research debates expanded into concerns with the mechanics of the forces of nature more generally and, eventually, to human beings and the functioning of their bodies and minds.

Two points are crucial in understanding the influence of the conservation of energy. First, far more was at stake than the efficient development of machines, as important as that motive was at the height of the Industrial Revolution. Equally important, scientists were motivated to discover the general laws of nature as a whole and, ultimately, God's role in the creation of the world:

*The concern with engines and the interest in conversion processes were both aspects of the same preoccupation with getting work out of nature as efficiently as possible. . . . [T]here was a theological motive to all this. It made sense that the Creator had designed the natural economy as efficiently as possible (Bowler and Morus 2005, 85–86).*

Second, the "natural economy" extended to an understanding of the functioning of the human organism, and comparisons were frequently made between machines and the forces of nature, on the one hand, and human beings and their bodies on the other. "As the power to work is without question the most important of the products of animal life," German physiologist Mayer wrote in the mid-19th century, "the mechanical equivalent of heat is in the very nature of things destined to be the foundation for the edifice of a scientific physiology" (cited in Russett 1989, 107).

For sport and athletic training, the influence of the conservation of energy was critical. While athletes certainly trained in the late 19th and early 20th centuries, the term *training* was synonymous with *drill*, signifying the repetition of skills and movements to refine athletic technique and improve precision. From the turn of the century to as late as the mid-20th century, training and physical education manuals did not generally promote training programs designed to systematically boost or enhance the body's overall ability to generate power, speed, or endurance. Under the influence of the conservation of energy, the body was instead treated like a well-oiled machine with a fixed and limited capacity (Beamish and Ritchie 2005; Beamish and Ritchie 2006, 52–59). It would take years before this institutionalized mind-set experienced dramatic changes. Thus, despite the fact that experiments in human physiology dating back to the 1920s and 1930s demonstrated that the human body's overall energy could be expanded through systematic, specified, overload training, these basic principles—ones taken for granted today—were not applied until the Cold War created social and political conditions conducive to the progression of modern "high-performance" training. As Hoberman says, scientists "were preoccupied with discovering human potential rather than initiating attempts to modify it. Performance-enhancement meant tapping the hereditary potential of the human or animal organism rather than artificially manipulating the organism itself" (Hoberman 1992, 98). Following Kuhn, it would take a new social environment, of which Cold War Olympic sport was the most important element, to create a new paradigm of training and human performance, in which new scientific institutional settings—thus a new "normal science"—were created to enhance the athletic body's performance potential.[4]

---

[4] Discussion of the effects of the Cold War on sport and training is clearly beyond the scope of this chapter. For in-depth treatments, see Hoberman (1992), Beamish and Ritchie (2006), and the articles in Wagg and Andrews (2007). In terms of the new institutionalization of medical science applied to sport, Mignon writes that the 1960s "saw the emergence of a new type of individual, the 'trained athlete,' different psychologically and physiologically from the man in the street. There also developed medical routines specific to the sport person, with specific treatments for specific injuries, but also specific care for preparation. This went hand in hand with the development of medical staff as a necessary condition of sports preparation: biomechanics for exercises and massages; nutritional scientists for vitamins and complements; psychologists for personal discipline and meditation; pharmacologists for the use of different medicines on the market. This rationale could also come to encompass non-medical uses of medicine such as steroids, analgesics, stimulants or tranquilisers" (2003, 233).

The full influence of the transition to a new paradigm of human performance is clearly reflected in the running career of Roger Bannister. On one hand, Bannister lamented the appearance of a "new professionalism" in sport, "not only in the sense of direct and indirect payment for sport, but also in devoting unlimited time and energy to sport, to the total exclusion of any other career" (Bannister 1964, 71–72). Yet, ironically, Bannister did as much as any other single athlete to push sport toward the new form of professionalism he so condemned. Bannister used the most advanced technology, medical and scientific discoveries, and training regimens available in the 1950s. Realizing that the 4-minute barrier would not fall without the most up-to-date performance aids, Bannister used new "fartlek" and interval training methods; specially made lightweight shoes with spikes and graphite soles; pacemakers; and even the application of his working knowledge in human physiology, based in part on oxygen-enriched treadmill experiments he performed on himself and others. With a medical degree and a master's degree in physiology, Bannister pushed the boundaries of scientific knowledge of human performance; his approach, as Bascomb describes, was "decidedly scientific":

> *Few had examined the human body's capacity to withstand punishment as Roger Bannister had. . . . Arterial $pCO_2$, blood lactate, pulmonary ventilation, carotid chemoreceptors, oxygen mixes, hyperpnea, and gas tensions—this was how Bannister described the effects of training on his body (Bascomb 2004, 90).*

Bannister even wrote two papers, "The Carbon Dioxide Stimulus to Breathing in Severe Exercise" and "The Effects on the Respiration and Performance During Exercise of Adding Oxygen to the Inspired Air" (Bascomb 2004, 90–91). Bannister, in short, is perhaps more emblematic of the new paradigm of human performance than any other single individual.

While the "fixed energy" days of training in sport are long gone, the brief historical account presented here serves as a reminder of how much "sport" has changed within the last century alone. Using social theory and some of the basic premises of the sociology of science encourages us to think critically about changes that have occurred. From the late 19th century to the mid-20th century, scientists had one set of "truths" about how the body should be trained or should not be trained. Scientists from the mid-20th century on, however, have had a distinctly different set of assumptions. Neither was necessarily "right," but in both cases the social and political environment created the conditions that determined the underlying set of assumptions about what should "naturally occur" in the world of sport.

## UNDERSTANDING THE USE OF PERFORMANCE-ENHANCING SUBSTANCES

While it might not appear that the brief history of the emergence of a new paradigm of human performance presented here is relevant to the use of performance-enhancing substances in sport, there are in fact critical links, and two of them stand out.

First, the new paradigm of intensified competition and the use of scientific training methods to expand human performance potential, on the one hand, and the use of performance-enhancing substances to increase that same potential, on the other hand, both emerged out of the same conditions and the same social "logic." The decades immediately following World War II were critical ones. Several developments combined to forever change the nature of sport: the entry of the Union of Soviet Socialist Republics into the Olympic Games in 1952; the postwar partitioning of Germany and accelerated competition between the newly formed Federal Republic of Germany and German Democratic Republic; the intensified state-run or combined state- and privately run sport systems that emerged in Eastern Bloc and Western Bloc nations, respectively; the heightened awareness of Olympic competition, owing in part to television coverage and advancements in television technology; the new commercial motivations for sporting success; an accelerated emphasis on world records as a reflection of national prestige; and a general desire to push the limits of human performance. While the new paradigm of training was one reflection of these and other factors in the postwar era, so too national sport systems in Eastern and Western Bloc countries, coaches, sport administrators, sport physicians, and other medical practitioners, as well as athletes themselves, turned to performance-enhancing substances in several sports. And while today many consider it an inherent "truth" that the use of performance-enhancing substances is contrary to the fundamental principles or ethos of sport, in the immediate postwar era there was little moral condemnation of that sort. The use of performance-enhancing substances was part and parcel of this accelerated emphasis on extending the limits of human performance, and while the International Olympic Committee acted to prohibit certain substances and practices in the 1960s, the fact that those enhancers were part of the same fundamental structure and logic of "sport" in the postwar era has led to contradictions in the rules and prohibitions against performance enhancers that continue to the present day (Beamish and Ritchie 2006; Dimeo 2007).

Second, the fundamental justification for the prohibition of performance-enhancing substances is that those substances contradict the essential purity, essence, or, in the vernacular of the World Anti-Doping Agency (WADA), the "spirit" of sport. As WADA's code says in no uncertain terms in a section titled "Fundamental Rationale for the World Anti-Doping Code," "Anti-doping programs seek to preserve what is intrinsically valuable about sport. This intrinsic value is often referred to as the 'spirit of sport'; it is the essence of Olympism" (WADA 2003, 3). The claim that the use of performance-enhancing substances contradicts the "intrinsic value" or "spirit of sport" is based on an assumption that sport has a transhistorical and ideal form or "essence." In reality, however, this assumption is misguided. First, sociologists are acutely aware of the fact that sport varies between cultures and over time; sport is an ever-changing enterprise, and the values that surround sport today are different—often vastly different—from those that pervaded sport during, say, ancient, medieval, or early industrial times, and, as we have seen, the values of "training" have varied considerably within the last century alone.

Also, if sport had an eternal essence and if it was so plainly obvious that the use of certain performance-enhancing substances contradicted the "spirit" of sport, rules would have existed in the past to prohibit those substances. Good scholarship in sport history and sport sociology, however, has shown that the last 40 years or so represent an entirely unique era in terms of attitudes toward the use of performance enhancers. While different substances were used in the early 20th century, the late 19th century, and as long ago as ancient times, when the original Olympic Games were first held in Greece (776 BCE–393 CE), there is no evidence that rules existed to prohibit the use of those substances or, more important, that there was any general moral condemnation or public outcry when athletes were thought to be taking substances to boost their performances (Dimeo 2007; Waddington 2005; Yesalis and Bahrke 2002). Recent scholarship has only begun to unpack the history of, and reasons for, the prohibition of certain substances in international sport in the postwar era (Beamish and Ritchie 2006; Dimeo 2007).

## CONCLUSION

The sociological study of training presented in this chapter, one informed by the sociology of science, has demonstrated that, even within the last century, sport has changed—and changed dramatically—in terms of scientific approaches to training and understanding of the "normal" functions of the body in general and, more specifically, the performance of the human body in sport. Like other theoretical perspectives used in sociology, the sociology of science provides enlightened perspectives that allow us to understand sport in terms of its social environment. Despite the fact that authors O'Neil and Holland described important events in the changing world of sport in the 1950s in the first edition of *Sports Illustrated,* they could not come anywhere close to imagining the full, dramatic changes that would occur in sport's future. And, while sociological theory can never fully anticipate sport's future or even fully explain past events, this chapter demonstrates that understanding one theoretical tradition—the sociology of science—gives us significant insight into some of the important factors underlying sport's dramatic changes over time.

## Suggested Research

1. Following Kuhn, scholars might examine long-term paradigm changes in the application of science to sport and what those changes reveal in terms of social and political dimensions of sport, as well as ethical dilemmas.

2. Following Latour and Woolgar, scholars might study specific institutional settings in which sport is studied from a scientific perspective and in which sport practices, especially high-performance training and competition, are altered based on scientific findings.

3. Following Merton, scholars might explore specific sociopolitical contexts in which sport science is practiced and how those contexts manifest themselves in the norms of scientific practice.

## Additional Resources

### Theory

Bowler, P.J., and I.R. Morus. 2005. *Making modern science: A historical survey.* Chicago: University of Chicago Press.

Bowler and Morus provide an excellent survey of major events and issues in the philosophy and history of science, including a history of major scientific disciplines and discoveries.

Kuhn, T.S. 1970. *The structure of scientific revolutions*. 2nd ed., enlarged. Chicago: University of Chicago Press.

> A classic in the history and philosophy of science, Kuhn's book focuses on broad historical trends in science, in which paradigmatic assumptions form the basis for scientists' questions and studies within a particular discipline.

Latour, B., and S. Woolgar. 1979. *Laboratory life: The social construction of scientific facts*. London: Sage.

> Based on a 2-year participant-observer study of a neuroendocrinology laboratory in California, Latour and Woolgar demonstrate that scientists explain away or rationalize inconclusive data in order to remain consistent with scientific projects' original theories and premises.

Merton, R.K. 1973. *The sociology of science: Theoretical and empirical investigations*. Chicago: University of Chicago Press.

> Merton is the most important figure in the historical development of the sociology of science, and in this classic functionalist account he highlights the norms of scientific inquiry.

## Sport Topic

Beamish, R., and I. Ritchie. 2005. From fixed capacities to performance-enhancement: The paradigm shift in the science of "training" and the use of performance-enhancing substances. *Sport in History* 25:412–33.

> Beamish and Ritchie narrate details of significant changes in early to mid-20th century sport in which scientific approaches to athletic training shifted from ones based on assumptions of the "fixed capacity" nature of the human body to ones based on the idea of unlimited production of energy.

Hoberman, J. 1992. *Mortal engines: The science of performance and the dehumanization of sport*. Toronto: Free Press.

> Hoberman recounts late-19th- and early-20th-century studies of athletes, demonstrating that biomedical scientists were not interested in boosting athletic performance until the appropriate sociopolitical context emerged, much later in the 20th century, and encouraged them to do so.

Yesalis, C.E., and M.S. Bahrke. 2002. History of doping in sport. *International Sports Studies* 24:42–76.

> A good general historical account of drug use in sport from the 19th century through the 20th century.

# 5 | Political Economy

## Sport and Urban Development

*Kimberly S. Schimmel, PhD*

---

**Social theory:** Urban political economy and urban regime theory

**Proponents of the theory:** Harvey Molotch, John Logan, Clarence N. Stone

**What the theory says:** Urban development is fraught with conflict concerning the use of space. The burdens and benefits of urban development are unequally distributed, and politics and human agency matter in the economic and development outcomes of cities.

---

If you look around almost any city in the United States today, it is difficult not to notice sport. Sports fans don the jerseys and hats of teams, thus advertising the city and connecting the team to the territory. Domed stadiums dot the skylines of urban areas and proclaim a city's "big league" status. Even in small towns, local chambers of commerce place road signs that announce to visitors that the town is "Home of the Champions" in some type of sport. Government subsidies of high school and college sports are anchored, in part, in the belief that success in sport brings recognition to host cities and creates a sense of solidarity among local citizens (Coakley 2007). This rationale extends to elite-level sport as well. One of the reasons that state and local tax monies are invested in professional team franchises is the belief that they serve as catalysts for civic community building. Sport mega-events serve similar functions at a global level. Cities spend enormous amounts of money to bid on and host large, high-profile sport events as a way to promote a city's "image" to the rest of the world. Sports stadium and infrastructure construction are connected to urban regeneration schemes through the belief that elite sports teams and events stimulate the local economy and create jobs.

Scholars who study sport-related urban development, however, refute the notion that this type of civic investment provides real benefits for a city as a whole. Empirical evidence shows that while some groups in a city may profit, others are burdened (Schimmel 1995, 2001, 2006). The rich, diverse literature of sport studies explores the connections between sport and city, including analyses of how sport has been used by urban elites in pursuit of nonsporting goals such as place promotion and real estate development. The overarching theoretical perspective for examining the effects of political decision making upon urban development, however, is found in urban studies. In the next section, I present a brief overview of the urban political economy paradigm within urban studies and highlight the position of urban regime theory within the paradigm. I then provide an example of regime theory application and extension in sport studies research.

## URBAN POLITICAL ECONOMY AND URBAN REGIME THEORY

The term *political economy* refers to a broad scholarly paradigm in which scholars from a wide range of disciplines and subdisciplines generate questions related to the interactions of economic, political, and cultural affairs. Continuing the legacy of Karl Marx, political economists examine how material processes of production and exchange shape, and are shaped by, decisions made in economic and political institutions. In *urban political economy*, this concern centers on "material productions of and within cities" (Nevarez 2005, 5122). This leftist-oriented urban framework emerged in the United States in the 1970s as a challenge to mainstream urban social science, which assumed that participation by city governments, urban planners, and businesses in local development policy was inherently "apolitical" (see, especially, Peterson 1981, 142). As a result, mainstream urban studies scholars were unable to adequately explain or critically understand problems such as "white flight," uneven urban development and urban poverty, and political unrest in urban centers. In a direct challenge to mainstream social science, urban political economists stressed class struggle for the control and enhancement of urban space and emphasized the role of economic structure and social power in explaining social relations (Nevarez 2005).

In the late 1970s and early 1980s, scholarship in urban political economy flourished in the United States, as a number of scholars—influenced by the work of French sociologist-philosopher Henri Lefebvre; British geographer David Harvey; and Spanish-born, French-trained sociologist Manuel Castells—began articulating a paradigm that emphasized the importance of analyzing particular features of capitalism in any assessment of urban life. The richness and depth of Marxist thought inspired a variety of neo-Marxist approaches to urban analysis. Scholars debated the relative significance of the economy, the social production of space, competition for capital investment, significance of political processes, and the role of the state in urban development (see Feagin 1988; Nevarez 2005; Schimmel 2002).

As Nevarez (2005) explains, although urban political economy traces its concern for the structural dynamics of capitalism to Karl Marx, it is Max Weber's legacy that provides the conceptual vocabulary with which to understand how humans creatively and intentionally organize their social relations to accomplish a wide variety of objectives—and how these actions both support and reproduce dominant authority structures. Just as neo-Marxist urban theory developed as a critique of mainstream sociology, so too emerged an alternative to the view that cities are "held captive" (Peterson 1981) to the capitalist mode of production. The neo-Weberian question, "Who governs the city?"—posed in the 1950s and 1960s by community power scholars—was reintroduced by urban political economists who criticized the "capital logic" perspective for introducing politics only after the fact, as an urban reaction to economic forces. Thus, urban political economists adapted "neo-Weberian premises to the neo-Marxist problematic and identified the social production of urban space—that is, city building—as the institution that organizes the material interests and galvanizes the political dominance of urban elites" (Nevarez 2005, 5123).

Among the various perspectives for understanding the nature of place-based political economy, perhaps none has been more influential than Harvey Molotch's growth machine thesis. Appearing in 1976, his paper "The City as Growth Machine" was a watershed event in the history of urban political economy. Unique in both scope and vision, it established and propelled a research agenda that now extends across multiple disciplinary boundaries; it also provided a basis for critical reevaluation of work on the politics of local urban development. Jonas and Wilson (1999) point out that, at various stages in its development, the growth machine thesis has drawn conceptual support from a complex mix of scholarly traditions. It has been informed and inspired by critical understandings from urban ecology, community power analysis, and neo-Marxism and structuration theories. At the very center of Molotch's 1976 thesis is a fundamental insight that has stood the test of time: "Coalitions of land-based elites, tied to the economic possibilities of places, drive urban politics in their quest to expand the local economy and accumulate wealth" (Jonas and Wilson 1999, 3). Recently, McCallum, Spencer, and Wyly (2005) have argued that the growth machine concept endures, 30 years after its introduction, despite two important contextual shifts. First, contemporary elites are less place bound and therefore far less likely to be dependent on the fortunes of particular cities. Second, decline of industrial economy has resulted in changes in the specific strategies used by growth machines in their searches for capital investment and profit.

In light of these contextual shifts, contemporary research in urban political economy has developed the growth machine thesis further and addressed some details that were not originally fully theorized. The main focus has been on gaining better understanding of the members of growth machine groups, their relationships to one another, how they engage in the political-economic realm, under what conditions they cooperate, what resources they have available, and how effective they are at achieving political hegemony and in influencing local development. Since the late 1980s, these issues have been taken up by "urban regime theory," the most recent iteration of the growth machine perspective and now quite possibly the most dominant school of thought in urban political economy for the study of local urban development.

Sport studies scholars have dealt, either directly or indirectly, with some of the central concerns of the urban regime perspective of urban political economy. One of the most significant understandings that the sociology of sport has contributed to understanding contemporary urban development involves conceptualizing the ways in which sport *as a dominant cultural form* is mobilized by urban regimes in their attempts to construct and maintain the hegemony of a pro-growth ideology. This is achieved in part through a discourse trading in terms such as "community," "civic pride," "major league city," and "world-class city" (see Schimmel 2002). In the next section, I select samples from historically oriented scholarship in sport studies regarding the development of "modern" sport and offer the suggestion that, in mostly unintended ways, they provided the empirical and conceptual materials necessary to build a political-economic framework for understanding sport and urban development in contemporary U.S. society.

## SPORT DEVELOPMENT AND URBAN DEVELOPMENT IN HISTORICAL PERSPECTIVE

Historians widely agree that most current major sports evolved, or were invented, in the city (Adelman 1986; Hardy 1982). Historians of sport have documented that the development of sport and the development of cities were intertwined and that early sport was promoted both as a means to escape urban problems and for building urban communities. Much of this scholarship exists as case studies focusing on *specific* cities. Steven Hardy (1982) and Melvin Adelman (1986), for example, consider sport as both cause and effect in the development of physical structures, social organizations, and ideologies in Boston and New York between 1820 and 1915. David Nasaw (1993) shows that cities were not just the problems for which sport provided a solution; but that only cities had the necessary conditions and elements to sustain the rapid growth of sport.

Stimulating and sustaining urban growth necessitated the mass production of agricultural and material goods, thus disrupting traditional patterns of work, leisure, and land use. In large cities, such as London and New York, immigrants with widely diverse sporting backgrounds adjusted to the routine of congested urban-industrial culture, which created both the demand and the means for the development and growth of sport. Cities were the sites of the dense populations, transportation networks, technological innovations, discretionary incomes, and entrepreneurial spirit necessary for the success of commercial sport. Additionally, cities were the focus of concerns for health, morality, and community which continually served as rationales for promoting sport to urban residents (for a review of historical literature on sport and the city, see Hardy 1997).

In addition to documenting early sport and urban development in specific cities, sport studies scholars have also contributed pieces of a broader conceptual lens through which to analyze historical sport–city connections, taking into account urbanizing landscapes and the expanding capitalist economic system that transformed the societies of Europe and North America and fueled the evolution of contemporary sport. For the purposes of this chapter, I select three such studies. One of these, Alan Ingham and Robert Beamish's (1993) essay "The Industrialisation of the United States and the 'Bourgeoisification' of American Sport," argues that previous sport studies scholarship had identified the conditions necessary for the creation of commercial sport (e.g., urbanization, industrialization, technological innovation), but that these conditions were not sufficient for the integration of sport into the market. Thus, Ingham and Beamish employ the concepts of "instrumental rationality" from Max Weber and "valorization" from Karl Marx to establish a general framework with which to explain the development of sport "in different places and at different times" (1993, 169). Their analysis focuses on the creation of the consumer market for commodified sport in the United States, but the overarching political-economic framework, they argue, explains the same changes throughout Western capitalist societies.

To Ingham and Beamish's valorization thesis, I add two selections from Steven Riess' research, and the combination provides an inception for a particular way to think about the role of sport in urban development. In *City Games: The Evolution of American Urban Society and the Rise of Sports* (1989), Riess emphasizes the spatial dimensions in sport and urban development through the mid-19th and early 20th centuries. He employs a "city-building" perspective to organize an analysis of the ways in which individuals and groups struggled for seizure of and ideological control over limited space. Riess shows that urban space is contested terrain and that labor, class, and ethnic social cleavages are both revealed and reproduced in geography. In *City Games*, he examines how elites, workers, reformers, and others used sport in attempts to build their communities, and he documents the ensuing struggles over playgrounds, clubhouses, and ballparks. In *Touching Base: Professional Baseball and American Culture in the Progressive Era* (1980), Riess focuses on urban elites and the development of baseball. He shows how the interests of baseball club owners mutually served politicians and transportation and real estate developers. Baseball club owners were given information regarding plans for public transit lines and real estate development, as well as special tax breaks and city services. In return, these early urban "political machines" reaped the rewards of increased patronage on the trolley lines they operated and the improved public image that hosting a baseball club offered.

The sport studies scholarship I have selected thus far can be seen as providing the beginnings of a political economy framework focused on sport studies and urban studies which has made an important contribution to our overall understanding of sport and urban development. Although none of these selected works was aimed specifically at establishing a political-economic theoretical framework per se regarding the ways in which sport is used in urban development, they all contribute empirical and conceptual building blocks to it. As Stephen Hardy (1997) illustrates, the "urban paradigm" has dominated sport historiography since the early 1900s and has provided sport scholars with numerous detailed texts that describe the ways in which sport emerged in various cities and came to be valued both for its own sake and also as a means to other desirable ends, both tangible and intangible. Ingham and Beamish employed concepts from Marx and Weber and contributed an organized theoretical analysis of the broader context, forces, and dynamics that underlay the emergence of consumer sport in capitalist societies. Stephen Riess' work emphasized the contested nature of urban space and revealed the intimate connections between sport club and franchise owners and political and economic actors, thus describing early examples of the inclusion of sport in urban growth and development coalitions.

Altogether, the political-economic interpretation that emerges in this historically oriented scholarship acknowledges the extension of capitalism's production–consumption relations into the realm of sport culture and identifies powerful elites who make decisions and act in ways that advance their own interests. They make a profound impact on the development of sport and the development of cities, and their decisions are experienced at local levels in a variety of ways. My point is this: Sport studies scholarship can count among its strengths a body of literature that addresses some of the very issues identified by urban studies scholars as constituting important elements of an urban political-economic framework. Sociologists of sport have elaborated the growth machine thesis and provided empirical support for the idea that urban growth regimes form and act in ways that benefit themselves and certain parts of the city to the detriment of others. In some cases, rather than being sideline players, sport-related actors (for example, professional sport franchise owners) have become members of urban growth regimes. In these cases, urban development plans center on a specific type of urban project that utilizes more city space, leverages more public funding (thus requiring more ideological support), and alters the landscape more than perhaps any other development project: sports stadium and related sports infrastructure construction. The research tactic used by these social scientists is the analytic case study, which provides an integrated view of the historical, social, economic, and political forces that contour urban development planning and implementation. Data for these cases studies are drawn from numerous sources, which may include (but are not limited to) personal interviews with government, corporate, and community actors; planning documents; descriptive statistics published by government agencies; media reports; and city advertising, public relations, and image-making materials.

In the following section, I highlight application of urban regime theory in constructing a case study of urban development in the city of Indianapolis, which today is widely touted by city boosters, in mainstream media, and in travel, convention, and trade publications as the "Cinderella of the Rustbelt" and the "Comeback City." One basic tenet of urban regime theory is that rather than being inevitable, strong governing arrangements are difficult to achieve. Questions that are central to urban regime theory analysis include the following: What is the character and composition of local governing arrangements? What are the relationships between the members that strengthen or weaken the group? What resources are available to governing groups as they pursue their agendas? What factors shape the direction of urban development plans? As opposed to the more "apolitical" (see Peterson 1981, 142) perspectives on urban development, urban regime theory focuses on political arrangements and recognizes local variation (e.g., from one city to another) in them and thus provides the conceptual tools for exploring a political-economic interpretation of the Indianapolis "growth success" story. Indianapolis has generated much attention among urban studies scholars, especially within the last 10 or so years (see especially McGovern 2003; Ritchie and Kennedy 2001; Wilson and Wouters 2003). However, it was in the sport studies literature that an analysis of sport and urban growth and capital investment in Indianapolis first appeared (Schimmel, Ingham, and Howell 1993). Subsequent and more detailed case study research analyzed Indianapolis growth politics from a regime theory perspective; the following discussion is a summary of some of those results (see Schimmel 1995, 2001).

## SPORT, URBAN REGIME, AND URBAN DEVELOPMENT IN INDIANAPOLIS

Indianapolis is a Midwestern U.S. city that, like many others in the mid-1970s, was facing a complex set of social and economic challenges. The backbone of the local economy was heavy manufacturing; especially prominent were factories connected to the automobile industry, a fact that made the city vulnerable to capital disinvestment and industrial mobilityspurred by national economic downturns and foreign competition. In order to regenerate "Naptown," civic leaders argued, it would be necessary to build and promote a new image of the city. Local growth advocates decided to attempt to transform Indianapolis from a sleepy Midwestern town into a white-collar tourist and corporate headquarters center and to target the nation's expanding service sector economy as a way to redevelop the city's downtown. Local elites collaborated on an agenda to use sport as a foundation upon which to build an amenity infrastructure and entered the 1980s with a determination to put their city "on the map."

It was also significant that Indianapolis was (and is) the corporate headquarters of Eli Lilly and Company, one of the largest pharmaceutical concerns in the world; indeed, Eli Lilly's influence upon the planning and implementation of Indianapolis' growth agenda cannot be overemphasized. Lilly Endowment Inc., the philanthropic arm of the company, contained over US$1.2 billion in assets in 1970, making it the second-largest charitable foundation in the United States (Nielsen 1985). In the late 1970s, board members of Eli Lilly and Company had become increasingly concerned about the condition of Indianapolis. As one of the city's largest employers (7,442 in 1989) and a Fortune 500 company, Eli Lilly took a keen interest in the community with an eye toward enhancing its ability to recruit top executives and management-level employees, a process that was becoming increasingly difficult. Jim Morris, a Lilly representative and former aide in the Mayor's office, met informally with public officials and corporate elites who also had an interest in planning and implementing a strategy designed to enhance the city's "quality of life" for middle- and upper-class populations. One important meeting occurred in the late 1970s: Jim Morris from Lilly and Robert Kennedy, director of the Indianapolis Department of Metropolitan Development, met privately to discuss the city's direction. During that meeting, Morris handed Kennedy a one-page list of big-ticket projects that Morris said the endowment would consider funding.

In 1980, the Regional Center Plan, prepared for the Indianapolis Department of Metropolitan Development by Hammer, Siler, George Associates, outlined the city's revitalization objectives to the year 2000. With the realization that the Lilly Endowment's considerable financial resources were available for development projects, discussions concerning a growth strategy became more enlivened and more frequent. Representatives from the Greater Indianapolis Progress Committee, the Corporate Community Council, the mayor's office, the Department of Metropolitan Development, and the Lilly Endowment met formally and informally throughout the 1980s to devise and implement the city's agenda for development. In addition to these institutional groups, an informal but exclusive group of young executives began meeting regularly with Jim Morris to discuss the way in which downtown revitalization and economic development should proceed. Members of this group, which was active throughout the 1980s, called themselves the City Committee. Between 1978 and 1988, when the City Committee was most active, the Lilly endowment spent US$140 million on downtown construction projects. Although local public relations campaigns were successful in attributing the city's growth strategy to (then) Mayor William Hudnut, growth coalition insiders say that it was Jim Morris who determined that sport should be used as an urban growth vehicle. His vision got fleshed out through the City Committee and public (i.e., visible) organizations—some of which were born out of City Committee meetings.

The agenda for urban redevelopment in Indianapolis emerged and evolved from a long tradition of alliance building between corporate elites and eminently skilled mayors who were able to combine their financial, bureaucratic, and political resources behind big-ticket development projects. By 1991, more than US$168 million was invested in downtown state-of-the-art sports facilities. Among the most expensive were a US$21.5 million, 5,000-seat swimming and diving complex; a US$6 million, 20,000-seat track-and-field stadium; a US$2.5 million, 5,000-seat velodrome; and a US$77.5 million, 60,300-seat domed stadium, which was used to entice the National Football League's (NFL's) Colts franchise to relocate to Indianapolis from Baltimore. Funding for these projects was provided by public and private sources.

The city, state, and federal governments provided grants, tax abatements, and industrial revenue bonds, and the Lilly Endowment contributed philanthropic grants.

Designed to enhance the city's quality of life for middle- and upper-class residents, sports projects were presented to the local community as a "public interest" that would benefit the city as a whole. However, as Clarence N. Stone, whose case study of Atlanta (1989) was foundational in the construction of regime theory, has long argued, the "public interest" that is supposedly addressed in development policy cannot be determined objectively. Public need gets defined through political arrangements made by urban elites who have similar interests and concerns. People whose needs differ from those within these elite coalitions are often excluded from the planning process. In this case, concerned that Indianapolis' "Naptown" image put them at a competitive disadvantage for specially skilled labor and capital investment, the urban regime fashioned a growth agenda that propagandized their visions of a good business climate and "quality of life" throughout the population.

Indianapolis is the location of one of the most intensive, successful, and long-standing growth regimes in the United States. Between 1974 and 1992, US$436.1 million in city funds was spent, and an additional US$2.2 billion from state and federal governments and private sources was leveraged in pursuit of the regime's downtown development agenda (McGovern 2003). The regime's activity in building new sports facilities, attempting to lure professional sports franchises and amateur sports organizations, and hosting sports events articulated with broader strategies for urban development. Indianapolis city boosters proclaim that they have had much to cheer when it comes to the so-called "success" of the sport strategy. In addition to serving as the annual host of premiere auto racing events including the Indianapolis 500, the Allstate 400 at the Brickyard, and the only Formula One race held in the United States, the city has hosted the 1982 National Sports Festival, the 1987 Pan American Games, the 1991 World Gymnastics Championships, and the Final Four of the NCAA Men's Basketball Tournament in 1980, 1991, 1997, and 2000 (and is slated to do so again in 2010). Numerous national sports-related organizations are located in Indianapolis, including the NCAA, USA Track & Field, and the American College of Sports Medicine. The city boasts five professional sport franchises, including the 2006 NFL Super Bowl Champion Indianapolis Colts. In 2003, *ESPN The Magazine* ranked Indianapolis as the "#1 Pro Sports City" in North America (Greater Indianapolis Chamber of Commerce 2009).

The sport strategy for development endures today in Indianapolis, as evidenced by the fact that the city is currently constructing a US$900 million sports stadium and expanded tourist infrastructure, which will replace the ones constructed to anchor downtown development and "convert" the city only two decades ago (Schimmel 2007). This development agenda continues despite the fact that urban and sport studies scholars have been highly critical of the Indianapolis "success story." The massive amounts of public and private resources invested in the sport agenda have not trickled down, percolated up, or spun across all segments of the population. The presence of teams, events, and facilities has not created a large number of new jobs, nor has it stemmed the loss of downtown residential population (Austrian and Rosentraub 2002). Poverty among ethnic minority groups continued to grow throughout the 1980s and into the 1990s (Wilson 1996), and members of the African American and working-class communities, who were excluded from the planning process, have felt that their needs were discounted in favor of (white and) upper- and middle-class collective-consumption privileges and "lifestyle" enhancements (Schimmel 2001; Wilson 1996). From 1991 through 1997, municipal debt increased dramatically, poor families were priced out of city swimming pools and golf courses, and the city lost market share in employment against national averages (Ritchie and Kennedy 2001). In 2004, municipal budget shortfalls were such that the city had to take out a US$10 million loan from its own sanitary district to "enable the continuation of essential police and fire services" (Minutes of the City-County Council August 2, 2004, 394). The point here is not that Indianapolis residents were (or are) worse off than those in other cities in the U.S. "Rustbelt" but rather that the sport strategy has not, as urban elites proclaim, made it *better for everyone*.

## CONCLUSION

Scholars working in the sociology of sport bring deep skepticism to any notion that sport can act as a solution to general urban problems. Although it may create a sense of attachment that is important at an interpersonal level, sport does not significantly change the economic, social, and political realities of everyday urban life. While acknowledging that sport is meaningful at interpersonal levels and can contribute positively to civic initiatives, it is important to keep in mind that a city is not a unitary entity that benefits uniformly from development policy. Featuring sport in urban development may be useful in constructing consensus for growth agendas and in providing a symbol for city residents to rally around. However, we should also be cognizant of the fact that such a powerful symbol of common interest may obscure other city investment concerns such as housing, schools, recreational space, and city services. City boosters and urban elites often frame development agendas as "the city's goals" and in ways that indicate a sense of territorial ambition through the use of slogans such as "Our city has big dreams!" But cities do not dream. Cities do not have aspirations. *People* do. *People* plan cities, and people share the benefits and bear the burdens of those plans unequally. As has been the case since the rise of sport in urban-industrial contexts, issues such as ethnic assimilation, class conflict, control of urban space, and ethnic and gender relations are inseparable from the promotion of contemporary sport.

## Suggested Research

1. Longitudinal analysis: A major sports facility has a limited "shelf life," and many that were built to attract or retain professional teams and major events are now being torn down and replaced. How does a regime form and then either hold together or fall apart as new urban challenges emerge, and what is its role in the long-term development of a city?

2. Cross-cultural analysis: Using new sports facilities and events to stimulate urban growth is not unique to the United States. Expanding the geographical boundaries of urban regime theory would both test the theory's assumptions and perhaps more thoroughly explain the conditions under

which growth regimes emerge and are effective. Can urban regime theory accommodate a double focus on broad context and narrow intragroup dynamics?

# Additional Resources

### Theory

Jonas, A.E.G., and D. Wilson, eds. 1999. *The urban growth machine: Critical perspectives two decades later.* Albany: State University of New York Press.

> This collection of 15 chapters examines the relevance of the "growth machine thesis" for research in the late 1990s. The conclusion, written by Harvey Molotch, suggests directions for future research.

Logan, J., and Molotch, H. 1987. *Urban fortunes: The political economy of place.* Berkeley: University of California Press.

> This foundational work in urban political economy focuses on class relations and political stakes underlying the activities of powerful elites, called "growth machines," that shape urban areas.

Stone, C.N. 1989. *Regime politics: Governing Atlanta, 1946–1988.* Lawrence: University Press of Kansas.

> This work establishes urban regime analysis as a theoretical lens through which we can examine how urban elites engage in the political process; it argues the importance of human agency and local particularities in the shaping of urban areas.

Stone, C.N. 2004. It's more than the economy after all: Continuing the debate about urban regimes. *Journal of Urban Affairs* 26 (1): 1–19.

> Stone defends regime theory against critique from theorists who argue for more emphasis on an economic imperative in examining urban development.

### Sport Topic

Gregory, H.D., and G.H. Mason. 2008. Urban regimes and sport in North American cities: Seeking status through franchises, events and facilities. *International Journal of Management and Marketing* 3 (3): 221–241.

> This article offers a broad overview of both the management of place by urban regimes and the use of sport in urban growth and status-enhancement initiatives in North American cities.

Henry, I., and J.L. Paramino-Salcines. 1999. Sport and the analysis of symbolic regimes: A case study of Sheffield. *Urban Affairs Review* 34 (5): 641–666.

> This research focuses on the political and ideological dimensions of urban regime activities in the context of a deindustrializing urban city in the United Kingdom.

McCallum, K., A. Spencer, and E. Wyly. 2005. The city as an image-creation machine: A critical analysis of Vancouver's Olympic bid. *APCG Yearbook* 67:24–46.

This article uses Molotch's "growth machine" thesis as a framework in a case study analyzing the visual narrative strategies used to craft a representation of Vancouver in the city's bid to host the 2010 Olympic Winter Games.

Nauright, J., and K.S. Schimmel, eds. 2005. *The political economy of sport.* London: Palgrave Macmillan.

This collection of ten chapters demonstrates the diversity of political-economic analysis applied to sport; three chapters are devoted to sport mega-events and urban development.

Sage, G. 2000. Political economy and sport. In *Handbook of sports studies*, ed. J. Coakley and E. Dunning, 260–276. London: Sage.

Sage provides an overview of the major paradigms within the political-economic framework and includes explanations of how these paradigms can be used to research sport-related topics.

St Petersburg Times/ZUMA Press/Icon SMI

# 6 | Institutional Logics Theory

## Examining Big-Time College Sport

*Richard M. Southall, EdD, and Mark S. Nagel, EdD*

---

**Social theory:** Institutional logics

**Proponents of the theory:** Peter L. Berger, Thomas Luckmann, Margaret C. Duncan, Barry Brummett, Roger Friedland, Robert R. Alford, Richard R. Nelson, Sidney G. Winter, Richard M. Southall, Mark S. Nagel, John Amis, Crystal Southall, Marvin Washington, Marc J. Ventresca

**What the theory says:** Within an organization or institution, institutional logics determine what practices and symbolic constructions—both of which constitute organizing principles available to organizations and individuals to guide the evaluation and implementation of strategies, establish routines, and create precedence for further innovation—are acceptable or unacceptable.

---

College sport occupies a significant place in the intricate cultural fabric of higher education in the United States. Some educators have praised intercollegiate athletics as an essential component in the development of well-rounded individuals (Bailey and Littleton, 1991; Chu 1989; Funk 1992; Maraniss 1999). Football coaches invariably speak of teamwork, discipline, and loyalty when discussing the benefits of their sport. To many, college sport is the symbolic "tie that binds" alumni to current students. Stadiums and coliseums—fixtures on major college campuses—consecrate the identity and remembrance of past athletic triumphs in ways impossible for classrooms and laboratories to match (Bailey and Littleton). College presidents, in the midst of their school's trip to a prestigious bowl game, cite the ability of collegiate athletics to attract people to the institution in a way that few things can (Putler and Wolfe 1999).

Chu (1989) discussed the historical acceptance of the integration of the mental, physical, and spiritual development of individuals as a consistent rationale for the appropriateness of college sport as an educational enterprise in the United States. Baxter and Lambert (1991) discussed the contention of many intercollegiate athletic administrators that "the commercial success of intercollegiate athletics . . . [is] related to the belief in the educational purpose of and high ethical standards of amateur competition" (184). While few still argue that college sport's sole purpose is character development (Bailey and Littleton 1991), National Collegiate Athletic Association (NCAA) and athletic department mission statements still contain language explicitly describing college sport's educational nature and expressing the preeminence of student-athlete welfare in organizational decisions.

However, as Gerdy (1997, 7) stated:

> *Organizations inevitably evolve to achieve that for which they are rewarded. Inasmuch as athletic departments have been rewarded principally for the purpose of winning games, they have evolved to emphasize achievement of this goal to the detriment of all others.*

In Gerdy's view, while Division I-A intercollegiate athletic departments exist, of course, within a university, many are differentiated from the university as a whole because their primary purposes seem to involve winning games and generating revenues (1997, 8). For the past 20 years, college sports' conflicted nature has been affirmed in numerous research studies and descriptions (Baxter and Lambert 1991; Baxter, Margovio, and Lambert 1996; Brown 1996; Case, Greer, and Brown 1987; DeBrock, Hendricks, and Koenker 1996; DeVenzio 1986; Eitzen 1987; Padilla and Baumer 1994; Sack 1987). In addition, several historical accounts of intercollegiate athletics (Byers 1995; Sack and Staurowsky 1998; Sperber 2000; Zimbalist 1999) have described "big-time" college sport as a long-standing, systemic process that places "the corporate needs of commercial sport over the academic needs of athletes" (Sack and Staurowsky 1998, xii). These portrayals of the NCAA and of college athletic departments describe organizations whose institutional logics seem to be contrary to those of colleges and universities.

However, a college sports fan, preparing to root for his or her favorite team during its season-ending football bowl game or March Madness basketball contest, may have little interest in examining whether there is an "educational purpose" to present-day, big-time commercialized college sport or in the extent to which the NCAA in particular achieves its stated purpose of retaining "a clear line of demarcation between intercollegiate athletics and professional sports" (Thomas 2006, 2).

In fact, big-time university athletic departments' commitment to educational principles may conflict with their need to maximize revenue streams derived from college sports fans' unwavering devotion to their favorite college basketball or football teams. Such loyalty to one college sport (men's basketball) has reached almost mythic proportions within a 25-square-mile area of North Carolina, where Interstate 40, known affectionately as Tobacco Road, connects the University of North Carolina at Chapel Hill (UNC), Duke University, and North Carolina State University (NCSU). According to Forbes' first financial ranking of college hoops teams, these three schools' men's basketball teams are among the most valuable "amateur" college basketball commodities; UNC tops the list, Duke comes in 5th, and NCSU ranks 13th (Schwartz 2008).

However, even as big-time men's college basketball has become a multimillion dollar enterprise on many NCAA Division I campuses, it pales in size, scope, media attention, revenues, and expenses to the college football landscape, in which lucrative contracts for coaches, changing conference affiliations, massive stadium expansions and renovations, premium seating and sponsorship agreements, and multimillion dollar network and cable broadcast contracts are the norm. These business tactics of NCAA Football Bowl Subdivision (FBS) athletic departments mirror strategies employed by National Football League (NFL) organizations that have seen team values rise into the hundreds of millions, and in some cases into the billions, because of successful revenue-generating activities over the past 25 years. As Schwartz (2007, paragraphs 1, 2) noted:

> *The game plan is working in college, albeit on a much smaller scale: Last year, 10 college football teams raked in at least [US]$45 million in revenues—among them, the University of Notre Dame, University of Georgia, Ohio State [University] and Auburn University—compared to none five years ago.*

As the Forbes rankings attest, big-time college basketball and football teams are increasingly viewed as valuable sport properties similar to NFL and National

Basketball Association (NBA) franchises. As a result, scholars and students examining college sport will inevitably encounter contradictions and conflicts, as well as identity dissonance—a condition which arises when trying to reconcile college sport's increasingly business-oriented identity with a preexisting, and possibly extinct, educational one (Brand 2006; Elsbach and Kramer 1996) within the college sport field. While many administrators at the NCAA and in university athletic departments claim that they are comfortable with "the juxtaposition of the NCAA's educational mission with a commercial entity" (National Collegiate Athletic Association 2002, paragraph 5), some NCAA staff members—such as Bob Lawless, NCAA Executive Committee Chair from 2001 to 2003—have identified a potential conflict of interest arising from the NCAA's increased emphasis on revenue generation associated with the NCAA's broadcast contract with CBS: "There's a realization that when you receive a certain amount of revenue from a network that they're going to generate revenue in order to meet the agreement of the contract" (National Collegiate Athletic Association 2002, paragraph 6). However, the existence of such identity dissonance has been repeatedly dismissed by NCAA Division I university presidents, who have publicly remained unperturbed with "a corporate partner essentially 'sponsor[ing]' the NCAA's educational mission," as long as it is "done well and tastefully" (National Collegiate Athletic Association 2002 paragraphs 2, 6).

While NCAA and university presidents proclaim, a priori, that this balancing act is being successfully performed, the theory of institutional logics provides a lens through which to examine empirical data from college sport television broadcasts for evidence of how colleges and universities, as well as the NCAA, are utilizing such broadcasts to represent college sport to the consuming public.

## THEORY OF INSTITUTIONAL LOGICS

Institutional logics have been defined (Friedland and Alford 1991; Scott et al. 2000) as belief systems that essentially work to constitute appropriate and acceptable courses of action for organizations and institutions. Friedland and Alford (1991) argued that all of contemporary Western society's major institutions, such as Christianity, capitalism, the family, democracy, and the bureaucratic state, have logics that guide action. Within an organization or institution, institutional logics determine what practices and symbolic constructions—both of which constitute organizing principles available to organizations and individuals to guide the evaluation and implementation of strategies, establish routines, and create precedence for further innovation—are acceptable or unacceptable (Duncan and Brummett 1991; Friedland and Alford 1991; Nelson and Winter 1982; Washington and Ventresca 2004). These logics become "encoded in actors' stocks of practical knowledge [that] influence how people communicate, enact power, and determine what behaviors to sanction and reward" (Barley and Tolbert 1997, 98). Such shared and generalized expectations allow individuals to engage in coherent, well-understood, and acceptable activities. Eventually, such institutional logics become unquestioned, taken-for-granted "facts" reflected in particular courses of action.

In a process similar to that associated with the development of a person's individual guiding philosophy, dissonance often arises between conflicting institutional logics. Over time, such contestation usually results in the emergence of a dominant institutional logic. This process works to establish local-meaning frameworks that guide institutional strategic planning and structural development by focusing the attention of decision makers toward those issues that are most consistent with the dominant logic and away from those issues that are not (Thornton 2002). As Silk and Amis (2000) demonstrated, at the field level such macropressures are exerted through coercive, mimetic, and normative mechanisms (DiMaggio and Powell 1983) that can be exerted formally (e.g., through established rules) or informally (e.g., by cultural expectations).

While field-level forces are important, it is also necessary to consider the cognitive, or microlevel, processes that emanate from the ways in which individuals interpret accepted rules in order to make sense of the world around them (Berger and Luckman 1967; Scott 2001). In this respect, activities become institutionalized through a process of "reciprocal typification of habitualized action" (Berger and Luckman 1967, 54) that results in repetitive, recognizable routines or patterns of interdependent actions involving multiple actors (Feldman 2000; Feldman and Pentland 2003; Nelson and Winter 1982). As these patterns or routines become established, they act as conduits through which acceptable courses of action are spread. The resulting shared belief structure leads to unquestioned and taken-for-granted established courses of action (Barley and Tolbert 1997; Jepperson 1991; Nelson and Winter 1982; Seo and Creed 2002; Zucker 1977). These pressures may also be coercive, mimetic, or normative, and can be exerted formally or informally (DiMaggio and Powell 1983; Scott 2001; Southall et al. 2008).

Such micropressures may be a basic pattern of organizational assumptions invented, discovered, or developed within an organization or institution by members' attempts to cope with problems associated with external adaptation and internal integration. Hofstede et al. (1990) described such micropressures within organizations as "broad, nonspecific feelings of good and evil, beautiful and ugly, normal and abnormal, and rational and irrational—feelings that are often unconscious and rarely discussible, that cannot be observed as such but are manifested in alternatives of behavior" (291). Since these assumptions have worked well enough to be considered true or valid, they are taught to new members as the correct way to perceive, think, and feel. While NCAA and college athletic administrators consistently espouse educational policies in public statements, the theory of institutional logics provides an objective framework from which to examine college sport and, specifically, evaluate the degree to which broadcasts of NCAA championship events, including games in the NCAA Division I Women's Basketball Tournament, reflect consistency with the organization's stated educational mission, goals, and values.

Based upon this theoretical framework, the case study presented here (which used both content and semiotic analyses) explored the ways in which a dominant commercial institutional logic shaped the (re)presentation of the 2007 NCAA Division I Women's Basketball Tournament. The case study provides empirical evidence of the existence of two perceived institutional logics—"educational" and "commercial"—within the college sport field, and supports the contention that big-time college sport reflects the dominant position of a commercial institutional logic. In addition, the study reflects how studying a specific sport-related issue can be guided and informed through the use of a robust and well-developed theoretical perspective.

## CASE STUDY: 2007 NCAA DIVISION I WOMEN'S BASKETBALL TOURNAMENT BROADCASTS

A primary justification for university sponsorship of athletics at the highly visible NCAA Division I level relates to fulfillment of the institution's "educational" mission (Gerdy 2006). Consistently, colleges and universities contend that their sponsorship of athletics is justified by such contests' ability to tell the institution's educational story to a public audience (Gerdy 2006), and for many college athletic departments television has become a prominent vehicle through which this educational purpose has been pursued. If college sports events are indeed educational in nature, it seems logical that broadcasts of those events would be designed to deliver educational messaging to the public, and it would follow that the content of televised college sports events—the images portrayed and messages conveyed—would highlight intercollegiate athletics' stated educational values. Therefore, one major factor in determining the return on educational institutions' investment in NCAA Division I athletics should be the extent to which televised athletic events, such as 2007 NCAA Division I Women's Basketball Tournament broadcasts, contain education-related messages that reflect or represent the NCAA and its members' professed educational institutional logic.

### Methodology

Utilizing the theoretical framework of institutional logics, televised college sport broadcasts can be viewed both as important marketing platforms and as reflections of big-time college sport's institutional logic. Within this research setting, we used a mixed-methods, directed-content-analysis methodology to quantitatively and qualitatively analyze a random sample of broadcasts from the 2007 NCAA Division I Women's Basketball Tournament ($n = 10$), as well as other primary and secondary documents from a variety of sources.

For purposes of this chapter, it is relevant to note that a directed content analysis relies on a developed theory or relevant research findings to provide guidance for developing initial content-analysis codes (Neuendorf 2002). This case study's coding schema was consistent with a protocol outlined by Madden and Grube (1994) and involved analysis of *nonprogram* (non-basketball-specific) broadcast content from pregame, in-game and postgame segments. Analyzed nonprogram content included traditional commercial advertisements (including network commercial time, local advertising spots, promotions, and "public service announcements" [PSAs]), as well as "nonstandard" in-game advertisements, graphics, promotional announcements, and game-announcer commentary (Gough 2006). In addition, nonprogram messages were categorized as either "commercial" or "educational" in nature.

Based on previous research (Southall et al. 2008 ), the nonprogram units that were developed included the following categories: standard commercial advertisements (ADV), NCAA public service announcements (NCAA), corporate-sponsor public service announcements (CORP), nonstandard sponsorship graphics without verbal commentary (GR), nonstandard sponsorship graphics with verbal commentary (GR/VER), verbal commentary (VER), academics-related player-information graphics with or without verbal commentary (GR/ACA), and positive or negative educational verbal commentary (ED).

In addition to a quantitative content analysis, a qualitative analysis was conducted that uncovered underlying messages that were not only represented during NCAA Division I Women's Basketball Tournament game broadcasts but also promoted in organizational documents, operational handbooks, and public statements (Bignell 1997; Creswell 1998; Neuendorf 2002; Patton 2002). Examining the data in this fashion allowed the researchers to establish various levels of analysis, ranging from individual words and images to overall concepts—words and visual images grouped in concept clusters—contained in broadcasts and documents (Bignell 1997; Strauss and Corbin 1990). Such analysis allowed the performance of both linguistic and visual examination to determine "what [was] portrayed and symbolized . . . and what [was] absent or silenced" (Rossman and Rallis 1998, 146).

Ryan and Bernard (2000) stated that quantitative content analysis utilizes "techniques for reducing texts to a unit-by-variable matrix and analyzing that matrix quantitatively to test hypotheses" (785). Such a matrix is produced by applying a set of codes to a qualitative text, which may consist of either a written text or an audiovisual media artifact. Once such codes are constructed, they must be investigated in order to determine whether coders are reliably applying them in a similar fashion. This investigative process is used to determine *intercoder reliability*.

In order to establish intercoder reliability and provide basic validation of the coding schema, researchers have proposed a number of reliability tests, including Scott's pi ($\pi$) and Cohen's kappa ($\kappa$) (Neuendorf 2001, 2002; Riffe, Lacy, and Fico 1998). A high level of agreement or reliability constitutes evidence that the developed code(s) possess external validity and in turn may be used in later theme development. Most researchers consider a resulting Scott's pi or Cohen's kappa of < .80 to .90 to be an adequate measure of intercoder reliability (Neuendorf 2001, 2002; Ryan and Bernard 2000). In addition, it is suggested that at least 15 percent of sampled broadcasts be subjected to intercoder reliability analysis (Neuendorf 2002, Ryan and Bernhard, Wimmer and Dominick 1994). Consistent with this accepted protocol, four sampled broadcasts (40 percent of study sample) were tested for intercoder reliability (Neuendorf 2002; Wimmer and Dominick). The resulting Scott's pi and Cohen's kappa (.98, 1.0) established acceptable intercoder reliability levels (Neuendorf 2002).

## Results

As one of the primary governing bodies in college sport, the National Collegiate Athletic Association asserts that its core purposes are to "integrate athletics into higher education" and to ensure that the "educational experience of the student-athlete is paramount" (National Collegiate Athletic Association 2008a, paragraph 2). In order to standardize advertising and promotional practices, the NCAA has developed championship handbooks, as well as advertising and promotional standards manuals for various sports in order to delineate television time-out format and state its intention to work with "those advertisements and advertisers that support the NCAA's ideals and *exclude* [emphasis in original] those advertisements and advertisers (and others who wish to associate with NCAA activities) that do not appear to be in the best interests of higher education and student-athletes" (National Collegiate Athletic Association 2008b, 1). The handbook also contains language suggesting that all advertisements should support the NCAA's mission and core values (NCAA 2006a).

The sampled 2007 NCAA Division I Women's Basketball Tournament games ($n$ = 10) involved Entertainment and Sports Programming Network (ESPN) broadcasts of games from all four tournament regions (Dallas, Fresno, Dayton, Greensboro) and included four first-round broadcasts, three second-round broadcasts, two fourth-round broadcasts, and the national championship game. All games occurred between March 17 and April 3, 2007.

In addition to utilizing previously established nonprogram content categories, the researchers determined that each broadcast sample unit would consist of an uninterrupted 2-hour block of broadcast time ($n$ = 10 games, 20 hours of game broadcasts). This predetermination was made based upon ESPN's use of "whip-around" coverage (i.e., coverage that rotates between various contests) for a number of sampled broadcasts. As a result of this limitation, the total number of content category units (e.g., commercials, public service announcements, educational messages) may be decreased, but the ratio of specific content categories to total nonprogram content will be unaffected.

Technological advances such as digital television recorders (e.g., TiVo) allow television viewers the option of fast-forwarding through standard commercial breaks. This capability has had the dual effect of increasing advertisers' propensity to look to sport properties because of their ability to draw "live" rather than "delayed" viewers and of increasing the use of within-game graphics and verbal references to decrease the chance that viewers will fast-forward past such commercial content. Reflecting this trend, in addition to standard commercial advertisements and public service announcements, sampled broadcasts contained substantial amounts of inserted advertising graphics, both with and without accompanying in-game comments. Table 6.1 summarizes the study's nonprogram content analysis results.

**Table 6.1** Nonprogram Content in 2007 NCAA Division I Women's Basketball Tournament Broadcasts

| Nonprogram categories | Study totals (in seconds) | Average seconds per broadcast | Average minutes per broadcast |
|---|---|---|---|
| ADV | 13,312 | 1331.2 | 22.19 |
| NCAA | 555 | 55.5 | 0.93 |
| CORP | 333 | 33.3 | 0.56 |
| GR | 1,964 | 196.4 | 3.27 |
| GR/VER | 1,284 | 128.4 | 2.14 |
| VER | 1 | 0.1 | 0 |
| GR/ACA | 10 | 1 | 0.02 |
| ED | 69 | 6.9 | 0.12 |

ADV = standard commercial advertisements; NCAA = NCAA public service announcements; CORP = corporate-sponsor public service announcements; GR = nonstandard sponsorship graphics without verbal commentary; GR/VER = nonstandard sponsorship graphics with verbal commentary; VER = verbal commentary; GR/ACA = academics-related player-information graphics with or without verbal commentary; ED = positive or negative educational verbal commentary.

One important focus of this research was to determine the amount of educational messaging related to the participating universities' academic missions. While no one is suggesting that the only purpose of broadcasting NCAA Division I Women's Basketball Tournament games is to highlight the integration of college athletics into higher education and ensure that the educational experience of the student-athlete is paramount, these goals are articulated in the *NCAA Division I Women's Basketball Championships Handbook* (National Collegiate Athletic Association 2006b). Thus, determining the amount of educational messaging is a relevant area of inquiry.

On average, each sampled broadcast contained 1 second (0.2 percent of nonprogram content) of academics-related graphics (GR/ACA) content per broadcast ($n = 10$ seconds). In addition, the 10 sampled broadcasts contained a total of 69 seconds of educational messages (an average of 6.9 seconds per broadcast, or 0.4 percent of total nonprogram content).

## Case Study Discussion

The production of an NCAA Women's Basketball Tournament broadcast, like any represented sport event, contains content that highlights and selects certain aspects of the specific sport event (Gruneau, Whitson, and Cantelon 1988). Decisions related to in-game announcer commentaries, as well as the number and type of advertising and sponsor graphics inserted within an NCAA women's basketball broadcast, result from negotiations (both contractual and cultural) between various tournament constituencies and are fundamentally driven by each institution's logics. In today's commercialized college sport setting, there is evidence of the apparent existence of two contradictory institutional logics: educational and commercial (Southall et al. 2008). In addition, there is strong evidence to suggest that a commercial logic has been dominant in college sport for almost as long as the NCAA has been in existence (Washington 2004; Washington and Ventresca 2004). Indeed, Washington and Ventresca (2004) have suggested that the initial motivation for American universities and colleges in creating college sport programs was the enhancement of financial resources and increased visibility. This motivation is exemplified by the aggressive pursuit of television rights fees by the NCAA and its members since the early 1950s, as well as the organization's willingness to position competitions strategically in order to maximize commercial revenue (see Washington 2004). As others have found in different contexts (e.g., publishing, financial services), the existence of a dominant logic has pronounced implications for the direction of strategic decision making (e.g., Thornton 2002).

Based on these results of the case study overall, the 2007 NCAA Division I Women's Basketball Tournament provided little evidence that an educational institutional logic was influencing broadcast decision making. Consistent with previous research (Southall et al. 2008), these broadcasts did little to promote educational themes or images. While it is understandable that any sport event is going to overwhelmingly consist of "primary" messages related to the athletic contest itself, there are also significant opportunities within a broadcast to convey nonprogram messages of the broadcast entity's choosing. However, in sampled 2007 NCAA Division I Women's Basketball Tournament broadcasts, which were 2 hours in length, educational messages (both verbal and visual) were rare (on average 7.9 seconds per game or 0.1 percent of total nonprogram content). In addition, within the broadcasts, discussions of higher education, academics, and other broader university missions of teaching, research, and service did not occur. While ESPN placed an average of two NCAA PSAs per broadcast segment, there were no instances of university-specific public service announcements in the sample. This lack of "ad buys" on the part of universities reflects the high cost of a 30-second commercial spot during NCAA tournament broadcasts (Vasquez 2005). NCAA and ESPN policies that prohibit free PSA time for participating institutions reflect the existence of a dominant commercial institutional logic within both organizations. Not surprising, this commercial logic reflects ESPN advertising executives' desire to maximize ESPN's return on investment (ROI) by selling any and all available advertising inventory. In addition, the existence of such policies reflects the NCAA's tacit endorsement, if not active support, of ESPN's revenue maximization logic. While it is understandable that ESPN, which in 2001 signed an 11-year, US$160 million contract to broadcast the women's tournament and other NCAA events ("The evolution of women's college sports" 2001), has little incentive to give away such advertising inventory, the fact that the NCAA has made the strategic decision to acquiesce to such a policy is indicative that a dominant commercial logic also exists within the NCAA.

In addition to having no standard advertising presence within broadcasts, universities were rarely mentioned per se (e.g. "the University of Tennessee," "the University of North Carolina at Chapel Hill"). Instead, athletic monikers, nicknames, and quasi-franchise or "program" references were the norm when referring to athletic teams (e.g., "Tennessee," "the Vols," "North Carolina," "the Tar Heels").

It is no secret that administrators from the NCAA and from member university athletic departments recognize that "television networks are trying to do everything they can to add value and increase advertising sales to be able to pay the ever-increasing rights fees we ask for. . . . We are the ones driving their needs to do these types of things" (Weiberg 2001, paragraph 3). Contrary to then-president Cedric Dempsey's claim that "in actuality what we've done is provide more money without increasing ad time during events" (Brown 2002, paragraph 44), documentary analysis revealed that the NCAA has increased the length of "full television time-outs" in its television commercial format. It is not public knowledge whether this change was made unilaterally by the NCAA or whether ESPN or CBS exerted pressure on the NCAA to increase advertisement time during sports broadcasts.

NCAA administrators have contended that, "to be sure, the NCAA isn't yet guilty of having sold its soul" (Brown 2002, 1), and that selling a sport event (e.g., NCAA men's and women's basketball tournaments) "doesn't render the NCAA a commercial opportunist" (2). In addition, NCAA members have contended that television broadcasts provide great opportunities to tell "the truth—over and over again—through promotional platforms gained in [such] agreement[s] . . . [about] the partnership between intercollegiate athletics and higher education" (3).

However, this case study offers little evidence that such truth-telling took place during broadcasts of the 2007 NCAA Division I Women's Basketball Tournament. Although David Goldfield (faculty athletic representative at the University of North Carolina at Charlotte has said, "There's nothing wrong with money and making it, especially if you can use it to further your mission" (Brown 2002, 4), it should be noted that he also warned, "It's easy for the NCAA's credibility to be compromised when the public is bombarded with mixed messages" (4). Goldfield's concern reflects the possibility that an educational institution's academic credibility may be compromised when members of it have adopted a dominant commercial logic: "The problem comes when the money diverts you from what you're supposed to be doing" (4).

This case study's results suggest that such a dominant commercial logic exists within the NCAA and within member athletic departments involved in big-time college sport. Similar to broadcasts of NCAA Division I men's basketball broadcasts (Southall et al. 2008), the 2007 NCAA Division I Women's Basketball Tournament broadcasts did not bombard the viewing public with "mixed messages." Overwhelmingly (99.8+ percent of the time), nonprogram messages within such broadcasts were commercial in nature. While the NCAA clearly promotes its commercial "brand," education is rarely, if ever, represented.

## CONCLUSION

Specific to the NCAA Division I Women's Basketball Tournament, a commercial logic is so dominant within the NCAA that, in concert with activity by the NCAA's business partners, it inevitably shapes the logic of the universities whose teams are part of the field. Although ESPN contractually controls the commercials and, in fact, all nonprogram content associated with the tournament broadcasts, the NCAA continues to assert that it controls NCAA championship events and that all decisions regarding its championships are first and foremost made on the basis of ensuring student-athlete welfare (National Collegiate Athletic Association 2006a, 2006b). In official documents, the NCAA notes that even though a broadcast partner has purchased rights to a sport event, all television rights (whether over the air or via cable), both live and delayed, still fall under the NCAA's jurisdiction (2006a). Regardless of this level of control that so far the NCAA has managed to retain, the broadcasts' content offers strong evidence that a commercial logic has come to dominate the NCAA Division I field.

Every 2007 NCAA Women's Basketball Tournament game broadcast by ESPN provided an opportunity for the NCAA to highlight the integration of college sport with the organization's educational mission, on which its tax-exempt status rests. However, despite the NCAA's claim that it exerts control over the representation of tournament games, educational messages were barely noticeable in this study. Though many observers may not care that the NCAA appears to be saying one thing and doing another, this inconsistency is potentially related to public policy and legal issues. The public and the U.S. government have long adopted a laissez-faire attitude toward NCAA business practices, but the landscape of multibillion-dollar, big-time college sport has begun to attract increased congressional and media scrutiny (Thomas 2006). As college sport revenue streams and broadcast platforms continue to expand, more disgruntled fans, journalists, and members of Congress will begin not only to question why taxpayers should subsidize such commercial activities but also to demand increased accountability regarding the distribution of these subsidized revenues.

Though current NCAA president Myles Brand continually espouses educational values, there are some who suggest his rhetoric reflects simply ceremonial conformity to what he perceives as a requirement for institutional legitimacy (as well as a way to provide "cover" from scrutiny by the Internal Revenue Service). This study offers strong evidence that NCAA educational pronouncements are not reflective of the NCAA's organizational behavior (Meyer and Rowan 1977). In essence, Brand's use of collegiate and amateur nomenclature seems to be a point of competitive brand differentiation designed to distinguish the NCAA in an increasingly crowded sports marketplace. While some NCAA officials, industry analysts, and members of the general public may proclaim the preeminence of educational values, this is little more than—depending on one's viewpoint—a naive interpretation or a deliberate attempt to mislead.

## Suggested Research

1. There is clearly a need for additional ceremonial-facade research (Meyer and Rowan 1977) to evaluate the extent to which other televised college sports events convey messages consistent with those found in our research. We suggest that analyses of such broadcasts along a possible spectrum of "commercialization" (e.g., Division I football bowl games, Division I women's basketball tournament games, Division I Men's College World Series games, Division I women's softball national championship games, any Division II national championship games, and Division III national championship games that are broadcast, though there are few and these are primarily limited to football and men's basketball) would be useful in determining whether all such broadcasts exhibit the same corporate, commercialized form found in this study.

2. Further analysis should be conducted to determine the extent to which a commercialized institutional logic (evident in the broadcasts of NCAA Division I men's and women's basketball tournament games on CBS and ESPN) has been adopted in the production of college sports events on other broadcast networks. Specifically, the emergence of CBS College Sports Network and ESPNU as additional interactive new-media platforms for delivering "nonrevenue" college sporting events to consumers offers a potentially useful setting for such analyses.

3. Extend the work of Green, Costa, and Fitzgerald (2003) to examine the effectiveness and value of the NCAA logo's visual exposures during event broadcasts (see Debner and Jacoby 1994; Shapiro, MacInnis, and Heckler 1997). Further studies should also qualitatively assess the perceptions and motives of broadcasters in representing college and professional sports events to determine whether differences exist between such broadcasts.

4. Research that probes consumers' perceptions of the educational importance of events such as March Madness and Division I football bowl games might reveal the effectiveness of NCAA public relations activities attempting to reinforce the "educational" aspect of big-time college athletics.

# Additional Resources

**Theory**

Friedland, R., and R.R. Alford. 1991. Bringing society back in: Symbols, practices, and institutional contradictions. In *The new institutionalism in organizational analysis*, ed. W.W. Powell and P.J. DiMaggio, 232–262. Chicago: University of Chicago.

> Friedland and Alford discuss institutions as the substance out of which social constructs and politics are made. They emphasize that within organizations and fields, multiple and competing logics may exist. Since institutions or organizations are social constructs, they may exert profound influence on individual preferences and actions. The concept of logic generally refers to broader cultural beliefs and rules that structure cognition and guide decision making in a field. At the organization or institutional level, logics can focus the attention of key decision makers on a delimited set of issues and solutions leading to logic-consistent decisions that reinforce extant organizational or institutional identities and strategies.

Meyer, J., and B. Rowan. 1977. Institutional organizations: Formal structure as myth and ceremony. *American Journal of Sociology* 83:340–363.

> Meyer and Rowan detail how formal organizational structures often reflect rationalized institutional rules. The elaboration of such rules results in expanded and increasingly complex structures. Meyer and Rowan contend that such institutional rules function as organizational myths, which gain legitimacy through an organization's use of them to retain resources, increase legitimacy, and ensure organizational stability.

Scott, W.R. 2001. *Institutions and organizations.* 2nd ed. London: Sage.

> This book is an excellent source for the scholar or student new to the theory of institutional logic because it provides an historical overview of the development of the theory as well as an extensive review of the theoretical and empirical literature on institutions and organizations. Scott offers an extensive review and critique of institutional analysis in sociology, political science, and economics as it relates to recent theory and research on organizations.

Washington, M. 2004. Field approaches to institutional change: The evolution of the National Collegiate Athletic Association 1906–1995. *Organization Studies* 25:393–414.

> Washington examines the NCAA as an example of an interest association that demonstrates how institutional change may occur. An interest association plays a vital role in the social control and evolution of organizational fields. After a discussion of the theoretical literature on institutional change, Washington examines how the NCAA—as it competed for dominance in the U.S. collegiate athletic field with a contender institution, the National Association of Intercollegiate Athletics (NAIA)—changed by altering its membership criteria.

**Sport Topic**

Byers, W. (1995). *Unsportsmanlike conduct: Exploiting college athletes.* Ann Arbor: University of Michigan Press.

> This book details the "untold" story of the NCAA. Walter Byers was the executive director of the NCAA from 1951 to 1988, and his book provides a history of the growth of the NCAA from small office to its current multibillion dollar operation. Despite being one of the most important architects of the current big-time college sport environment, Byers provides criticisms regarding NCAA operations—particularly of the "exploitation" of college athletes.

Gerdy, J.R. (2006). *Air ball: American education's failed experiment with elite athletics.* Oxford: University Press of Mississippi.

> As a former college athlete and administrator, John Gerdy has seen the inner workings of big-time college athletics. Since resigning his position with the Southeastern Conference, Gerdy has written extensively about the structure, operation, and impact of intercollegiate athletics. This book details the detrimental effects that college athletics has had upon all levels of education and the continued threat to the American educational system if the present emphasis on athletics is not altered.

Sack, A.L., and E.J. Staurowsky. (1998). *College athletes for hire: The evolution and legacy of the NCAA's amateur myth.* New York: Praeger Publishers.

> Former Notre Dame football player Allen Sack and former college athletic director Ellen Staurowsky detail the history of the NCAA and provide insights regarding its current operation. The book provides an invaluable examination of the formation of the NCAA and its key strategic decisions. The authors provide evidence that the NCAA has repeatedly acted in the best interests of the NCAA rather than those of the college athletes the NCAA claims to support.

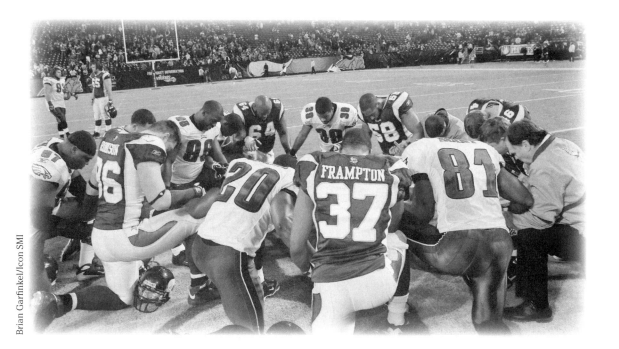

Brian Garfinkel/Icon SMI

# 7 | Playing for Whom?

## Sport, Religion, and the Double Movement of Secularization in America

*David Yamane, PhD, Charles E. Mellies, BA, and Teresa Blake, BA*

**Social theory:** Secularization theory

**Proponents of the theory:** Robert Bellah, Peter Berger, José Casanova, Mark Chaves

**What the theory says:** Secularization theory achieved paradigmatic status in the sociology of religion in the 20th century. Scholars built upon the ideas of the founding theorists of sociology to understand how religion is transformed in the modern world. Yamane stresses the *double movement of secularization*: the broad movement in the history of the West toward a decline in the scope of religious authority vis-à-vis secular authorities and the persistence or reemergence of religious organizations under the secularized conditions established in the first movement. We can see how sport as a social institution has been largely secularized so that religious groups which seek to be effectively involved in sport are constrained to work in ways that articulate with and are accommodative of the reality of a secular society. At the individual level, we may find some people who integrate their religious beliefs and athletic practices, but for most people religion and sport offer separate, even competing, roles.

W ith a gold cross dangling from his ear, Barry Bonds hits another home run; when he touches home plate, he points to the sky. U.S. soccer star Landon Donovan makes the sign of the cross prior to taking penalty kicks, as do countless baseball players before stepping into the batter's box, American football kickers prior to attempting field goals, and basketball players before shooting free throws. After leading the St. Louis Rams to a Super Bowl victory, quarterback Kurt Warner was asked by an interviewer on national television, "Kurt, first things first. Tell me about the final touchdown pass to Isaac [Bruce]." Warner responded, "Well, first things first, I've got to thank my Lord and Savior up above. Thank you, Jesus!" After getting injured in the first game of the season, Wake Forest University quarterback Riley Skinner thanked God for the opportunity to play college football.

These scenes from contemporary American life seem very much at odds with what the founding theorists of sociology would expect to find in a modern society, but they are readily understood through an updated version of the dominant theoretical perspective in the sociology of religion: secularization theory.

## THE DOUBLE MOVEMENT OF SECULARIZATION

Early interpreters of the emerging modern social order held that the "acids of modernity" were destructive of religion, especially the supernatural beliefs that undergird it. According to Emile Durkheim (1912/1995, 425), "the former gods are growing old or dying." In Max Weber's (1958, 139) famous phrase, the modern world is "disenchanted." Or, as Karl Marx (1978, 476) put it, somewhat more poetically, "All fixed, fast-frozen relationships, with their train of ancient and venerable prejudices and opinions, are swept away, all new-formed ones become antiquated before they can ossify. All that is solid melts into air." This is the experience of modernity (Berman 1988).

This view was taken up into contemporary sociology under the banner of "secularization theory," which achieved paradigmatic status in the sociology of religion in the third quarter of the 20th century (Tschannen 1991). Unlike the founding theorists of sociology, secularization theorists stressed the *transformation* of religion in the modern world rather than its ultimate death (Yamane 1997). In particular, the secularization paradigm holds that, over time, the place of religion in the social order, the structure of religious organizations, and the orientation of individuals to religion all *change*. The primary direction of this change, according to Bryan Wilson (1982, 149), is toward "diminution in the social significance of . . . religious institutions, actions, and consciousness." But the scope and intensity of religious activity witnessed in the final decades of the 20th century raised questions about the very reality of secularization, especially in the most modern of all Western societies, the United States. This development led some scholars to call for the abandonment of the "old" secularization paradigm in favor of a "new paradigm" for the sociological study of religion in American society (Warner 1993).

For secularization theorists, however, the question was how to reconcile the obvious vitality of religion in America with the strong expectation that the social significance of religion would decline as society modernized. Advocates of what Yamane (1997) calls "neosecularization" theory have focused attention on the core tenets of the paradigm (e.g., Chaves 1994). According to Tschannen (1991, 403), although the secularization paradigm "is not completely represented in any one of the theories" of its various carriers, "its core element—*differentiation*—is shared by them all." The notion of institutional differentiation highlights the fact that, in the course of modernization, "specialized institutions develop or arise to handle specific features or functions previously embodied in, or carried out by, one institution" (Wallis and Bruce 1991, 4). As a consequence, in a highly differentiated society, the norms, values, and practices of the religious sphere have only an indirect influence on other spheres such as business, politics, education, and leisure (see Casanova 1994, 37).

Unfortunately, some observers jump too quickly from this core thesis of secularization to a corollary that sees religion not only as differentiated from the secular sphere but also as wholly privatized. Thus, to highlight decline in the scope of authority of religion is to tell only part of the story of the place of religion in modern society. Secularization does not simply *constrain* religious activity in differentiated societal spheres. Secularization also *enables* religious activity. Yamane (1997) calls this dual nature of secularization—both constraining and enabling—the *double movement* of secularization.[1] The *first moment* of this double movement focuses not on the decline of religion per se but on the broad movement in the history of the West toward a decline in the scope of religious authority vis-à-vis secular authorities

---

[1] I stole the term *double movement* from Karl Polanyi, who used it in a different context and sense in *The Great Transformation* (1944).

in the process of institutional differentiation. The *second moment* recognizes the reemergence of religious organizations in other societal spheres—but under the secularized conditions established in the first moment. Put more concretely, under conditions of societal-level secularization, where the scope of religious authority over sport has diminished, religious groups which seek to be effectively involved in sport are constrained to work in ways that articulate with and are accommodative of the reality of a secular society. At the individual level, we may find some people who integrate their religious beliefs and athletic practices, but we will find that for most people religion and sport offer separate, even competing, roles.

## SOCIETAL-LEVEL SECULARIZATION: THE DIFFERENTIATION OF SPORT FROM RELIGION

The vast amount of religious activity we see in and around sport today can obscure from view the long-term trend toward the secularization of sport. In fact, however, secularism is a key characteristic that distinguishes modern sport from ancient athletics (Guttmann 1978). Secularism particularly concerns the changing purpose of modern sport. From the beginning of human history, people aimed to please the gods through ceremonies, dancing, and athletic activity. Originally, athletic competitions were fundamentally religious enterprises, meant to show special talents to the gods, express thanks to them, or implore them to take certain beneficent actions such as assuring the earth's fertility (Guttmann 1978, 18).

Examples abound. The Mayans and Aztecs erected stone ball courts next to their places of worship and often used stories of athletic competition to explain nature, believing, for example, that the sun and moon were results of a game between the gods and a set of twin brothers during the creation of civilization. As a result of losing, the twin brothers lost their heads as a sacrifice, and this tradition continued, with one player from every game being sacrificed. The secular Olympic Games we know today were created as an exercise of devotion to the Greek god Zeus. Athletes had to swear on the highest deity that they had been training for at least 10 months and would abide by the rules of competition, and violations of this oath led to fines which were used to construct statues of Zeus. The original Olympics lasted 5 days, of which only 2½ were used for competition; the entire first day was devoted to religious ceremonies. Native American tribes used sport to explain nature and please the gods. Southwest Apaches used unwed males in relay races in honor of the masculine sun and the feminine moon (Baker 2007).

In the Western world, athletics began to be approached more secularly by the Romans, and their principal purpose became not religious expression but entertainment. Roman athletes focused on fighting, as in gladiator contests, and Roman sport often pitted the members of the lower classes against each other as entertainment for the elites. Victory usually allowed the competitor to survive and was therefore emphasized over simply participating (Guttmann 1978). Modern sports, though less extreme, have taken a more Roman approach to sport in their secularism. According to Kliever (2001, 43), this movement parallels the general pattern of societal-level secularization under which religion "has lost effective control over vast areas of cultural life that were once conducted under its watchful eye." As with other institutional spheres—science and the arts, politics and economics, health care and social welfare—sport "operates under its own rules and pursues its own ends" (Kliever 2001, 43).

This institutional differentiation between religion and sport is a long-term trend that Yamane characterizes as the first moment in the double movement of secularization. As with the differentiation between religion and politics that Yamane (2005) has previously examined, the differentiation between religion and sport creates the context within which religious activity can take place in the differentiated societal sphere—and this religious activity constitutes the second moment of the double movement.

Once sport loses its fundamentally religious character, it becomes a separate institutional sphere which can be a target of regulation by religious authorities. But as secularization proceeds, that regulation becomes less effective and hence less common. For example, citing sport as too "self-indulgent" and as an activity wherein most participants and spectators were more interested in drunkenness and sex than exercise, the Puritans banned athletic competition (Baker 2007, 15). Indeed, as Price (2001, 17) observes, "Before 1850 most Protestant groups condemned sports because sports diverted attention and consumed energy that could have been spent in the exercise of faith." But in the 100 years that followed, there was a sea of change in that orientation. This change was driven in large part by the importance of sport in Christian colleges. With the rise of Harvard, Yale, and Princeton, sport became inevitable (Putney 2001). Despite each college's early attempts to limit athletic activity, college students were hell-bent (so to speak) to use sport to determine superiority over rival schools. In the South, sporting events such as horse racing and cockfighting became popular social events. The farther south and west one went, the more lewd drunkenness would increase; in the mountains, no-holds-barred fighting was the sport of choice, and plenty of alcohol was present to entertain the crowds (Baker 2007).

As noted later, the present reality is that religious organizations seeking to engage in sports rarely challenge their fundamental structure and purpose. The more fundamental pattern is of engagement through accommodation. As Price (2001) puts it, Sabbath prohibitions have given way to "Super Sunday" celebrations. An oft-cited line by sports commentator Frank Deford makes the point well: "Sport owns Sunday now, and religion is content to lease a few minutes before the big games" (qtd. in Coakley 2007, 558; Price 2005, 198).

## SPORT AS CIVIL RELIGION?

Under conditions of societal-level secularization, there is not simply a division of functions between various institutions. Rather, institutions can overlap or even compete in fulfilling various functions. For example, religion historically was a primary institutional agent of socialization into societal values. Today, many people in American society look to sport to inculcate values. "Sport builds character" is something of a mantra today. Indeed, if our dominant cultural value is competitive individualism (Bellah et al. 1985), sport seems much better suited to socializing individuals into this value than does religion. Because of the centrality of sport in American society, some scholars have gone so far as to suggest that sport functions as a "civil religion."

*Civil religion* refers to the cultural beliefs, practices, and symbols that relate a nation to the ultimate conditions of its existence.[2] The idea of civil religion can be traced to the French philosopher Jean-Jacques Rousseau's *The Social Contract* (1762/1968). Writing in the wake of the Protestant–Catholic religious wars, Rousseau maintained the need for "social sentiments," outside of organized religion, "without which a man cannot be a good citizen or faithful subject." The broader question motivating Rousseau concerned political legitimation without religious establishment. Emile Durkheim's work in *The Elementary Forms of Religious Life* was clearly influenced by his countrymen's concern for shared symbols and the obligations they articulate. Recognizing that "the former gods are growing old or dying," Durkheim sought a more modern basis for the renewal of the collective sentiments that societies need if they are to stay together. He found that basis in the "hours of creative effervescence during which new ideals will once again spring forth and new formulas emerge to guide humanity for a time" (Durkheim 1912/1995). Civil religious ideals arise from national civil religious rituals.

Robert Bellah's (1967) essay, "Civil Religion in America," brought the concept into contemporary sociology. Like Rousseau and Durkheim, Bellah sees legitimation as a problem faced by every nation, and he sees civil religion as one solution, under the right social conditions. Bellah (1980) argues that in premodern societies, the solution consisted either in a fusion of the religious and political realms (in the archaic period) or in a differentiation but not separation (in the historic and early modern periods). Civil religion proper comes into existence only in the modern period, when church and state are separated as well as structurally differentiated. That is, a civil religion that is differentiated from both church and state is possible only in a modern society.

Sport is often looked to as a sort of civil religion that can be used to legitimate the state and to create social solidarity. Whether it does so well is another issue. Although the United States hockey team's defeat of the Soviet team at the 1980 Winter Olympics was a moment of national effervescence that attached itself to the flag in an instance of national legitimation, such moments are few and far between. Indeed, sport is more apt to create solidarity *within* groups than *across* groups. Consider, for example, Warren St. John's (2005) account of Alabama football in *Rammer Jammer Yellow Hammer*. Alabama football is a sort of folk religion among its fans (Mathisen 2006), but this also creates divisive in-group-versus-out-group dynamics, as between Alabama fans and Auburn fans. So, while sport may have the potential to create group solidarity, it does not generally serve the function of creating social solidarity writ large. Although many examine the civil religious dimension of sport, it cannot, according to any strict definition, play this role. As Mathisen (2006, 291) puts it, "sport is also something like a civil religion, but not quite."

---

[2] In this section, I borrow from my encyclopedia entry on civil religion (Yamane 2006).

# ORGANIZATIONAL INNOVATION CONNECTING RELIGION AND SPORT

Societal-level secularization changes the overall relationship between sport and religion as social institutions in a way that diminishes the religious significance of sport. At the same time, the free market for religion created by the institutional differentiation of religion from other social institutions creates a fertile soil in which organizations can freely compete for attention and adherents. Evangelical Christians, in the United States in particular, have been very adept at using sports organizations to advance religious ends—from the YMCA of yesterday to the sports ministries of today.

## Muscular Christianity and the YMCA

The idea of "Muscular Christianity," a Christian commitment to health and "manliness," can be found in sections of the New Testament, but the term was not coined until the mid-1800s. Indeed, many Puritans were suspicious of sport for moral reasons. Like dancing, playing games was considered sinful—as an idle waste of time that could be better spent working or worshipping. Eventually, even these Protestant sects came to embrace sport, in part through the ideology of Muscular Christianity. Religious leaders who supported connecting religion and sport promoted the idea of the body as a temple as part of a framework in which the combination of a sound mind and body became essential in worship. The term *Muscular Christianity* was coined by the press to describe the work of authors Charles Kingsley and Thomas Hughes. Their "adventure novels replete with high principles and manly Christian heroes" sparked a discovery of the social benefits of athleticism, and "chief among these was its ability to ameliorate English class differences" (Putney 2001, 12–13). Muscular Christianity placed an emphasis on fellowship, honor, and service while teaching "English boys that one can be the best looking, best playing, and most popular, and still be humble" (William McKeever, qtd. in Putney 2001, 15). Its main focus was to address the concerns of boys directly, not abstractly, so that they could apply religion to their lives. The idea did not catch on quickly in America, but over time it has become one of the most notable tools employed in Evangelical Protestant outreach ministries.

The Young Men's Christian Association (YMCA) was started in England with strict religious ideals. Appalled at city lifestyles, George Williams created the YMCA as a place where men could fellowship together. The YMCA's initial activities in England were Bible studies, Christian readings, and prayer; all amusements were prohibited. The YMCA was designed to educate and promote Christian responsibilities in a world of temptation and self-indulgence (Baker 2007, 47). Card playing, billiards, secular reading, and physical activity were forbidden by early English leaders, only to become a vital part of the American YMCAs.

In 1851, under the leadership of Captain Thomas Sullivan and the Reverend Lyman Beecher, Boston became the first city in the United States to open a YMCA. The Boston Association modeled its facilities after those of its English counterparts and emphasized the library and reading rooms where Bible classes could be held (Putney 2001, 65). By 1856, there were over 50 YMCAs in the United States, from Georgia to California (Baker 2007, 48). In time, U.S. YMCAs began recruiting young men from all walks of life and employing a more secular approach than that of their English counterparts. Cards, secular novels, and athletic competition began to bring young men into the building, where leaders could preach the Word. Whereas English YMCAs acted as safe havens for Christian young men, American YMCAs used popular activities to recruit and convert non-Christians. In 1860, the annual convention of the U.S. YMCA decided that gymnasiums should be built at all YMCA locations, and by 1890 more than half of the 400 YMCAs in the United States had on-site gyms (Baker 2007, 50), which were soon followed by bowling alleys, boxing rings, and swimming pools. Through use of these facilities, as well as camping trips and baseball leagues, the YMCA used sport and teamwork to expose young men to Muscular Christianity and lead men to Christ.

It is difficult to underestimate the contribution to modern sport made by individuals associated with the YMCA. The term *bodybuilding* was first used in 1881 by Robert Roberts, a devout Baptist and gymnasium superintendent at the Boston YMCA, and William Morgan invented volleyball while serving as an instructor at the Holyoke, Massachusetts, YMCA in 1895 (Young Men's Christian Association 2009). But the YMCA's greatest contribution to sport came from James Naismith, a Presbyterian seminary graduate who was in residence at the YMCA Training School in Springfield, Massachusetts, when he developed the modern game of basketball in 1891 (Baker 2007, 61). The sport's popularity grew exponentially over the years, and it has become the most popular organized YMCA sport. It has also become one of the leading evangelical tools for other Christian organizations such as Athletes in Action.

Sport remains integral to YMCA programming today; the "Y" sponsors leagues for baseball, soccer, tennis, football, basketball, volleyball, and gymnastics. The prevalence of these secular activities marks a dramatic change in the means employed by YMCAs today as compared with those at the time of their founding. But what of the ends? Although the mission of the YMCA remains "to put Christian principles into practice through programs that build healthy spirit, mind and body for all," there is little organized effort at the Y to proselytize today. According to William Baker (2007, 55), "in 1888, most YMCA men agreed with Luther Gulick, who reminded them that the gymnasium should always be a means to the end 'of leading men to Christ.'" More than 100 years later, that end has long been lost at the YMCA as the organization has internally secularized.

## Evangelical Protestant Sports Ministries

As the YMCA decreased its emphasis on sport as a method of bringing young men to Christ, other organizations arose to fill the void. Professional athletes began openly sharing their testimonies, a practice that opened the door for many prominent religious leaders to use famous athletes in their efforts to attract young people to meetings. The first of several evangelical sports organizations, Sports Ambassadors (SA), was established in 1952. SA took the use of athletes as spokespersons for Christ to the next level by organizing exhibition games in order to draw large crowds; during halftime, players would share their personal testimonies (Ladd and Mathisen 1999, 129).

As the popularity of sports grew on college campuses, so did the opportunity for ministry. The Fellowship of Christian Athletes (FCA) was created in 1954 as a student-athlete Christian ministry and grew into an organization of summer camps and retreats designed to promote Christian ideals among high school and collegiate athletes (Ladd and Mathisen 1999, 130). Campus Crusade founder Bill Bright envisioned a more evangelical Christian ministry that he hoped would travel the world and preach the Gospel through sport. This approach became the focal point of its offshoot, Athletes in Action (AIA), founded in 1966 and intentionally positioned to the theological "right" of FCA. Today, AIA has a presence on nearly 100 U.S. college campuses and 35 professional sports teams. It fields summer teams in baseball, basketball, soccer, tennis, volleyball, wrestling, track and field, power lifting, and sports medicine to promote the Christian message and personal testimonies of Christian athletes (Athletes in Action 2009).

As Mathisen (2006, 299) observes, the founding of SA meant that "an entirely new genre of religious organizational forms was created, with sport occupying an essential presence." SA, FCA, and AIA are the "Big 3" Protestant sports ministries. Unlike in the formative years of the YMCA, which used religion to legitimize sport, the roles are now reversed: these organizations use sport to legitimize religion, which suggests the increasing social significance of sport and the relatively decreasing social significance of religion.

These Christian sports ministries do not generally attempt to reform sport; rather, they work within the existing framework of the meaning, purpose, and organization of modern sport. They accommodate themselves to their secular reality, and this process exemplifies the double movement of secularization: Secularization at the societal level allows for the proliferation of religious activity at the organizational level, but those religious organizations that seek to engage other social spheres must do so on the other spheres' terms. In this way, Christian organizations engaging with sport are no different from the religious organizations, which Yamane (2005) studied, that are engaging with legislative politics.

## RELIGION AND SPIRITUALITY AT THE INDIVIDUAL LEVEL

In American society, religion as an integrative force and source of collective identity has given way to a more individualized approach to faith centered on personal autonomy, resulting in "both an enlarged arena of voluntary choice and an enhanced freedom from structural restraint" (Hammond 1992, 10–11). According to Robert Bellah (1964), religious life in earlier times was a "one possibility thing"; in modern society, it becomes an "infinite possibility thing." This description of the move from religious identities being "ascribed" to their being "achieved" reflects developments taking place in modern society generally. Not only is religious identity increasingly chosen, but so are family, ethnic, and other identities. According to Anthony Giddens, in societies based on tradition individuals have relatively clearly defined roles, but in societies in which modernity has taken root individuals have to establish their roles for themselves. "Modernity," Giddens (1991, 20) writes, "is essentially a post-traditional order. The transformation of time and space, coupled with the disembedding mechanisms, propel social life away from the hold of preestablished precepts or practices." Modernity creates a situation of unprecedented choice. Indeed, according to Peter Berger (1980, 14), because "modernity pluralizes," it also universalizes *heresy*, or choice. Berger (1980, 25) concludes, "Modernity creates a new situation in which picking and choosing becomes an imperative."[3]

In a secularized society, people can choose *whether* to be religious and, if so, *how* they are religious. They can choose to make religion part of their identity as an athlete, or to make athletics part of their religious identity—or not. As the examples that opened this chapter suggest, many individuals do visibly choose to connect religion and sport. Unfortunately, in both the sociology of religion and the sociology of sport, efforts to systematize this relationship have lagged behind its visibility. Without question, there are a number of parallels between religion and sport at the individual level. Both evoke emotions and inculcate values. And we can easily find times and places in which individuals *use* religion in sport. For example, Coakley (2007) notes that religion can help athletes cope with uncertainty and give meaning to their activities or put them in perspective. But for every Bob Cousy, who made the sign of the cross before shooting free throws, how many Catholic professional basketball players do not? And of all individuals who shoot free throws, how many make a religious sign prior to shooting?

To push the study of religion in sport forward, we need to be more concerned with generalizability than with visibility. In this case, *data* is not simply the plural of *anecdote*. Unfortunately, there is a scarcity of good data to use in systematically investigating the connection between religion and sport in the lives of individuals. Some smaller-scale studies suggest a link. For example, Storch and his colleagues (2004) compared 57 intercollegiate athletes and 169 nonathlete undergraduates at the University of Florida and found that athletes had higher levels of conventional religious faith. There are good reasons to expect this finding. Sport shares many of the same values as certain religions, particularly Evangelical Christianity (Mathisen 2006). Overman (1997) highlights the connection between sport and the Protestant ethic of success, self-discipline, and hard work. The Protestant ethic is especially conducive to participation in organized sporting competition rather than in free and expressive play (Coakley 2007, 538).

But how generalizable are the findings of Storch and his colleagues? Two of the authors of this chapter, Yamane and Blake, have lately been analyzing data collected by UCLA's Higher Education Research Institute which speak to the question in a systematic way.[4] Using multiple regression models that control for several other variables, Yamane and Blake (2008) find that college athletes are *less* religious than college students in general. Some suggest that there is a value conflict between sport and religion that could lead to the lower levels of religious commitment we find, but we believe that a more accurate view is to see sport as a *secular competitor*

---

[3] Berger (1980, 24–25) notes that the word *heresy* "comes from the Greek verb *hairein*, which means 'to choose.' A *hairesis* originally meant, quite simply, the taking of a choice."

[4] Complete descriptions of the sample, data, and measures, as well as results from our regression analyses, are available in Yamane and Blake (2008).

to religion for people's time and attention. Religion and sport, in this view, are part of a zero-sum game, since both require investments of time and energy. Indeed, the most visible manifestations of religion in sport—wearing religious symbols or making religious gestures—require no real religious commitment by the individuals in question; think Barry Bonds. Generally, when push comes to shove for college athletes, sport wins out over religion.

Of course, in the contemporary United States, it is important to distinguish between religion and spirituality. Whereas religion is often associated with inherited tradition and dogmatic beliefs, spirituality is seen as a quality of an individual, particularly as relates to his or her personal experience. Spirituality is seen as a more primary and pure relationship to the divine than is religion (Yamane 1998). This distinction raises the possibility that college athletes are perhaps spiritual but not religious. If so, this might be accounted for by two reasons. First, one can more easily be spiritual on one's own terms, making it easier for athletes to accommodate spirituality in their busy lives. Second, for some, athletics itself can be a form of spiritual practice (Hoffman 1992), and their peak or flow experiences during performance (Jackson and Csikszentmihalyi 1999) may sensitize them to a spiritual dimension of life in general.

We find, however, no general support for this position. Our analyses of the UCLA data suggest that college athletes are *less* spiritual than students in general (Yamane and Blake 2008). Why? According to Mathisen (2006, 288), modern sport is the antithesis of play: "If play is free, sport is highly structured; if play is outside the ordinary, sport has become worklike; and, importantly, if play is intrinsic, sport is extrinsic." Therefore, as Mathisen (2006, 287) notes, it may be precisely *outside* of formally organized sporting activity that we may see the true "signals of transcendence" that Peter Berger spoke of when examining not sport but *play*. Kliever (2001) also emphasizes the notion that a modern ethic of work in sport trumps the ethic of play.

Although we found college athletes generally to be less religious and spiritual than their fellow college students, one important exception emerges in our analyses. Evangelical Protestant athletes are *more* religious *and* spiritual than college students in general. This is not surprising given the history of "Muscular Christianity" in the United States, as well as the popularity of groups such as AIA and FCA on college campuses (Cherry, DeBerg, and Porterfield 2001, 27). The theology of Muscular Christianity allows Evangelical Protestants to sacralize sporting events and also provides a framework that allows athletes to negotiate conflicts between sport and their religious beliefs (Coakley 2007, 556). This theology gets activated by AIA and FCA ministers and groups that provide strong systems of social support for belief and practice—"plausibility structures" (Berger 1967)—that are key to sustaining religiosity.

Of course, more systematic studies on more general populations are necessary in order to draw conclusions with certainty. For now, we would provisionally say that religion and sport in the lives of individuals are separate spheres of existence that connect at some times and for some people. But, as we would expect from the theory of secularization, there appears to be no inherent connection between them today.

## CONCLUSION

The theory of secularization highlights how sport and religion today exist as differentiated social institutions that can at times interact but which operate according to distinct norms. Thus, to characterize the relationship between religion and sport in modern America as a "fusion," as does Price (2005, 196), is an overstatement. At certain times and places, religion and sport do have a close relationship. But this is not the same as saying that sport has a constitutionally religious dimension, as in Mayan ball games or sumo wrestling under Shinto. The idea that sporting activity is fundamentally religious, or that religious authorities can regulate sporting activity, is a thing of the past. The secularization of sport as a social institution is thus a reality.

The fact that religion no longer fundamentally legitimates sporting activities and that sporting activities do not fulfill the legitimating function of a civil religion in American society does not mean that religion does not matter to sport or vice versa. In fact, sociologists of religion have increasingly noted the religious vibrancy that can be unleashed by macrolevel secularization. Secularization at the societal level can be a sort of liberation for religion, allowing it to multiply in form and content and to diffuse throughout society in a more liquid fashion. The sacred is no longer confined to certain places or times and is no longer controlled by certain people. It is democratized. The true vitality of religion in American sport obtains not at the institutional or civil religious level, then, but at the organizational and individual levels.

Religion and sport have both been marginalized in sociology, which is odd and unfortunate given the large number of people who regularly participate in religious and sporting activities. This dual marginalization perhaps explains the relative inattention to the nexus between religion and sport. In this chapter, we have tried to suggest that examining this connection can be beneficial to both the sociology of sport and the sociology of religion, specifically through the application of a revised theory of secularization at three levels of analysis (institutional, organizational, and individual). In conclusion, we hope this chapter offers sport scholars some insights into how some sociologists of religion think, and stimulates them in turn to bring their own insights to the attention of students of religion.

### Suggested Research

1. Neosecularization theory suggests that religious organizations should undergo some internal secularization in the process of engaging the world of sport. Researchers should focus attention on the following question: Do sport-based religious ministries simply lend legitimacy to competitive sport, or do they challenge in any way the fundamental logic of competitive sport?

2. Neosecularization theory suggests that religion is marginalized in the world of sport, since sport operates according to its own norms, which are differentiated from religious norms. Researchers should consider whether the same is true of *play*. That is, is the role of religion in relation to *play* different from its role in relation to organized and competitive sport?

3. Yamane and Blake found the connection between participation in athletics and religiosity or spirituality to be focused on a particular socioreligious group: Evangelical Protestants. Building on Yamane and Blake's research on a representative sample of college athletes, researchers should consider whether there is a systematic relationship between participation in athletics and religiosity or spirituality beyond college athletes.

## Additional Resources

### Theory

Bellah, R. 1964. Religious evolution. *American Sociological Review* 29:358–374.

Berger, P. 1967. *The sacred canopy*. New York: Doubleday.

> Bellah and Berger provide two of the most important modern statements of the theory of secularization. Both attempt to understand the effect of the modern era (or "modernity") on religion. Bellah argues that in the primitive religious world view, life is a "one possibility thing" and completely organized by the religious symbol system. By the fifth (modern) stage of religious evolution, the religious symbol system becomes "infinitely multiplex" and religious life is an "infinite possibility thing." Religion no longer has the capacity to organize all of life. Berger argues similarly that religion historically provided a "sacred canopy" under which all of reality was subsumed but that in modern society this canopy has lost its plausibility and has religion become a matter of individual choice rather than societal legitimation. Both Bellah and Berger firmly root their work in the social theories of Emile Durkheim and Max Weber; Bellah was also heavily influenced by Talcott Parsons, and Berger was influenced by the German phenomenological tradition (e.g., Alfred Schutz).

Chaves, M. 1994. Secularization as declining religious authority. *Social Forces* 72:749–774.

Yamane, D. 1997. Secularization on trial: In defense of a neosecularization paradigm. *Journal for the Scientific Study of Religion* 36:107–120.

> In the face of criticisms of the theory of secularization, Chaves articulates a revised perspective that focuses on secularization as a process not by which religion itself disappears but by which religious authority declines in the course of societal modernization. "Declining religious authority" must be analyzed on three levels: societal, organizational, and individual. Yamane grounds his argument in Chaves' work and codifies what he calls the "neosecularization" paradigm. As is evident in this chapter, Yamane also stresses the *double movement of secularization*: the broad movement in the history of the West toward a decline in the scope of religious authority vis-à-vis secular authorities and the persistence or reemergence of religious organizations under the secularized conditions established in the first movement.

Guttman, A. 1978. *From ritual to record: The nature of modern sports*. New York: Columbia University Press.

Mathisen, J. 2006. Sport. In *Handbook of religion and social institutions*, ed. H.R. Ebaugh, 285–303. New York: Springer.

Guttman and Mathisen, respectively, put sport in its proper historical and social context. Guttmann's book traces the history of modern sport, distinguishing it from ancient and medieval sport. Modern sport has seven key characteristics: secularism, equality (both of opportunity to compete and in the conditions of competition), specialization of roles, rationalization, bureaucratic organization, quantification, and the quest for records. As Guttman himself recognizes, these are key characteristics of modern society, generally, as described in the work of social theorists Max Weber and Talcott Parsons. Mathisen's chapter is a comprehensive overview of the state of the art in the sociology of religion and sport, with emphasis on folk religion and Muscular Christianity (about which he has written elsewhere).

### Sport Topic

Athletes in Action (www.aia.com) and Fellowship of Christian Athletes (www.fca.org).

Athletes in Action and the Fellowship of Christian Athletes are the two oldest, largest, and best-known sport-based ministries in America today. Both are rooted in the Evangelical Protestant tradition. Their Web sites provide glimpses into their guiding theologies and the range of activities in which they engage.

Catholic Athletes for Christ (www.catholicathletesforchrist.com), Sports Faith International (www.sportsfaithinternational.com), and Pontifical Council for the Laity, Church and Sport section (www.vatican.va/roman_curia/pontifical_councils/laity/).

These three Web sites represent organizations that come out of the Roman Catholic tradition as distinct from the evangelical Protestantism of AIA and FCA. Catholic Athletes for Christ (CAC) is a newer sport-based ministry that is meant to do what AIA and FCA do but from a Roman Catholic perspective. As is evident from the CAC Web site, the organization's activities are more limited, but the theological rational is similarly robust. Sports Faith International, founded in 2008, is "dedicated to inspiring and transforming our culture through the world of sports." The Church and Sport section of the Pontifical Council for the Laity reflects the Roman Catholic Church's official voice worldwide on this issue.

# PART

# Theories of Inequality

One finding from the collection of research in the sociology of sport over the years is that the "playing field" is still not level (Zimbalist 1999). Several chapters in part III address lingering inequities head-on.

## Feminist Theory

Addressing one of the biggest concerns of the 21st century for feminist sport scholars, Angela Hattery writes in "Feminist Theory and the Study of Sport: An Illustration From Title IX" that feminist theory applied to sport attempts to explain the power differential between men and women inside the institution of sport. One glaring example of continuing inequity illustrated in the chapter is the annual salary differential between the winningest coach in the history of intercollegiate basketball (men's and women's), the University of Tennessee's women's basketball coach Pat Summitt, who is paid $1 less than men's coach Bruce Pearl. Even though Summitt "lives" in the basketball world of luminaries such as Dean Smith, John Wooden, and Bobby Knight, whereas Pearl does not and probably never will, salaries were set by the administration according to the old rule: Women earn less than men, even when they are clearly more qualified. Summitt's lower salary is a symbolic reminder that women's sports—indeed all things associated with women—are considered second-class.

## Social Reproduction Theory

In "Social and Cultural Capital: Race, School Attachment, and the Role of High School Sports," Rhonda Levine zeroes in on an issue clearly in need of exploration. Is the high school a place of academic learning or, as it seems, a place where boys and, increasingly, girls go to play sports? The role of the high school today is examined using the theoretical work of sociologists such as Bourdieu and Coleman to address issues of the social reproduction of advantages and disadvantages that accrue over generations by race, ethnicity, gender, and social class.

## Race, Class, and Gender Theory

Along with Benny Cooper, I take on a very understudied social problem in sport: the violence perpetuated against women by their intimate partners. In "Race, Class, and Gender Theory: Violence Against Women in the Institution of Sport," we argue for (a) more exposure of these acts, (b) stiffer penalties, and (c) more even application of penalties—regardless of the status of the athletes who psychologically or physically maimed their partners. One recent case is illustrative: A judicial hearing board found Syracuse University basketball player Eric Devendorf guilty of violating the university's student code of conduct—he was accused of physically assaulting a woman—and applied the penalty of indefinite suspension for the rest of the 2008–2009 academic year (Cole 2008). Devendorf was suspended from Syracuse University on December 10, 2008. On December 27, 2008, ESPNews carried the story that Devendorf was reinstated from the suspension. The initial finding by police that he had beaten his girlfriend was apparently misunderstood and was now recharacterized as a case of verbal abuse. The case resonates with points made in the chapter.

## Hegemonic Masculinity

Clemson University's Bryan Denham takes us inside the gym in "Masculinities and the Sociology of Sport: Issues and Ironies in the 21st Century" for a look behind the scenes at the sport of male bodybuilding. Denham utilizes the framework provided by hegemonic masculinity theory to examine the men who participate in bodybuilding in order to better understand the athlete who is said to be "stoic and self-reliant, athletically rugged, strictly heterosexual, and void of complaint." The examination in this chapter demonstrates "the paradoxical, strained nature of masculinity in contemporary society," revealing that few of these men ever reach their ideal goal and that, as a result, they tend to "question their self-worth and live in perpetual fear of failing to meet the expectations both of women and of other men."

## Structuration Theory

In this chapter, titled "Getting Girls in the Game: Negotiations of Structure and Agency in a Girls' Recreational Sport Program," Cheryl Cooky uses ethnographic study at an after-school program for "at-risk" girls to look at how structure "shapes the production and reproduction of social interactions." Specifically, Cooky attempts to understand culture and agency. She looks at "youth as constructed within the context of cultural discourses on 'at-risk' youth and girls in sport." Moreover, she discusses "the ways in which adult organizers and girl participants, through their everyday interactions, negotiated the tensions that surfaced between the program's primary objective to empower girls and the girls' resistance to the program."

Brand X Pictures

# 8 | Feminist Theory and the Study of Sport

## An Illustration from Title IX

*Angela J. Hattery, PhD*

**Social theory:** Feminist theory

**Proponents of the theory:** Claudia Card, Susan Bordo, Joan Acker, Cynthia Fuchs Epstein, Judith Lorber, Susan Griffin, Susan Brownmiller, Emily Kane, Mary K. "Mimi" Schippers, Patricia Hill Collins, Rebecca Walker, Jennifer Baumgardner, Patricia Yancey Martin, Charlotte Perkins Gilman

**What the theory says:** Feminist theory aims to understand the nature of inequality; it focuses on gender politics, power relations, and sexuality. While generally providing a critique of social relations, feminist theory focuses largely on analyzing gender inequality and on the promotion of women's rights, interests, and issues. Themes explored in feminism include art history, contemporary art, aesthetics, discrimination, stereotyping, objectification (especially sexual), and oppression. Patriarchy is conceptualized as a system of power and oppression that values men and male activities and qualities over women and their activities and qualities. Feminists argue that gender is a core organizing principle of social life, that it exists across time and geography, and that it both creates and requires gender difference—and as a result essentializes masculinity and femininity.

Feminist theory traces its ancestry to social philosophers such as John Stuart Mill, who advocated human rights and liberty for all people and penned *The Subjection of Women*. The development of feminist theory is generally understood to have a synergistic relationship with the "feminist movement" that has occurred across three "waves." Specifically, feminist theory developed alongside the issues that were seen as most compelling for women at particular points in history. Thus, in order to develop a good understanding of the historical movement of feminist theory, it must be contextualized by a discussion of theory as a response to social issues that created the various "waves" as social movements. Because the institution of sport was not viewed as central to the lives of men or women—men's primary participation would have been limited to those privileged enough to attend elite, men-only colleges such as Harvard and Yale—sport as an institution did not receive attention from first-wave feminists. Yet in working to understand the development of feminist theory and its later application to sport, a brief review of the history of feminism is instructive.

## THE FIRST WAVE

The first wave of feminism focused on two key issues: (1) the status of women in the family (marriage, economic self-sufficiency, reproductive rights)—an issue that continues to be important and is now examined in terms of "gender roles"—and (2) women's suffrage. Early feminist theorists, who wrote pamphlets and letters about contemporary issues, were also active in the social movements for suffrage and reproductive rights. Suffragists such as Elizabeth Cady Stanton and Susan B. Anthony wrote about and agitated for women's right to vote. Emma Goldman, one of the early feminist writers, along with the Grimké sisters and Margaret Sanger, viewed marriage and reproduction as the key institutions in the subordination of women. They wrote about and agitated for women's rights to choose both marriage and motherhood.

Goldman put it succinctly:

> *I demand the independence of woman, her right to support herself; to live for herself; to love whomever she pleases, or as many as she pleases. I demand freedom for both sexes, freedom of action, freedom in love and freedom in motherhood (qtd. in Wexler 1984).*

These early feminists understood the importance of economic and political freedom and believed that it could be achieved only by gaining control over all aspects of one's sexuality and reproductive capacity. Goldman argued, much as Engels (Engels and Leacock 1972) had, that marriage was less often a relationship of love and more often a relationship of exploitation that allowed men to extract resources—including labor power and access to sexuality—from their wives.

> *Marriage is primarily an economic arrangement, an insurance pact. It differs from the ordinary life insurance agreement only in that it is more binding, more exacting. Its returns are insignificantly small compared with the investments. In taking out an insurance policy one pays for it in dollars and cents, always at liberty to discontinue payments. If, however, woman's premium is a husband, she pays for it with her name, her privacy, her self-respect, her very life, "until death doth part." Moreover, the marriage insurance condemns her to life-long dependency, to parasitism, to complete uselessness, individual as well as social. Man, too, pays his toll, but as his sphere is wider, marriage does not limit him as much as woman. He feels his chains more in an economic sense (Goldman 1911, 240).*

After the first battle of the 20th century was won—when the 19th amendment to the U.S. Constitution, passed in 1920, gave women the right to vote—the feminist movement took a hiatus of sorts, but it reignited during the tumultuous period of social upheaval that characterized the 1950s and 1960s. Feminists adjusted their sights, as the issues facing women remained the same, yet also changed.

## MODERN FEMINIST THEORY: THE SECOND WAVE

Following in large part on the heels of the Civil Rights Movement of the 1950s and 1960s, when African Americans were using diverse tools in their efforts to obtain civil rights—sit-ins, lawsuits, challenges to the U.S. Constitution—feminists began to agitate once again to expand the rights of women. Feminist activism of the late 1960s and early 1970s focused on constants such as reproductive rights (*Roe v. Wade* was decided in January 1973), economic freedom (proposed legislation included the Equal Pay Act, which was signed into law in 1963 but is still not enforced successfully),[1] and the Equal Rights Amendment (which has never passed), as well as

---

[1] In June 2007, the U.S. Supreme Court ruled in a case that put significant time limits in place for filing pay discrimination suits. This ruling will make enforcing the Equal Pay Act considerably more difficult.

on new goals inspired by the civil rights legislation of the 1950s and 1960s—specifically, equal access, which culminated in Title IX.

Feminist theory responded to the changing landscape and developed into several strains, the two most common of which are liberal feminism and radical feminism (Jaggar 1983). Liberal feminism assumes that the key problem of gender inequality is the domination of institutions by men. Men control the economic sphere, the political sphere, the judicial sphere, the educational sphere, the medical sphere, and so on. Liberal feminism focuses primarily on transforming these existing structures so that membership and power inside these institutions are shared across gender lines (Jaggar 1983). Many feminist social movements—including the movements for reproductive rights, the Equal Rights Amendment, and Title IX—involve strategies proposed by liberal feminist theory. Thus, liberal feminists would invest in a policy such as Title IX as a strategy for achieving gender equality in sport.

In contrast, radical feminism assumes that the very structures themselves have been so poisoned by patriarchy that they cannot be transformed but must be completed eradicated and rebuilt from the ground up (Jaggar 1983). For example, many radical feminists believe that the entire economic system—capitalism—which they argue has been built fundamentally on the exploitation of women (for an excellent discussion, see Acker 2006), must be destroyed and replaced with an alternative economic system; most radical feminists favor some version of socialism. In terms of sport, radical feminists would argue that the entire system of organized sport—high school, intercollegiate, and professional—would have to be destroyed and replaced with a system that is not fundamentally based on the exploitation and dominance of women as cheerleaders, wives, sex objects, and victims of sexual and intimate partner violence (see Smith and Cooper in chapter 10 in this volume). Thus, in order to establish gender equality in sport, the entire institution of sport would have to be dismantled and rebuilt from the ground up, and this rebuilding effort would hold gender equality as its core organizing principle.

## POSTMODERN FEMINISM: THE THIRD WAVE

One of the primary criticisms of second-wave feminists and the feminist movement was that it rested on the assumption that gender was the key status around which all oppression was organized. Primarily due to pressure by feminists of color, who felt that second-wave feminism rendered variations by race and class invisible, the third wave has focused on the ways in which race, class, and gender—and other statuses---are part of a complex system of oppression that results in variations in gender oppression. This newest form of feminism involves a fusion of feminist theory with critical race theory. The product—race, class, and gender theory—assumes that multiple systems of domination create inequality, both alone and as a result of interactions with each other.

The race, class, and gender framework was largely developed by black and multiracial feminists (Andersen 2001; Baca Zinn and Dill 2005; Collins 1994, 1998, 2004; Davis 1983; King 1988). This theoretical paradigm rests on the assumption that systems of oppression and domination (i.e., patriarchy, capitalism, and racial domination) exist independently and are woven together in what Zinn and Dill (2005) refer to as a matrix of domination. They and others argue that many phenomena—including child rearing (Hill and Sprague 1999), the wage gap (Padavic and Reskin 2002), incarceration (Hattery and Smith 2007; Western 2006), and intimate partner violence (Esqueda and Harrison 2007)—are best understood when we consider the independent and interdependent effects of these systems of domination (see also Crenshaw 1991; Smith 1998). However, though second-wave liberal feminists attended to the institution of sport, very little is written about sport from the perspective of third-wave feminists. Their focus has been primarily on access to power, relationships in the family, reproductive rights, and economic self-sufficiency—all of which vary by race and class. Thus, though the institution of sport is filled with discussions of race as it pertains to male athletes, very little attention has been paid to racial variation and how it shapes the experiences of women athletes and gender more widely.

Additionally, drawing both on radical feminism and on race, class, and gender theory, postmodern or third-wave feminism is especially concerned with power and the ways in which it simultaneously shapes and is shaped by gender (Acker 2006; Epstein 2007; Lorber 1995). This focus on power makes the theoretical framework provided by postmodern feminism useful in examining the ways in which gendered power shapes the institution of sport, as well as the constructions of masculinity and femininity that are applied to athletes—and, to a lesser extent, coaches—themselves.

## TITLE IX AND GENDER EQUITY IN INTERCOLLEGIATE SPORT

The illustration or case study for this chapter comes from a larger project on gender equity that is reported in Hattery, Smith, and Staurowsky (2008). The case study provided here allows us to examine the degree to which the tenets of Title IX legislation—equal access regardless of gender—are met with respect to intercollegiate sports in the United States. The case study also allows us to test the utility of various forms of feminist theory in examining gender and sport, specifically as they relate to Title IX.

### Title IX

*Title IX* refers to a relatively simple law with unbelievably complex implications:

> *No person in the United States shall, on the basis of sex, be excluded from participation in, be denied the benefits of, or be subjected to discrimination under any education program or activity receiving Federal financial assistance. . . . (Carpenter and Acosta 2005).*

Enacted in 1972, Title IX was one of a series of laws and legal decisions that resulted from the women's movement, or second-wave feminism. As previously noted, the Equal Pay Act had been passed in 1963, and *Roe v. Wade* would be decided in 1973. However, though we most frequently think of and debate Title IX in terms of its effect on female (and male) participation in high school and collegiate athletics, the original statute made no reference to athletics. The legislation covers all educational activities, and complaints under Title IX alleging discrimination in fields such as science or math education, or in other aspects of academic life (e.g., access to health care and dormitory facilities), are not unheard of. The law also applies to nonsport activities such as participation in school bands and cheerleading.

Because the primary focus of Title IX is *access*, the majority of the research on gender and Title IX has focused on *participation* by girls and women—specifically, counting how many girls and young women play organized sports and how many women coach sports teams.[2] Title IX was written to provide equal access by gender, and the majority of research on Title IX has limited the discussion of equal access simply to participation. My intent in this chapter is to move beyond assessing Title IX based simply on participation and to examine its effect on providing *equal opportunity*. Drawing on the work of contemporary feminist scholars, I focus on Title IX as contested terrain, where the issue is not so much one of participation but rather one of power—namely, the power to control the institution of sport and allocate its most highly guarded resource: money.

## Feminist Theory and Title IX

Contemporary feminist theorists such as Joan Acker (2006), Judith Lorber (1995), and Cynthia Fuchs Epstein (2007) argue that patriarchy—the system of power that privileges men and male activities and qualities over women and their activities and qualities—both *creates* and *requires* gender difference and, as a result, essentializes masculinity and femininity. As Lorber writes,

> *I see gender as an institution that establishes patterns of expectations for individuals, orders the social processes of every day life, is built into the major social organizations of society, such as the economy, ideology, the family, and politics [and sport], and is also an entity in and of itself (Lorber 1995, 1).*

Sport, feminists argue, has been socially constructed as hypermasculine, and as a result, access to this closed world has been more or less limited to men. Evidence for this view can be found in the incredible resistance to including women, on the part both of individual men and of institutions. Augusta National, the golf club that is the home of the Masters Tournament, does not allow women as members. When women have attempted to join, or even just protested outside the grounds, the reaction has bordered on violence. A key question, then, is this: If sport is so good for men, why have men, and institutions, been so resistant to offering all that is good in sport to women? Epstein's presidential address to the American Sociological Association offers important insight:

---

[2] Carpenter and Acosta have put together a comprehensive count of female athletes and coaches every year since 1973. Furthermore, they track trends by individual sports and by level (high school versus college). Their reports are the best source available for tracking trends in participation and coaching by gender.

*The enforcement of the [gender] distinction is achieved through cultural and ideological means that justify the differentiation. This is despite the fact that, unlike every other dichotomous category of people, females and males are necessarily bound together, sharing the same domiciles and most often the same racial and social class statuses. . . . It is important to note that women's inequality is not simply another case of social inequality, a view I held in the past (Epstein 1970). I am convinced that societies and strategic sub-groups within them, such as political and work institutions, maintain their boundaries—their very social organization—through the use of invidious distinctions made between males and females. Everywhere, women's subordination is basic to maintaining the social cohesion and stratification systems of ruling and governing groups—male groups—on national and local levels, in the family, and in all other major institutions. Most dramatically, this process is at work today in the parts of the world where control of females' behavior, dress, and use of public space have been made representations of orthodoxies in confrontation with modernism, urbanism, and secular society. But even in the most egalitarian societies, such as the United States, women's autonomy over their bodies, their time, their ability to decide their destinies, is constantly at risk when it intrudes on male power (Epstein 2007, 4).*

Epstein argues several key points that are important to our discussion here, the first being that, of all statuses, gender is the only one for which status groups (men and women) have continuous experiences with cross-status intimacy—in this case, cross-gender intimacy, as intimate partners, in child–parent relationships, in cross-gender sibling relationships, and so forth—and these experiences occur in all societies, regardless of the culture's norms surrounding sex segregation. Second, this intimacy requires the hypermaintenance of gender boundaries; in other words, it requires that we define clearly what it is to be a man and what it is to be a woman and that these qualities be nonoverlapping and mutually exclusive. Furthermore, access to institutions will be strongly shaped by gender, such that many institutions, especially those with any significant power, will be highly segregated. Third, women's ability to control their own "destinies is constantly at risk when it intrudes on male power." In other words, the more power women gain in society—for example, being elected to the U.S. Senate, being appointed CEO of a Fortune 500 company, having access to a safe and legal abortion—the more frequently men will attempt to articulate gender differences and enforce gender boundaries.

What does all of this have to do with sport? I frame the analysis presented in this case study—an examination of the resources allocated to women intercollegiate athletes and women's intercollegiate sports programs—through the lens provided by Epstein. I suggest that the more access women have to sports participation and coaching, the more media exposure women athletes have, the more important it becomes for men to remind women that they are still just women. One way to articulate gender is to focus on gender differences: Women can't dunk the basketball. Women's sports are less interesting to watch. And one way to enforce gender boundaries is to allocate resources according to power rather than need. In other words, I hypothesize that since the passage of Title IX, as women's athletics has encroached on the territory previously reserved exclusively for men, the resources allocated to women athletes and programs at the intercollegiate level vary as much by gender as they do by sport, and that this variance has less to do with the inherent costs of supporting a sport than it does with the gender of the athletes playing it.

## The Case Study

This case study is based on examining resource allocations to men's and women's intercollegiate sports using data that is federally mandated by Title IX through the Equity in Athletics Disclosure Act (EADA). Data on participation and resources—both expenses and revenues—must be reported yearly by each college and university athletic department. Data can be requested through the Freedom of Information Act. My collaborators and I contacted 27 Division I Bowl Championship Series (BCS) athletic departments and requested their EADA 2006 reports; these reports constitute the data analyzed in this study. Specifically, this analysis compares the funding received by men's and women's teams. Additionally, using data compiled from the official Web site of the NCAA (www.ncaa.org/wps/portal), college and university Web sites, and local media reports, I examine the roles that success, the coach's gender, and the gender of the athletes being coached play in determining salaries awarded to top coaches.[3]

## Findings

The most basic focus is on the degree to which gender differences in resource allocation continue to exist. To answer this question, I examined resources allocated to all sports teams for which institutions had both a men's and a women's team.[4] Next, the analysis was narrowed to two key sports: basketball and soccer. These two sports were chosen for several reasons. First, the majority of schools in the sample had basketball and soccer teams for both men and women, and, as noted by Carpenter and Acosta (2006), basketball and soccer are two of the sports offered most commonly for intercollegiate women. Second, many people, such as Glenn B. George, have identified soccer as a sport in which gender equity has been achieved (Glenn B. George, personal communication, 2007). Third, because basketball is a high-profile, revenue-generating sport—increasingly so for women as well as men—and soccer is not (for either gender), I was able to explore the presence (or absence) of gender equity in resources in a high-profile sport as compared to that in a nonrevenue sport.[5]

---

[3] For a detailed discussion of the methods, see Hattery, Smith, and Staurowsky (2008).

[4] Data not shown.

[5] Though in various regions of the country different sports are considered high-profile—for example, ice hockey is a high-profile sport in Wisconsin—basketball is the only sport we could identify that is high-profile across all regions of the country. It is also the only high-profile sport that consistently offers teams for both men and women. The obvious high-profile sport that does not is football.

The data presented in table 8.1 are reported as the average difference between the resources allocated to men and men's teams and those allocated to women and women's teams. The data were generated by subtracting the average resources allocated to women and women's teams from the average allocated to men and men's teams. Thus, a minus (-) indicates that the average resources allocated to women and women's teams were greater than the average resources allocated to men and men's teams. Positive numbers reflect the reverse.

The data in table 8.1 indicate several important measures of continued gender inequity in resource allocation. To summarize:

- Male student-athletes receive, on average, US$598 more in scholarship aid per year than do female student-athletes.
- Coaches of male teams earn, on average, US$190,310 more than coaches of female teams earn.
- Men's teams have, on average, US$271,490 dollars more to spend on recruiting than do women's teams.

When we examine the data more closely, we see that there is considerably more gender equity in the nonrevenue sport—soccer—than in the high-profile, revenue-generating sport of basketball.

In particular, I note that, on average, women's soccer players and women's soccer teams receive *slightly greater* resource allocations than do male soccer players and male soccer teams. In contrast, gender inequity clearly persists in basketball, where men's basketball players and teams continue to benefit considerably from athletic department resource allocations as compared with women's basketball players and teams. Of particular importance is the fact that the average gender differences in basketball are *more than 10 times greater* than the slight advantage seen in women's soccer. Overall, the data in table 8.2 (on p. 106)—which reports the average difference between, on one hand, men and men's teams, and, on the other hand, women and women's team—document the fact that gender equity in

**Table 8.1**   Gender Differences (Men's Resources Minus Women's Resources) in Expenditures*

|  | Soccer operating expenses | Soccer per capita spending | Basketball operating expenses | Basketball per capita spending | Scholarship aid per capita | Head coach salary | Recruiting spending |
|---|---|---|---|---|---|---|---|
| Mean | - US$22,708 | - US$901 | US$275,050 | US$12,303 | US$598 | US$190,310 | US$271,490 |
| Median | - US$4,100 | - US$165 | US$211,559 | US$8,786 | US$430 | US$154,779 | US$225,818 |
| Stan. Dev. | 89149 | 2737 | 280371 | 21271 | 3752 | 195104 | 210586 |

* Data on aid (scholarships), salary, and recruiting expenses are reported in aggregate and are not available by team.

**Table 8.2** Gender Difference (Men's Resources Minus Women's Resources) in Soccer Versus Basketball Expenditures

| Soccer | | Basketball | |
|---|---|---|---|
| Operating expenses | Per capita | Operating expenses | Per capita |
| - US$22,708 | - US$901 | US$275,505 | US$12,303 |

resource allocation is being achieved in nonrevenue sports such as soccer but that gender *inequity* persists and is substantial in the high-profile sport of basketball.

## Success

Next, I examined the degree to which success "pays off" in resource allocation in intercollegiate athletics. It is logical to conclude that successful programs and successful coaches can demand greater resources for themselves and their teams. We certainly have evidence for this among the ranks of football and men's basketball head coaches. For example, in 2007, Nick Saban signed an 8-year, US$32 million contract (i.e., paying US$4 million per year) with the University of Alabama. Furthermore, the relationship between a player's success and compensation is evident in contracts such as that of Alex Rodriguez, who signed a 10-year, US$275 million contract in late 2007 with the New York Yankees.

In light of such evidence, I examined the relationship between success and resource allocation in women's soccer by considering the case of the University of North Carolina at Chapel Hill (UNC), which is by all measures the most successful of women's intercollegiate soccer programs. The Tar Heels have won 18 national championships and have produced the most talented women's soccer players in U.S. history, including Mia Hamm. The data in table 8.3 examine gender differences in resource allocation for women's soccer at UNC as compared with the sample mean.

The data in table 8.3 reveal *smaller* gender differences in resource allocation for soccer (men's as compared with women's) at the University of North Carolina at Chapel Hill than the mean for the sample. As an advocate for gender equity, I view this as good news, yet it is also interesting to note that the women's soccer program at UNC—arguably the best women's soccer program in the country— experiences *less* of an advantage over the UNC men's program than the sample mean. Though this may indicate an overall level of gender equity in intercollegiate soccer, it also suggests that there is *no resource advantage for winning in women's intercollegiate soccer.*

**Table 8.3** Gender Differences (Men's Resources Minus Women's Resources) for Soccer at UNC Versus Sample Mean

| | UNC | Sample Mean |
|---|---|---|
| Operating expenses | - US$22,708 | - US$35,443 |
| Per capita spending | - US$901 | - US$1,088 |

Next, it was important to examine the role of success on resource allocation in women's basketball. Because women's intercollegiate basketball has a tournament structure that is modeled after the men's Final Four, I created a scale on which each team received 1 point for each Final Four appearance. (The Final Four in women's intercollegiate basketball has existed for 26 years.) In order to test the relationship between success in women's basketball and gender differences in resource allocation for basketball, I correlated the number of Final Four appearances (the independent variable) with each dependent variable measure. Of all the variables tested, only two correlations were statistically significant: gender differences in per capita spending and gender differences in recruiting.

Interpreting the data in table 8.4, we see that success in women's basketball results in a slight *advantage* in per capita spending for women's basketball teams and a significant *disadvantage* in recruiting spending relative to men's teams at the same institution. I suspect that the major item contributing to the slight advantage in per capita spending in successful women's basketball programs is the salary of the head coach. At many of the most successful women's basketball programs—for example, the University of Tennessee, Duke University, the University of Connecticut—the head coach of the women's basketball program earns a salary commensurate with the salary of a moderately successful men's basketball program at the same institution. For example, Pat Summitt, head coach of the University of Tennessee Volunteers, has made 18 Final Four appearances and won 8 national championships and earns a bit over US$1 million per year. Because coaches' salaries are captured in the per capita measure, I suspect that successful teams have coaches who make high salaries and thus their per capita spending is slightly higher than the sample average. In addition, at institutions with the most successful women's basketball teams—which consequently also have the highest-paid coaches of women's teams—the coaches of the men's teams are paid salaries that are *slightly higher* than those of the coaches of the women's teams.[6] This difference persists even when the coaches of the women's teams are

**Table 8.4** Relationship Between Success in Women's Basketball and Gender Differences in Resource Allocation for Intercollegiate Basketball Teams

| | **Final Four Appearances** |
|---|---|
| Gender differences in per capita spending (male spending minus female spending) | - .842* |
| Gender differences in recruiting spending (male minus female) | .767** |

\* Significant at the p<.01 level
\*\* Significant at the p<.05 level

[6] Note that we cannot talk about this issue in terms of the gender of the coach, because some of the most successful women's basketball teams, including the University of Connecticut, have male coaches. Thus in this analysis we must talk about the gender of the players, not the gender of the coach.

more successful than the coaches of the men's teams. For example, Bruce Pearl, head coach of the men's basketball team at the University of Tennessee, slightly out-earns Pat Summitt, who is the winningest coach in intercollegiate basketball history—men's or women's—eclipsing even Dean Smith, the legendary coach at the University of North Carolina at Chapel Hill.

It's also interesting to note that success in women's basketball depresses recruiting money. I suspect that this results from an assumption on the part of athletic directors that because success in women's basketball is heavily concentrated in a handful of programs—there is little parity relative to men's basketball—highly successful programs sell themselves on the court and thus can save money on recruiting. In comparing highly successful programs with less successful programs, the EADA data reveal two important things. First, less successful programs have even smaller recruiting budgets; less successful women's programs have only 60-70% of the recruiting budgets available to highly successful programs. But, second, overall, regardless of the success of the womens' programs, their recruiting budgets are *always* only a fraction of the budgets allocated to men's teams for recruiting purposes. The point is that athletic directors don't reward highly successful women's programs with big recruiting budgets most likely because they don't feel it is necessary for continued success. In contrast, there is more parity in men's programs and thus there are many more successful teams vying for the same top prospects. Presumably this is part of the justification for large recruiting budgets for men's basketball teams.

## DISCUSSION

> As women gain recognition and status in sport, they will threaten the established order of male dominance. For example, in 1995, at the University of Connecticut,[7] both the women's and men's basketball teams were ranked number one in the country, and both teams enjoyed capacity crowds during their respective games. However, the men's head coach, Jim Calhoun, clearly resented the women's success. He told a reporter that having his team's accomplishments compared with those of the women's team was like having "mosquito bites"—in other words, irritating. It was also reported that when Calhoun encountered the crowd departing from a women's basketball game, he remarked that the university would have to set up a senior citizens home and day-care center for the fans attending the women's game (Kane 1996).

How can we interpret the findings that have been presented here? Overall, 35 years after the passage of the landmark civil rights legislation that is Title IX, intercollegiate sports can hardly be described as gender equitable. Though rates of participation have skyrocketed for women, the level of resources allocated to their teams leaves much to be desired.

---

[7] The UConn women's and men's teams each won the national basketball championship during the 2003–2004 season—the first time that both titles were won by teams from the same school.

Here, I suggest several reasons for this persistence in gender inequality in resource allocation. First, regardless of what anyone looking through rose-colored glasses may say, money talks. We invest both personally and institutionally in things that we value. Jonathan Kozol is fond of saying that nothing provides a clearer measure of the value we place on children's lives than what we invest in their education (2001, 2005). I suggest that the same holds true in intercollegiate athletics. One of the clearest indications we have of the value we place on women's sports is not the level of participation—though we feel good that we "let" girls play sports—but the resources we invest in their enterprise.

> *Sport is one of the most important institutions in American culture, as is demonstrated by the vast resources spent on sport-related enterprises. With respect to discretionary spending alone, billions of dollars are spent annually on the sale of licensed sports products. In spite of the all-pervasive influence of sport, however, academic scholars have largely ignored its significance. But if sport is "just a game," why are so much time, money, and cultural support invested in this particular institution? (Kane 1996).*

One advantage of the case study presented here, in addition to the fact that it is one of the few that examines the implementation of Title IX by analyzing resource allocations, is the research design, which allows for comparison of the same type of allocation for the same sport at the same institution. This design allows the researcher to control for variation in the costs of certain sports, as well as institutional differences. When we control the analysis in this way, the only viable explanation for gender differences is discrimination. By comparing, for example, men's basketball to women's basketball at the same institution, we can determine whether or not women are getting fair and equal treatment. The answer is no. I am hard-pressed to identify *any* reason why the per capita budgets and operating budgets for men's basketball are, on average, *more than 10 times greater* than for women's basketball at the same institution when tuition costs, facilities costs, travel costs, equipment costs, and staff costs ought to be the same, or at least comparable. And, the answers of course lie in several places, the most significant of which are salaries for head coaches.

Anecdotally, I know, as a professor on a Bowl Championship Series (BCS) college campus with student-athletes in my classes, that there are many other differences as well, including the cost of the pregame meal, the number of new shoes allocated per player per season, and the cost of travel. On my campus, the men's basketball team flies a charter plane to all games outside of the state, whereas the women's team travels by coach bus. Not only are these vastly different experiences in terms of *quality*—as is required by Title IX—but they also produce different outcomes. In short, charter air travel allows the men to be away from campus for a shorter period of time and thus miss fewer classes. Yet, I remind the reader, for all of this investment and rationalizing about the need to pay for charter air travel so that the institution can minimize the time that the men spend away from campus—and thus miss fewer classes—men's basketball players post the lowest graduation rates of all male student-athletes, and their rates are significantly below those posted by women's basketball players. So I ask yet again: How is this investment justified? It is often justified by the myth that men's sports, especially football, bring in considerable revenue to the university. In fact, according to research complied by Mark Aleysia at the *Indianapolis Star* and reported by Earl Smith (2007), fewer than 10% of all universities reported that their football teams made a profit.

That said, how can we explain the relative equality in soccer? I suggest that the situation with soccer is similar to that of most nonrevenue sports: In the overall athletic hierarchy, these sports are already so devalued and receive so much less funding that there are not many ways to invest even less in the women playing these sports. As Billy Preston once sang, "Nothing from nothing leaves nothing." And, in analysis that is not reported in this paper, I found that the less money invested in men's sports, the narrower the gender differences. For example, in examining track and field, we find that there is almost no funding for any athlete and that the gender differences are minute.

Finally, I ask, if the goal of intercollegiate sports is to provide an opportunity to get a college education while simultaneously having the opportunity to have a rich athletic experience, how can we justify investing so much less in the experiences of women than in those of men? Anyone who has watched the documentary *A Hero for Daisy* or followed the plight of the Yale women's crew team must ask the question: Why did women like Chris Ernst and her team have to fight just to have the right to the same warm shower the men got after practice?

## CONCLUSION

The analysis in this chapter focused on gender differences in resource allocation at Bowl Championship Series (BCS) institutions. Specifically, I compared resource allocations at institutions that fielded teams for both men and women in the same sport. In order to examine the role that prestige plays in shaping gender differences, I narrowed the analysis to soccer (a lower-prestige sport characterized as gender equitable) and basketball (a highly prestigious, masculinized sport).

In sum, the average women's soccer team had *slightly greater* resource allocation than the average men's soccer team (calculated by institution), whereas the average men's basketball team had *significantly greater* resource allocation than the average women's basketball team (calculated by institution). The average gender difference in basketball was 10 times greater than the average gender difference in soccer. In other words, gender differences were minimal in soccer, which is considered to be a relatively gender-equitable sport, and they were huge in the highly prestigious, highly masculinized world of intercollegiate basketball.

Finally, I examined the role that success played in gender differences in resource allocation for the most successful women's soccer and basketball teams. For the most successful women's soccer program—the University of North Carolina—success reduced the slight advantage that women's soccer teams hold, on average, over men's teams at the same institution. In contrast, success in women's basketball—as demonstrated by the University of Tennessee program—only very slightly reduces the average enormous gender differences that exist in the resource allocations to the women's team as compared with those to the men's team. In other words, success in women's basketball and soccer have very little effect on a team's access to the resources available to men's teams at the same institution. In short: Winning doesn't pay much in women's intercollegiate sports.

As noted in the discussion of feminism, one of the characteristics of a patriarchal culture such as that which exists in the United States, is the devaluing of women and women's activities. Furthermore, Epstein has argued that the more women gain access to and power in prestigious male institutions—such as politics, the economy, institutions of higher learning—the more important it is for men to enforce gender boundaries. If Epstein is right, then we can predict that—as the data presented here demonstrate—the more competitive women's basketball players become, and the more attention they take from men's basketball, the more important it is to enforce gender differences and gender boundaries. One way to accomplish this—in short, to remind female student-athletes that, after all, they are still "only girls"—is to invest less in their experience. Talk to any woman basketball player on almost any Bowl Championship Series (BCS) college campus and she'll tell you that no matter how many games she and her teammates win or how many postseason tournaments they appear in, they are well aware that men playing the same sport on the same campus get more perks: better food, nicer hotels, better travel, and more sneakers. These are potent reminders of their subordinate place in the gender hierarchy (Acker 2006).

Thus postmodern feminist theory enables us to go beyond a more simplistic understanding of gender and the institution of sport by moving us beyond focusing on participation—which has largely been achieved and is the focus of liberal feminism—to a discussion of power (operationalized here as resources), which is the primary focus of postmodern feminist theory. When we apply a postmodern theoretical framework to the study of gender equity in sport, we come to the conclusion that, as demonstrated here, there is little evidence for gender equity in sport, and when it is found it is least likely to occur in the sports that are highly masculinized and highly prestigious.

## Suggested Research

1. Expand the analysis beyond soccer and basketball to sports, such as track and field, that are given even fewer resources.

2. Expand the analysis to hockey, which is highly masculinized and very prestigious—and was integrated only recently—yet is highly localized in the upper regions of the United States.

3. Expand the analysis to a site of significant power by considering women's access to the role of athletic director.

4. Expand the analysis to examine gender differences between athletic directors. Do differences exist in salary, responsibilities, who one reports to, and the prestige of the institutions where women and men are hired as athletic directors?

# Additional Resources

**Theory**

Acker, J. 2006. *Class questions, feminist answers*. New York: Routledge.

Acker's book explores the relationship between two key institutions: patriarchy and the economy. She examines the ways in which patriarchy provided gender-based oppression and inequality that were central to the development of capitalism, especially in the Western world. This is an excellent resource for exploring one form of postmodern feminism.

Epstein, C.F. 2007. Great divides: The cultural, cognitive, and social bases of the global subordination of women. *American Sociological Review* 72:1–22.

Epstein's speech, published as an essay, explores the way in which gender is socially constructed in such as manner as to essentialize masculinity (and maleness) and femininity (and femaleness) as binary and diametrically opposed. Epstein's piece is also instructive in exploring the ways in which segregation is employed as a strategy to deal with the conflict inherent in the need to maintain a gender hierarchy while having a high level of intimacy across status groups.

Jaggar, A. 1983. *Feminist politics and human nature*. Lanham, MD: Rowman & Allanheld.

Jaggar's book provides an excellent history of the feminist movement and the development of theory. Her book also contains an excellent summary of the primary tenets of the various forms of feminist theory that predominated during the second wave—specifically, liberal and radical feminisms.

Baumgardner, J., and A. Richards. 2000. *Manifesta: Young women, feminism, and the future*. New York: Farrar, Straus & Giroux.

Walker, R. 1995. *To be real: Telling the truth and changing the face of feminism*. New York: Anchor Books.

Baumgardner and Walker are considered to be two of the leading contributors to third-wave feminist theory. Both of these books explore key concepts of third-wave feminism, provide critique of second-wave feminist theory, and offer resources for further exploration and reading.

**Sport Topic**

Women in Intercollegiate Sport (http://webpages.charter.net/womeninsport/).

This Web site, provided by R. Vivian Acosta and Linda Jean Carpenter, offers all 35 years' worth of their "gender report card" that documents women's participation as athletes and coaches in high school and college sports.

National Association of Collegiate Women Athletics Administrators (http://www.nacwaa.org/rc/rc_titleix_main.php).

> NACWAA's Web site is a rich source of data for a variety of issues related to Title IX, gender, and sexuality in all aspects of sport. This site also contains links to many other sources on Title IX itself (the legislation), studies focused on Title IX, and other issues related to Title IX, particularly sexuality.

NCAA (http://www.ncaa.org/wps/portal).

> The official Web site of the NCAA contains both data and resources related to women in athletics and Title IX.

Equity in Athletics Disclosure Act (http://ope.ed.gov/athletics/).

> This Web site houses the EADA data that is reported for each college and university annually. It is a wonderful source of data for researchers interested in exploring the effect of Title IX on athletics.

# 9 | Social and Cultural Capital

## Race, School Attachment, and the Role of High School Sports

*Rhonda F. Levine, PhD*

---

**Social theory:** Social reproduction theory with emphasis on social and cultural capital

**Proponents of the theory:** James Coleman, Pierre Bourdieu

**What the theory says:** Social reproduction theory seeks to explain how inequality and the class structure are generationally reproduced. *Social capital* refers to how social networks can provide resources that help in the attainment of upward mobility. *Cultural capital* refers to the general knowledge, experience, style, and self-presentation that one has acquired through the course of his or her life that enables him or her to succeed in certain social settings to a greater extent than does someone with a less experienced background.

---

A number of ethnographic studies in recent years have brought a wealth of rich data to bear on the project of explaining the high school experience and academic achievement of African Americans and other racial and ethnic groups (Carter 2005; Conchas 2006; Dance 2002; Ferguson 2000; Flores-Gonzalez 2002; Lewis 2003; Lopez 2003; O'Connor 1997). Studies that focus primarily on social structural factors, including class relations, poverty, inadequate school funding, disinterested teachers, and inadequate curricula (Noguera 2003; Noguera and Wing 2006; Rothstein 2004), have been augmented and enriched by these detailed examinations of cultural and individual-level factors—such as values, aspirations, meaning, and social identity—to help explain persistent racial and ethnic achievement differences in high school. Unpacking the long-standing and puzzling achievement gap between blacks and whites in high school is all the more compelling as a project when we recognize that educational attainment is a key factor in closing the widening racial gaps in employment, income, and wealth.

This chapter contributes to the growing ethnographic literature by focusing on the role that sports play as a mediating factor that can lead to a positive school experience, greater school attachment, and greater academic achievement. Moreover, through a nuanced analysis of the actual experience of high school athletes, participation in sports can be seen as providing low-income African Americans with the social and cultural capital which they often lack and which is so important for positive school outcomes. The structural and cultural factors often given to explain the high school experience and academic achievement of African Americans regularly highlight the lack of adequate social and cultural capital, especially when they are compared with their white counterparts.

## THEORETICAL FRAMEWORKS

Two concepts from the literature on social reproduction are useful in analyzing and understanding the experiences of the young men whose lives I followed at Parlington High School.[1]

---

[1] All names of places and people have been changed to protect anonymity. The opening photo is for illustrative purposes only and does not represent any of the athletes in this chapter.

The concept of social capital was initially used by economists such as Loury (1977) but has become more widely utilized by sociologists since its influential development and application by James Coleman (1988). *Social capital* refers to social networks or connections between individuals that provide access to information, support, advice, and so forth. These social ties and networks affect most aspects of our daily lives, from finding housing to finding employment to finding an intimate partner. According to Coleman (1988, 101), "the function identified by the concept of 'social capital' is the value of these aspects of social structure to actors as resources that they can use to achieve their interests."

Social capital can simply be understood as resources that are gained through participation in social networks (Bourdieu 1986; Coleman 1988). Family ties, friendship ties, and, in the case of the male athletes at Parlington High, sports ties, can provide resources such as the inside track to jobs or even knowledge about educational programs through which one can eventually improve one's standing.

*Cultural capital* involves the knowledge, experience, and connections one has had through the course of life that enable him or her to succeed to a greater extent than does someone from a less experienced background. Bourdieu and Passeron first developed the concept in *Reproduction in Education, Society and Culture* (1970), where they were attempting to explain differences in educational outcomes in France during the 1960s. For Bourdieu, cultural capital acts as a social relation within a system of exchange that includes the accumulated cultural knowledge that confers power and status.

In a very general sense, *cultural capital* refers to general knowledge, taste, and basic ways of presenting oneself. Schools are known to favor the cultural capital of the middle class, thus putting low-income students at a marked disadvantage. For example, two sources of cultural capital are (a) basic knowledge of the significance of standardized tests for college admission and (b) how to navigate a course curriculum that would put one on the college track.

Between the summer of 2001 and early 2006, I followed the lives of 28 African American teenagers, 20 of whom were high-profile high school athletes, in a diverse small-city high school in the Northeast. The city, which I call Parlington, is located about 200 miles from a major metropolitan area and is home to a population of about 60,000 people; the racial breakdown of students in the high school is approximately 70 percent white, 20 percent black, 5 percent Hispanic, and 4 percent Asian. Nearly 50 percent of the approximately 1,800 high school students are eligible for free or reduced-cost lunch.

Some of the male athletes ran track and weight lifted, but my main interest for this chapter was in participation on the football or basketball team. These two sports are not only high-profile but also more popular among African American high school students. They have been found to have both negative and positive consequences on school attachment and academic achievement (Eitle and Eitle 2002). Through a theoretical lens provided by the concepts of cultural and social capital, this chapter discusses two basic findings pertaining to male athletes. First, high school sports in general may provide a means for greater school attachment and an incentive for academic achievement, but the degree to which it does so is dependent on the coach–player relationship. For most of the male students I talked with and observed, sports provided the promise of a path to a college education, yet few realized this promise. Nevertheless, sports may have been a key reason that they lasted as long as they did in high school (most of them graduated). Second, coaches function as an important source of social and cultural capital for some student-athletes (there is variation by athlete and sport).

## SPORT PARTICIPATION, ACADEMIC ACHIEVEMENT, AND SCHOOL ATTACHMENT

Whether or not sports meant a greater likelihood of having white friends and moving in and out of a white world with ease, sport participation did provide an incentive to do well in school and was seen by most black athletes as their ticket to a college education. Although all the athletes played high-profile sports and were stars or starters, none had any illusion of playing professional sports, though many did see playing at a Division I college as a reachable goal. Most, however, saw sports as their ticket to college, and all saw a college education as a vehicle for upward mobility—as providing what was necessary to get a good-paying job. Their coaches agreed.

Of the 20 athletes with whom I spoke, only three ended up going to college on a sports scholarship, and only Marques went to a Division I school. College recruiters were interested in both Izzy and Ray, but neither had the minimum grades to even get accepted as a coach-supported athlete, though Izzy eventually went to a community college on the West Coast on a football scholarship, thanks to Assistant Coach Gunning. Izzy's brother Eugene told me when he was in the ninth grade that he planned to attend college on a football scholarship, then proceeded to tell me what he had to do in terms of NCAA rules. He said that where he applied would depend on which schools might be interested in him. When I asked him if he ever just thought about applying to college without thinking about going to play a sport, he said: "I don't know. Honestly, I've never really thought about it like that. Like whenever I think of college, I think of football."

Sometimes the connection between sports and college could be a source of great disappointment, as Mr. Brenner, a former basketball coach, told me. When Roland was cut from the varsity basketball team because of "getting into trouble," he said, "I sat there and I cried. I broke down. I was like, 'Are you serious?' You know what I'm saying. This is my life. How else am I going to play Division I basketball without playing for a high school team?"

Most of the boys also saw sports as providing them with an alternative to the "street" and an incentive for doing well in school, whether they actually stayed out of trouble and academically achieved or not. Marques stated it best when he said:

> If I didn't play sports, I'd probably be another one of those black kids, probably smoking, drinking, you know, walking the streets. I really think, honestly I really think so, you know what I mean, because if you think about it, what else is there for you to do, if you're like in Parlington and like if you hang out with all the black kids, you know what I mean, you're going to get caught up in that stuff, you're going to start doing stuff.

Marques thought that sports gave him an incentive to do well in school and stay out of trouble. When I asked him after his first year of high school whether his grades were as good as they were in middle school , he said, "Yeah. It's because I, during the first marking period [which was ] the football season, we had to do good, and so I was really hitting the books." His grades dropped, however, during his sophomore year, especially when he got cut from the basketball team because of summertime conflicts with the coach.

Like Marques, many of the other athletes I spoke with expressed the belief that their desire to play football or basketball meant that they had to stay out of trouble and also do well in school. Dwayne told me, "For football I stopped everything, smoking weed, yeah. I wanted it." Eugene said he had to stay out of trouble because he had a "responsibility on the field and off the field, 'cause I'm not just like the captain of the football team and captain of the weight lifting team. I'm a role model, and I go to school, I talk to younger kids." Byron also thought that school athletes were role models for younger students because, as he put it, "They see all these popular sports guys and they want to be like them, so they see, they come to like a varsity game and they see all of us doing good. I mean, just hear people talking about us, so they want to be like that too." These athletes also knew they still had to do well in school, even though they were outstanding athletes. Byron knew that "you won't go anywhere if you don't go to class. No colleges will look at you." And Ray said more directly that his love for basketball provides his incentive to do well in school:

> I would not mess up in school because I love basketball too much, and [the coach] said, he told me straight up, the teachers would go and tell him and . . . he was like, "Well, if you plan on doing that this year, I'm just going to kick you off the team." And he told me that straight up, so I'm like—'cause I was slacking for about 2 or 3 weeks, and he benched me, you know what I'm saying.

Although Eugene and Byron may have expressed to me that they saw themselves as role models and that they had a responsibility to stay out of trouble and do well in school, neither of them were stellar students. Eugene's grades dropped during his sophomore and junior years and improved only during the later part of his senior year. Byron stopped going to school after basketball season during his senior year and did not graduate for another 2 years. However, basketball was his reason for going back to school and graduating, which made it possible for him to attend a community college and star on the basketball team. As for Ray, he was suspended from school during his senior year for sexual assault and never graduated from Parlington High.

Clearly, sports did not prevent everyone from getting into trouble. During the football season of Izzy's first year, when he was playing on the junior varsity team, he held up a white couple with a BB gun as they came out of a restaurant one block away from his house. Because he was only 15 at the time, he ended up being released, even though the arrest was for armed robbery. Instead of detention, he was put on probation for the rest of his high school years. Although he received favorable notice as an athlete during his sophomore year and was a starter on the varsity football team, he was also selling drugs and eventually established an operation that included both drugs (mostly pot and crack) and prostitutes. Izzy went on to have a terrific football season during his junior year but continued to cut classes, do poorly in school, and deal drugs after school. Most of this came to an end during the spring of his junior year, when the police raided his "crack spot"—the house where he and others were dealing drugs and running prostitutes. The police found guns, as well as drugs, and Izzy was in the house at the time. He was arrested but spent only 6 hours in jail, then received another probation. Now saddled with a record that included armed robbery at age 15 and an arrest in a crack raid at age 17, Izzy said he decided to stop selling drugs "because I was nervous and I was thinking like, yeah, I could really go somewhere with football."

Like Izzy, his older brother Curtis sold drugs while attending high school and playing football. Curtis found it a bit ironic that the week in which he was kicked off the football team was the very same week in which he was arrested for a drug-related armed robbery. When I asked him why he got kicked off the football team, he said:

> Because I wasn't going to gym class. I didn't really get kicked off, or I got suspended, but there was a week left, so I got kicked off. There wasn't no hope for me anymore that year.

The degree to which sport participation had an association with staying out of trouble and achieving in the classroom had much to do with the role that coaches played and how they were perceived by their players. So although it would appear, for example, that Izzy and Curtis were on a fast track to prison, Izzy eventually went to a community college on the West Coast to play football and Curtis not only went on to be an assistant coach for the JV football team but now works as an anti-gang advocate. The role that coaches played in their turnarounds cannot be underestimated.

## ROLE OF COACHES

Most of the research on the high school experiences of African Americans that views sports as a positive mediating factor fails to pay sufficient attention to the role that coaches play (Braddock 1981; Braddock et al. 1991; Eitle and Eitle 2002; Harris 1995, 1998a, 1998b; Miller et al. 2005; Roderick 2003; Sabo, Melnick, and Vanfossen 1993). The exception to the literature is Reuben May's *Living Through the Hoop: High School Basketball, Race, and the American Dream* (2008). May's ethnographic study of a high school basketball team illustrates, though with ambivalence, both the important role of the coach in the lives of poor black males and the manner in which participation in sports can provide an alternative to gangs. For the high school athletes I spoke with, their coach, rather than merely their participation in sports, seemed to be the main factor that accounted for their academic performance and post–high school prospects.

The football coaches not only played a positive role in terms of school experience and academic performance; they also contributed greatly to personal development, and their relationship with their players went well beyond the playing field. Whether they played the role of big brother, father, or mentor, these coaches provided not only the support needed in order for players to have a positive school experience but also the social capital for potential success after high school (whether or not the players ultimately took advantage of the opportunities).

Similar to Reuben May's Coach Benson, the football coaches at Parlington viewed their role as more than coaching a sport. Head Football Coach Moriarty expressed how he tried to make playing sports a productive experience for his players:

> *We try to make it productive. I think that's when a lot of kids get into trouble. They just have too much idle time. So sports also gets rid of the idle time. It forces them to be productive. You've got 2 hours of practice, then you've got to get something to eat. You know you better get some homework done because I'm going to check on that to see if you did your homework, or you're getting up and coming to class.*

The trust and rapport that the coaches built with their players were essential if they were to have any influence on players' behavior and academic performance. Coach Moriarty said to me that he was a father figure to his players and that in this role he was "firm." He knew that many of his players did not have fathers living with them, that they were living in less than the best of economic situations, and that many of them had experienced racism.

Once trust is developed and mutual respect is established between player and coach, the coach is able to have a greater effect on a player's school behavior. Marques told me that when his grades began to drop after he got cut from the basketball team, Coach Moriarty called him in and told him he expected him to raise his grades—and he did. When I asked him what made him buckle down, he said, "Because Coach Moriarty, really, he started to get on my back and I was wanting him off my back, so I just really tried to put my head in the books." Marques went on to tell me that Coach Moriarty would keep tabs on him, calling him down to his office from time to time just to see how he was doing in his classes and telling him that he would arrange for a tutor if Marques needed one in order to bring up his grades. Even Coach Gunning would get on his case, especially if Marques "didn't do good on a test, then like he'll call me after class and tell me like I need to get my head straight and stuff like that, because sometimes he sees me slouching in class and stuff like that." Coach Gunning reinforced this view: "Well, if you look at a lot of these kids, their grades were probably the best during football season."

Not only did the coaches play an important role in terms of players' school behavior and academic performance; they also became an important source of social capital. All of the athletes I spoke with would be the first in their family to go to college if they made it. The football coaches became their main source of information about when to take tests and how to fill out applications. Coaches also circulated their names to college coaches for possible football scholarships. Coach Moriarty explained to me that at the beginning of every school year the coaches meet with the high school's college advisors; at this meeting, they are given the dates of SAT tests, as well as information about financial aid forms, college applications, and the like. Coach Moriarty then explained to me that he would

> *have a kid do a resume at the end of the football season—seniors—and say, okay, what are your interests? What's your grade point average, what's your SATs, etc. and so forth, and then we have a constant parade of coaches coming through here. We probably see what, about 15 or 20*

*coaches every winter? And they come through with their catalogs, and we call the kids over here and say, "We want you to sit down and listen to this, about this school." Then if a kid has an interest—and I'm not just talking about athletics, but an interest in the school—we say, "Okay, we got to get you to [the college advising office]" and say, "I want you to call this kid down and fill out financial aid forms or fill out the college application form."*

Marques, the only one to be accepted to a Division I school on a football scholarship, was well aware of the role Coach Moriarty played in his receiving a football scholarship:

*Without Coach Moriarty, like trying as much as he does, I don't think I'd be getting these scholarships right now for football. Yeah. I mean, even though I'm good at football or whatever, I mean, there's tons of kids that are good at football, but their coaches really don't, like, look out for them, like try and do as much as they can, like to talk college for them. But without Coach Moriarty, I don't think I'd really probably be getting any scholarships for football right now. Honest to God!*

In addition to helping his players fill out applications and sending information to college coaches, Coach Moriarty drove Marques to various colleges to look at their campuses and also to attend summer football camps. During Marques' first year of college, Coach Moriarty took a first-year football player along with him to visit Marques and told this young player that if he played his cards right, worked hard, stayed out of trouble, and did well in school, he too could attend this prestigious Division I private college. But it was not only Division I prospects whom Coach Moriarty and his staff looked out for. When Ray was suspended from school during his senior year and eventually went to live with relatives in another state, Coach Moriarty looked into potential prep-school postgraduate programs for him to attend so he could get his grades up and become eligible for a 4-year college. However, even though Coach Moriarty made himself as available to Ray as he was to Marques, Ray never took advantage of the opportunity. Coach Moriarty was also in contact with a football coach from a nearby state college who was very interested in Izzy, but Izzy's admission was blocked because he did not have a 70 average at graduation. Even so, Coach Gunning had contacts at a community college in a Western state and arranged for Izzy to go there and even live with the football coach.

Sometimes the coaches went all out for a player and got burned. Through his own prep-school connections, Coach Reguiro heard of a program at an elite boarding school that had scholarship money for a postgraduate year for African American students. One of his players had experienced problems in the past but now seemed to be a perfect candidate for such a program. Coach Moriarty got in touch with the necessary people, and he and Coach Gunning helped the player fill out applications, bought him clothes to wear to his interview, and drove him to the school, which involved a 6-hour drive from Parlington. Seeing an opportunity that does not come often, the coaches gave their student the hope of a bright future, but, much to their disappointment, he left the program after only a month because he missed his girlfriend and felt out of place.

In addition to helping players have a positive school experience and providing them with the necessary resources for a successful life after high school, the coaches also gave them a tremendous amount of support, both moral and material, that was absent from their home life. As Byron put it, the coaches "make you want to do good stuff. They really, I mean, like certain people's households, it's horrible, so they get the football coach as your real family sometimes." Nowhere was this more evident than in the relationship between Coach Moriarty and the Shadrick brothers, Dwayne and Craig. Coach Moriarty saw this relationship as a matter of providing a support system:

> *You know what I think it is? The kids need a support system. They need that, and I don't think it can be a group setting. I think it's got to be as personal as it can possibly be, where something is kind of sometimes, "Come on, I'm going that way, I'll give you a ride home." "No, no," and I'll say, "Get in the car. I'm not taking no for an answer." I think the way I deal with these kids is I won't take no for an answer, if I want to do something nice for them. And a good example of that is, you know, I'll get people to say, "You know what, I want to donate a Christmas dinner to a needy family." So when [Dwayne and Craig] were juniors, I called them and said, "Hey, what are you guys doing for Christmas dinner?" "Well, it's just another day to us." I said, "Well, I've got someone that's donating a turkey and everything. . . . We'll go pick it up." "No, we're not going to do that. We don't accept charity." "This is not charity!" You know, and I didn't sweet talk them. I said, "You dumb shits, it's not charity." I said, "Somebody's doing . . ." "Coach Moriarty, you don't understand, we won't take it." I said, "Well, I'll bring it to your house," and they said, "We'll just leave it on the street." I mean, so we had some arguments, but . . .*

Dwayne and Craig were very thankful for all that Coach Moriarty did for them. As Dwayne, now a college graduate and a future elementary school teacher, said,

> *Coach Moriarty used to take me and he would try to dig and find out what's going on with me, what's going on, like talk to me. "I'm here for you, like step into my office and talk to me."*

Craig, who joined the Army Rangers after a year of college, said that Coach Moriarty understood what he and Dwayne were experiencing. According to Craig,

> *See, he actually understood that I was—you know what I'm saying?— we're poor. Electricity was getting cut off every once in a while, you understand? Especially during football. . . . He took care of us. Bought us some food, you know what I'm saying? He took care of us.*

In Coach Moriarty's words:

> *Yeah, I knew they didn't eat, and they'd come to school, and I'd say, "What's going on?" And I think the other thing that happened is when you have that more personal relationship with kids, is you develop that trust that you're not going to judge them, and it sounds like a very cliché thing to say, developing trust, but it got to the point where they'd come*

*in in a bad mood, I'd say, "What's wrong?" "Well, we didn't have any lights last night." "What do you mean, didn't have any lights last night?" "They shut off the lights. My mom had to make a choice between buying food or paying the light bill." I said, "Okay, we'll get the lights turned on." And so I'd make some phone calls and get the lights turned on. And at first they wouldn't acknowledge it, you know. And then after a while, it kinda got to be a joke. And then I'd get them jobs.*

Again, here is Dwayne:

*Because we were, like, poor, and [Coach was] making sure we had enough food and that we could take care of ourselves, at least decently. So I told him, "Coach Moriarty, I really need a job." He was like, "Come to my office tomorrow." I went to his office, it's like I got a job where you have to go down at 12:30, I most of the time had to go down, and I've been like that ever since. Whenever I say I need a job, he's given it to me, and . . . yeah, he's everything to me.*

Both Dwayne and Craig worked hard for Coach Moriarty during the summers and even during the school year. Craig noted that he would always get jobs where he was a role model, which made him feel very good. Most of the jobs involved working with younger kids, many of whom were at risk. For both Dwayne and Craig, selling drugs (which they did in their early years of high school) was a thing of the past once they had jobs and were able to earn honest money. Coach Moriarty was also instrumental in helping Curtis find not only a job but, to put it perhaps more accurately, a career in becoming an anti-gang advocate.

Like Coach Moriarty, Coach Gunning and Coach Reguiro had relationships with their players off the field. Coach Reguiro recognized the role that coaches play in helping kids stay in school and said that part of this role involves building a relationship outside of school: "I can't tell you how many miles I have given in my car to pick a kid up and to take a kid home." Coach Gunning had a special relationship with Izzy, not only helping him get into the community college but also pulling him out of a jam. Izzy tells the story this way:

*Yeah, for a matter of fact, one of the days of my double session I missed and got in trouble 'cause I owed the person I was selling drugs for a couple hundred dollars, and I told my brother about it, and I missed weight lifting the next day because I was going to make the money up. I mean, I missed football practice because I was going to make the money up. And my brother kind of figured that, and brought him and my football coach out to find me, all over, and then they finally found me. . . . I stopped selling crack for a while. . . . [The coach] made me promise that I would never sell the drugs.*

Coach Gunning tried to steer Izzy in the right direction:

*Izzy hated it, but I used to go with him to his parole officer and I got his parole extended, you know. It used to drive him nuts. But Izzy knew that I was a balance in his life.*

## CONCLUSION

As the case of Parlington High demonstrates, sports may constitute an important mediating factor that plays a far more positive role in the lives of some black teenagers than is generally recognized. The examples presented in this chapter show, often poignantly, good reason to believe that sports increased the young black athletes' attachment to school rather than detracting from it. Although few of the athletes realized their dreams of winning a scholarship to college, almost all of the boys in my overall study did graduate from high school, and a few have gone on to college. Playing sports and going to college are closely intertwined in their minds. Playing sports provides a reason to be serious about school—a reason that may not be important in mostly white suburban high schools. The teenagers in my study may have seen sports as an avenue of mobility into college. In fact, based on my interviews (which yielded results similar to what May found in his 2008 study of high school basketball players), I would argue that sports often kept the students in school longer than they would have lasted otherwise.

Most of all, this chapter suggests new directions for further research through its finding that coaches can make a major difference in the lives of young black athletes, not simply through such traditional cultural clichés as instilling discipline and perseverance but also by providing moral and material support outside the sport setting (and thus well beyond what is formally expected of coaches). This finding confirms the work of Royster (2003), which provides excellent evidence that blacks with the same technical training as their white counterparts lose out in the job market because they lack referral networks and because employers prefer white employees. Coaches provide an important source of cultural and social capital. For example, coaches become a source of important information about applying to college (e.g., when to take tests and how to fill out application and financial aid forms). Most of the parents do not know how to gain entrance to college; they and the athletes themselves tend not to seek advice from school counselors about the college application process, and thus they become dependent on coaches for guidance. Furthermore, coaches serve as a source of social capital, providing access to post–high school education—college and prep schools—as seen in the case of Marques. Even with several boys who continued to misbehave in school or break the law (e.g., Curtis and Izzy), the coaches were finally able to help them by means of their social connections, steering Curtis into anti-gang work and Izzy into a community college in a faraway Western state. These are not rare examples, and several others can be drawn from my larger sample.

Coach Reguiro, a perceptive and caring young man in his 20s with a degree from an Ivy League college, may have hit the nail on the head when he said, "If you're a black high school kid that wants to succeed, get yourself involved in athletics and find a white coach that cares." He is saying that playing a sport is not enough, and that not just any coach will do. Students need a coach who cares—and who can be understood by the teenagers as caring.

Coach Reguiro's point fits in with a more general finding in the biographies of successful students of color. There is usually a mentor somewhere in the picture—often a teacher or counselor, or any caring adult who provides social and cultural capital. These mentors, including coaches, mediate school attachment and academic achievement, thereby helping overcome racial stigma and class disadvantages.

## Suggested Research

1. The role of the coach as a source of both cultural and social capital can be further researched with respect to girls' high school sports teams. Does the role of a coach vary by sport or gender (or player or coach)? Do sports and coaches play the same roles for girls that they do for boys in terms of mediating school attachment and academic achievement? Are only high-profile sports likely to provide the social and cultural capital to help offset racial stigma and class disadvantages?

2. Another direction for possible research is to examine the social relationships of a high school sports team. Do high school sports provide occasions for cross-race and cross-class friendships? And if so, do these friendships provide both social and cultural capital?

## Additional Resources

### Theory

Bourdieu, P., and L.J.D. Wacquant. 1992. *An invitation to reflexive sociology.* Chicago: University of Chicago Press.

> This book provides an excellent overview of Bourdieu's work. The middle section takes the form of a dialogue between Wacquant and Bourdieu in which they discuss major concepts and critiques.

Lamont, M., and A. Lareau. 1988. Cultural capital: Allusions, gaps and glissandos in recent theoretical developments. *Sociological Theory* 6:153–168.

> This article examines Bourdieu and Passeron's original work on cultural capital, compares the original formulation with American literature on cultural capital, and proposes a new definition of cultural capital.

Stanton-Salazar, R.D. 1997. A social capital framework for understanding the socialization of racial minority children and youths. *Harvard Educational Review* 67 (1): 1–40.

> This article develops a framework around the concept of social capital and shows how problematic it is for racial-minority youth to gain access to social capital and how they develop strategies to overcome various obstacles.

### Sport Topic

Bissinger, H.G. 200. *Friday night lights: A town, a team, and a dream.* New York: Da Capo Books.

> This book offers a journalistic account of one high school team's football season in a declining city in Texas. The book describes the manner in which football was significant not only for the players and coaches but also for the city itself.

Frey, Darcy. 2004. *The last shot: City streets, basketball dreams.* New York: Mariner Books.

> Written by a journalist, this book gives an up-close look at the lives of four exceptional high school basketball players, their coaches, and their families. It shows how sport participation can provide an escape from life in a poor inner-city neighborhood for some, but also that it has its cost.

May, R.A.B. 2008. *Living through the hoop: High school basketball, race and the American Dream.* New York: New York University Press.

> Through participant observation, May illustrates the meaning of playing high school basketball for a group of poor young black males. May shows how basketball may provide an alternative to gangs and street life, keep the youths in school longer than they might otherwise stay, and possibly even provide a path to college, though at the same time it may also give false hope for how far it can take them.

# 10 | Race, Class, and Gender Theory

## Violence Against Women in the Institution of Sport

*Earl Smith, PhD, and Benny Cooper, BA*

---

**Social theory:** Race, class, and gender

**Proponents of the theory:** Bonnie Thornton Dill, Michael Messner, Patricia Hill Collins

**What the theory says:** Race, class, and gender theory focuses on ways in which power, privilege, and oppression are organized by race, class, gender, and other systems of domination (e.g., sexuality, religion, age, ability status).

---

The race, class, and gender (RCG) theoretical framework was largely developed by African American and multiracial feminists (Anderson 2001; Baca Zinn and Dill 2005; Collins 1994, 2004; Davis, 1983; King 1988). This theoretical paradigm is built on the premise that systems of stratification built on hierarchies including race, gender and class create relationships of privilege and oppression. These systems of oppression exist independently and interact in what Baca Zinn and Thorton Dill (2005) refer to as a "matrix of domination."

RCG theory has been recognized by many scholars as not being limited to the concerns registered in its name. In other words, the framework itself can be expanded to include other systems of power, privilege, and oppression, including sexuality, religion, age, ability status, and region of the world. Audre Lorde, for example, writes about her experience as an African American lesbian (2007) and how that shapes her position in the world. In this chapter, we argue that what we refer to as *SportsWorld* (Smith 2007) is yet another system of privilege and oppression—based on power—that provides access to privilege for its members, particularly those who attain a high level of success. This privilege manifests in many ways, including (at its extreme) amnesty and (more commonly) tolerance and underplaying of the serious nature of crimes—especially against women—perpetrated by high-profile male athletes.

As a framework for examining the data in this study, the race, class, and gender paradigm is useful for several reasons. First, RCG theory provides a framework for understanding systematic differences in the treatment of men who perpetrate violence against women; specifically, it allows us to postulate reasons for differential treatment. Second, because the paradigm focuses on ways in which power, privilege, and oppression are organized by race, class, gender, and other systems of domination, it lends itself well to analyzing phenomena, such as violence against women, that feminists and other scholars agree constitute expressions of *power and domination* (Brownmiller 1975; Brush 2001; Brush, Raphael, and Tolman 2003; Griffin 1979; Hattery and Kane 1995; Koss 1985, 1994; MacKinnon 1991; Rich 1980, 1995). In this chapter, then, we utilize the race, class, and gender paradigm for examining and understanding the relationships between race, gender, and athlete status that shape men's treatment of women, as well as the consequent treatment these men receive from the criminal justice system. To be crystal clear, for this analysis, *race, class, and gender theory* specifically means that we will examine the ways in which the race of the athlete, the sport that he plays, and the intersection of race and the sport in question all shape the types of consequences that a male athlete faces when he engages in an act of violence against a woman—which, of course, is always an expression of his position as a male in the system of gender stratification.

## THE ISSUE

Violence against women—particularly rape and intimate partner violence (IPV)—is nothing new. There is resounding agreement among scholars of gendered violence that it exists, in varying levels and degrees, in virtually every known human society (Sanday 2007) and has existed for most of recorded history, including biblical times. Scholars of gendered violence agree that much of the cause of violence against women, as well as our cultural tolerance for it, is rooted in our beliefs about men, women, sexuality, and gender roles (Brownmiller 1975; Hattery 2008; Sanday 2007). In the United States, violence against women has not only been tolerated; it has rarely even been seen as a matter requiring the attention of the criminal justice system (Browne 1989; Hattery 2008; Sanday 2007). Until recently, intimate partner violence was considered simply a family matter, and similarly rape was generally perceived to be a problem associated either with "loose" women or with women's supposed propensity to cry "rape" the morning after a regretted sexual encounter.

Thus, violence against women by male athletes is hardly surprising, given that these athletes are first and foremost men who have access to the power and privilege granted to them by the system of patriarchy that defines gender relations in the contemporary United States. We also note that the exploitation which men of color may otherwise face because of their race does not limit their use of violence against women (Hattery 2008; Hattery and Smith 2007; Collins 1994, 2004; Hill and Sprague 1999; Smith 2008). Indeed, in an analysis of a large-scale data set that examined rates of IPV by African American and white men, the first author and a colleague (Hattery 2008; Hattery and Smith 2009) demonstrated that there were few significant differences between the violence perpetrated by African American men and that perpetrated by white men.

On the one hand, male athletes are just men, and thus we might expect their levels of violence against women to be similar to that of men in the general population. Yet, as Sanday (2007) argues with regard to the sex-segregated institution of fraternities, and as Benedict argues with regard to the special privileges accorded athletes (Benedict 1999, 2005), there is reason to believe that male athletes may engage in more violence against women because of their segregation into another highly masculinized institution: SportsWorld.

As the first author has argued elsewhere (Smith 2007; Smith and Hattery 2006), SportsWorld is a highly segregated institution where men have very little access to women other than in some women's role as cheerleaders. Especially in high-profile sports, male athletes are rarely coached by women, women do not administer their governing bodies (e.g., as athletic directors or league presidents), and the athletes rarely work for women (women rarely serve as team owners); indeed, overall, these male athletes spend very little time with women as equal peers. The majority of the time they do spend with women occurs either in the context of family life or in contexts where women are defined as creatures whose very existence is to serve them, whether as personal assistants, cheerleaders, or groupies. Thus, it is perhaps not surprising that there is plenty of evidence to support the contention that SportsWorld is a culture characterized by misogyny. One example comes from a highly publicized incident involving football players at the University of Miami. The Hurricanes' college football program has been one of the most successful in the nation and has served as a "feeder" program for the National Football League (Smith 2007). In 2005, a 9-minute song, recorded to the tune of the popular song "If Your Girl Only Knew," was created and released on Internet sites such as MySpace. The lyrics are far too graphic and offensive to report here—as noted in an ESPN report, one could hardly even count the number of times women were referred to as "bitches and hos"—and the song also includes numerous references to gang rape and group sex involving members of the Miami Hurricanes football team. In fact, several of the performers were members of the Miami Hurricanes football team. Here is the text of the "refrain":

> *If your ho only know that she was getting fucked on the 7th floor*
> *If that bitch only knew that she was getting muddied by the whole crew*

Not only is SportsWorld a culture in which misogyny is rampant; there is also evidence (Benedict 1999, 2005) suggesting that when athletes, particularly high-profile athletes and those who have "value" to the team, are caught, they are treated with less severity than are other men in similar circumstances. A *Harvard Law Review* report (Schoen 1996, 1048) that examined cases in which high-profile athletes were charged with violence against women noted that they were treated with leniency; in fact, the charges were often dropped. We cite here the case of former football star Warren Moon, the first definitively successful African American quarterback to play in the National Football League.

> *On July 18, 1995, seven-year-old Jeffrey Moon called 911 to report that his parents were engaged in a violent confrontation. Felicia Moon told police in a sworn statement that her husband, Minnesota Vikings quarterback Warren Moon, had slapped her in the head, choked her until she "saw black and could not breathe," and pursued her in a high-speed car chase. Several days later, the Moons held a joint press conference, where the seven-time Pro Bowl quarterback announced plans to seek professional counseling, admitted that he had made a "tremendous mistake," and took "full responsibility for what happened." Moon was subsequently arrested for misdemeanor assault. Less than six weeks later, Moon threw for 247 yards as the Vikings lost to the Chicago Bears on opening day (Schoen 1996, 1048).*

We offer two more recent and more highly publicized cases—the murder trial of O.J. Simpson and the rape allegation against basketball star Kobe Bryant—to further illustrate the point. As with Warren Moon, while the legal system churned in Bryant's case, he was allowed to continue to play and even travel with his team, the Los Angeles Lakers. His ability to travel outside of the judicial jurisdiction of his case is rather unusual (Markovitz 2006). And, despite the fact that O.J. Simpson was detained during the trial in which he was indicted for murdering his ex-wife Nicole Brown Simpson, there was wide public support for "the Juice," and some indicated that the judge and other persons involved in the case were more interested in having "O.J." sign an autograph than in listening to the testimony.[1]

The subject of violence in sport—and, more specifically, violence against women by athletes—has not received systematic attention other than a few cases like those we cite above. Indeed, the majority of attention focused on the intersection of athletes, sports, and violence against women comes in the form of nonscholarly output—both within in the United States and internationally—from journalists fascinated with cases involving high-profile athletes. In fact, this attention by journalists is sparked by the two key incidents previously mentioned: (1) the O.J. Simpson murder trials—where journalists were intrigued by seeking to find out whether the famed football player killed his wife, Nicole, and her friend, Ron Goldman, and (2) the incident in which a young woman in Colorado accused Kobe Bryant of committing sexual assault (Beck 2004).

Attempting to fill the void, this chapter seeks to explain one type of violence by athletes: violence that athletes perpetrate against their intimate partners. To begin our quest, it is useful to review the theories of violence and deviance that have been developed by criminologists. Using the race, class, and gender paradigm as a framework for understanding power and privilege, we examine the treatment by the criminal justice system of college and professional male athletes (in football, basketball, and baseball) who engage in violence against women—rape, sexual assault, and domestic violence.

## METHODS AND DATA

Many acts of violence against women are committed each year. Only a small percentage are reported to the police, and only a small percentage of those reported cases go to trial (Hattery 2008). Thus, measuring acts of violence against women is complex. Because we were interested in the male athletes who engage in violence against women, the kinds of self-report data generated by asking victims would not be useful because it rarely, if ever, includes data on the individual men that are accused. Furthermore, certain standards must be met before a case is moved all the way through the criminal justice system, and because so few acts meet these standards (only about 25 percent of reported cases ever go to trial), and because court records can be difficult to obtain, we decided to use journalistic accounts of reported acts of violence as our data source. Because athletes are public figures and there is a great deal of general interest in them and in what they do, newspapers and online news sources are highly likely to include reports of athletes being accused—even unofficially—of violence against women. Such cases are deemed newsworthy. Furthermore, unlike court records, which can be difficult to obtain, access to journalistic accounts is relatively easy; it is also free and, because most news sources offer online access, data can be gathered even from distant locations. Finally, unlike many other sources of information, such as athletic department press releases, news accounts constitute a relatively permanent record and are

---

[1] Judge Lance Ito himself got caught up in the celebrity of the "trial of the century" and secured for himself an autograph from O.J. Simpson, the famous former collegiate and professional football player. See, especially, Hock (2008).

catalogued in a database (LexisNexis) that is searchable. This makes them a more systematic and reliable source of information, surpassed only by court records, which would have to be obtained by written permission—and often an in-person visit—to individual courthouses.

We searched sports databases such as SPORTDiscus and news databases such as LexisNexis for all cases of violence against women alleged to be perpetrated by college and professional athletes between 1995 and 2007. As the reader can see in figure 10.1, though we examined all types of violence against women reported in the media, the overwhelming majority of cases (80%) involved more severe types of violence—domestic violence and rape—whereas only 20% of the reported cases involved simple assault or harassment. We conclude that this is attributable to the adage, "if it bleeds it leads," thus the media is less likely to report minor acts of violence, even when they are perpetrated by high profile athletes.

The data set developed for the analysis this chapter, to our knowledge the first and only of its kind, includes incidents allegedly perpetrated by 90 athletes in the United States. In addition to cataloging the victim of the violence by relationship to the athlete (e.g., wife, girlfriend, woman with whom the athlete has an ongoing relationship), the data set also includes data on various outcomes, including dismissal of the charges, incarceration, probation, community service, fine, apologizing formally to the victim, and being referred to drug or alcohol treatment or anger management classes. This is important because many of these informal sanctions would not appear in a court record. Finally, the data set also includes background measures, such as the race or ethnicity of the athlete and the sport that he plays.[2] The data were entered in to SPSS (data analysis software), and all of the analyses were conducted using SPSS15 (a certain version of SPSS).

## Scale Analysis

When law enforcement authorities are alerted to an alleged crime (e.g., a victim or neighbor calls the police), the various possible outcomes range from the charges being dropped to the accused being charged with a crime; if a conviction is made, the penalty may range from a sentence with no jail time (e.g., probation, community service, or payment of a fine) to incarceration. In our initial analysis, we noted that there was *very little variation* in the types of punishment meted out to athletes who had been arrested on charges of violence against women.[3]

Therefore, we decided to create a variable that took into consideration all of the possible outcomes for each case. For every outcome—dismissal of charges, probation, community service, incarceration—each player was assigned 1 point when a punishment was assessed and 2 points when no punishment was assessed. Across 10 possible outcomes—and using binary coding on each outcome—the scale ranged from 10 to 20, with a 10 representing the case in which the athlete was charged and given every measured punishment (a "1" on each variable) and a 20 representing the case in which no punishment of any kind was assessed and the charges were dismissed. The mean for all athletes on the punishment scale

---

[2] For a list of the variables making up the data set, please contact the first author.

[3] Low variation makes statistical analysis very difficult because it can mask both real statistical difference as well as moderate differences that are not statistically significant.

was 18.1, which indicates that across the vast array of possible outcomes, athletes were, on average, given only one punishment—some were given no punishment and had the charges dismissed (scored as a 20)—and the most frequently assigned punishment involved being offered counseling or anger management classes.

## Findings: Race and the Likelihood of Various Criminal Justice Outcomes

Given the prolific literature on racial disparities in the criminal justice system—African Americans are more likely to be arrested, charged, convicted, and given longer sentences (Hattery and Smith 2007; Western 2006)—we were curious about whether the type and frequency of outcome in our data set was shaped by race and ethnicity (Hindelang 1978). The data in figure 10.2 demonstrate the racial distribution in our sample. As the reader can see, African Americans make up 70% of all athletes charged with violence against women in our sample.

Looking deeper, we see based on the data in figure 10.3 that the majority of offenders, regardless of race, are charged with the more severe forms of violence,

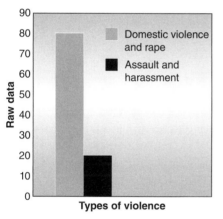

**Figure 10.1** Types of violence charged.

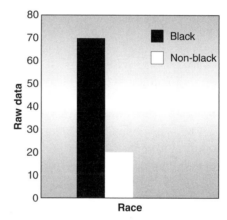

**Figure 10.2** Race of the offender.

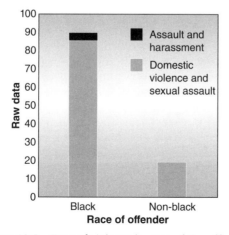

**Figure 10.3** Type of violence by race of the offender.

though a small number of African American men are charged with less severe forms of violence against women.

Overall, there were very few instances in which the outcome varied by the race or ethnicity of the offender, though both individually and in the combined scale there were slight differences in the likelihood of dropping the charges or incarcerating the offender based on his or her race. Of all the outcomes tested for individual punishments and the punishment scale overall, the only relationship that reached statistical significance was the impact of race on incarceration. White offenders were somewhat more likely to be incarcerated than their African American counterparts *when all sports were grouped together* (chi-square = 3.71, $p$ = .054). In light of the strong evidence for racial bias in the criminal justice system, and in order to "decode" this somewhat surprising finding, we examined the relationship between sport played and the likelihood of being incarcerated.

## Effect of Sport Played on the Treatment of Athletes of Various Racial and Ethnic Identities

As can be seen in figure 10.4, there is significant variance in the types of athletes who are most likely to be accused of acts of violence against women. More than 50% of our sample were football players, and approximately 15% played either basketball or baseball. The remaining category of "other" included boxers and athletes playing ice hockey and soccer. This distribution is not surprising for three reasons: (1) football rosters are significantly larger than any other sport, thus there are more athletes overall playing football, (2) there is literature that suggests that acts of violence against women are high among football players (see especially Benedict [1999] and Smith [2007]), and (3) the media is most likely to report incidents involving people who are "household names," and football players tend to have more name recognition than athletes playing many other sports. As with race, preliminary analyses that examined the effect of sport played on individual outcomes showed some slight trends, but none of the relationships reached the level of statistical significance.

The data in figure 10.5 reveals that the majority of violence perpetrated by athletes, *regardless* of sport played, falls into the more serious categories of violence. We do note that basketball players are slightly more likely to be charged with less severe acts of violence.

The same held true when we examined the relationship between sport played and the punishment scale. As with the analysis regarding race, the single trend that approached significance involved comparing the likelihood of incarceration based on the sport the offender played. Specifically, baseball players (who were predominately white and Hispanic) were slightly more likely to be incarcerated than were basketball or football players (who were disproportionately likely to be African American).

## The Interaction Between Race and the Sport Played

Suspecting a more complex situation, we then examined the relationship between race and punishment, controlling for sport played. The data in figure 10.6 illustrate the relationship between race and sport played. As the reader can see, African

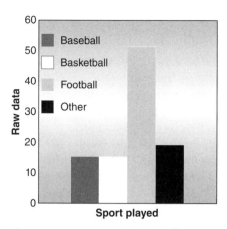

**Figure 10.4**  Sport played by offenders.

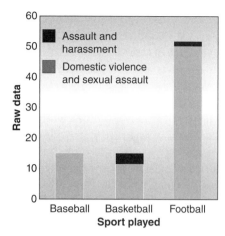

**Figure 10.5**  Types of violence by sport played.

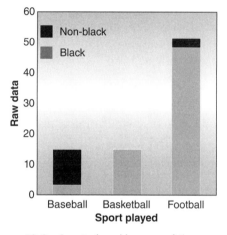

**Figure 10.6**  Sport played by race of the accused.

Americans in the sample were most likely to play football and basketball—in fact, no non-Black basketball players were charged with acts of violence against women—where as non-Black players were more likely to be represented among those baseball players arrested for acts of violence against women.

In the case of race and incarceration—the only test that proved to be statistically significant—we found that the relationship disappeared when the specific sport played (basketball, baseball, hockey, football) was added to the model. The same held true when we examined the relationship between sport played and punishment while controlling for race:

**Model 1**

  Independent variable: race

  Dependent variable: incarceration

  Control variable: sport played

**Model 2**

  Independent variable: sport played

  Dependent variable: incarceration

  Control variable: race

However, considering the trends in both models—none of the relationships were statistically significant—what we do find is that when African American baseball players are arrested, they are more likely to be incarcerated than are their white counterparts. But when African American male football or basketball players are arrested, they are less likely to be incarcerated than are their white counterparts.

Thus, we argue that the criminal justice system's treatment of athletes arrested for an act of violence against women is shaped by the interaction of their individual race and the sport they play. Of all the sports examined, baseball players were more likely to receive a punishment than were football or basketball players—a relationship that approached statistical significance. We argue that in the less prestigious sport of baseball, when an African American player is arrested, he is treated more or less as just an African American man. Thus he is more likely to be incarcerated than is his white counterpart, who, similarly, is treated simply according to his race. However, African American men playing higher-profile sports such as football and basketball are able to access the privilege of being associated with a more prestigious sport—and one that has a stronger fan following—regardless of their individual race. In this case, African American men are not only less likely to be incarcerated than their counterparts playing baseball but are also less likely to be incarcerated than white players playing the same sport.[4]

## DISCUSSION

It is rare to find data involving race and the criminal justice system in which African American men as a group fare better than white men as a group. This is precisely the kind of situation where it is useful to extend the race, class, and gender theory to conceptualizing sport as an institution of power, privilege, and oppression. As noted above, Baca Zinn and Dill (2005) make clear in their discussion of race, class, and gender theory that social institutions are combined in a matrix of sorts, such that status locations can be examined as consisting of both privileged statuses and oppressed statuses. The majority of Americans hold both positions of privilege and positions of oppression that work in complex and interconnected ways to shape our daily lives. As noted, for example, though African American men are oppressed by a system of racial domination, they are privileged by patriarchy and often by heteronormativity. Thus, as with their white counterparts, a large minority (25 percent) engages in physical acts of intimate partner violence.

Beginning with the matrix described by Baca Zinn and Dill (2000), we argue that the relatively lenient treatment that African American basketball and football players receive when they engage in violence against women can be best understood by expanding the matrix to include the institution of sport—especially high-profile sport. When we do this, we can understand findings that otherwise seem contradictory. By adding the institution of sport to the matrix, we add yet another status location in which an individual can either gain access to privilege or face oppression. When an African American man like Warren Moon beats his wife, he

---

[4] The cell sizes for white basketball and football players who were arrested for violence against women were very small, which results in difficulty in performing certain statistical tests.

enters the criminal justice system as (1) an African American, (2) a man, and (3) a high-profile athlete. Though his status as an African American will likely create harsher treatment, his statuses as a man and as a high-profile athlete—and, as Baca Zinn and Dill (2005) point out, the nexus of these two statuses is inextricably woven together—provide him with privilege that will shape his treatment.

The case of boxer Sugar Ray Leonard is an example of how the media—where it is impossible to cover up the story of an athlete abusing his spouse or partner—can spin the case to make it look like something it is not. To understand why so little is said or written about IPV in SportsWorld, it is important to look closely at how news reports can hide the story inside the story. In examining how sports reporters describe intimate partner violence when high-profile athletes are the perpetrators, the authors note that they hang a "tag" on the story that is more likely to be believed by the reading public—something like drug or alcohol use or abuse.

Messner and Solomon (1993, 123) put it this way:

> *Basic to the initial framing of this breaking story is the way in which the question of why Leonard abused his wife is answered. Juanita Leonard stated that she believed that Leonard's physical abuse of her was caused by his use of alcohol and cocaine. Sugar Ray Leonard also stated that the only times he hit her were when he had been drinking. But when he was asked directly if the "problems between you and your wife" were caused by "the fact that you drank or used drugs," he flatly stated, "No. There was a period in my life when my career had ended temporarily and I was going through a state of limbo, and I wasn't particularly happy with my marital situation." This is a strand of the testimony that apparently was ignored by the reporter who wrote the breaking story. Wife abuse was presented as a secondary issue, caused by the drug and alcohol abuse. Despite this initial drug story frame, the graphic, emotionally gripping testimony about domestic violence left open the possibility that this could have developed into a story about wife abuse. As the story broke, then, the drug story frame was still very fluid, still very much in the making.*

Not much has been written about the violent sport of boxing in regard to IPV (Oates 2006), but it is instructive to see that, even after his retirement from the ring, Leonard is still being protected because of his stature as a high-impact amateur and professional boxer. The case of Los Angeles Lakers basketball superstar Kobe Bryant is a bit different but is also definitely about privilege.

Although the Kobe Bryant case differs from Leonard's and is extreme in its implementation—the judge arranged court hearings, for example, around the Los Angeles Lakers' schedule—it is similar to the experiences of many basketball and football athletes who are accused of crimes of violence against women. In other words, African American basketball and football players pay a lesser penalty for being African American because of their status as high-profile, and often very popular, athletes. This finding raises questions about the ways in which power and privilege are accessed in the elite world of professional athletics and how this process may be quite different from that in the world in which the rest of us live—a world in which race trumps virtually every other social identity.

## CONCLUSION

In this chapter, we utilized media reports of violence against women to create a data set that allowed us to analyze the role that race played in the disposition of these cases in the criminal justice system. Our analysis revealed a complex relationship between race, sport played, and treatment in the criminal justice system. In sum, African American men who play baseball—where they are in the minority—received harsher penalties when they were accused of violence against women than did their white counterparts. In contrast, African American men who play football and basketball—where they are in the distinct majority—received more lenient treatment than did their white counterparts. Using and expanding the race, class, and gender paradigm, we argue that these findings can be explained by understanding "high-profile athlete" as a privileged status within the matrix of domination. That said, we also argue for more exposure of these acts of violence against women and for stiffer penalties against male athletes who psychologically or physically injure their partners. Unlike many other crimes, in cases of violence against women—primarily rape and intimate partner violence—where individuals are both the victims and the key witnesses, it is not uncommon for cases to be dropped because victims, who are often the intimate or ex-intimate partners of the defendants, refuse to testify. We suggest that just as with rules that call for an automatic appeal in death-sentence cases regardless of the convicted individual's desires, female victims of these violent acts should not be allowed to withdraw their testimonies after having been coerced by, more often than not, money.

Finally, no other single theoretical paradigm is able to provide a way of understanding such a complex and intriguing finding. Furthermore, the underutilization of RCG theory in research on sport—driven in part by the fact that much of this research is done by men who, in their position of male privilege, rarely look to such theoretical models—should be addressed. We suggest that there are likely many other phenomena in the institution of sport that we would benefit from examining through the lens provided by race, class, and gender theory.

## Suggested Research

1. Race, class, and gender theory is well suited to addressing inequalities in the workplace, in the military, and in a variety of sport-related settings, including sports administration. One area of inquiry involves pay disparities between female and male coaches. At the University of Tennessee, for example, the men's basketball coach, Bruce Pearl, makes more money than does the women's coach, Hall of Famer Pat Summitt, whose achievements far surpass Pearl's.

2. Another example of how race, class, and gender theory helps predict inequitable outcomes involves the professional field of law. More women than men attend and graduate from law school, yet in the professional field of law more men than women make partner. Much to-do has been made about the demanding hours involved in law practice and the idea that women have to care for children, but no such rationalizations can be verified empirically. See, especially, Guinier, Fine, and Balin's *Becoming Gentlemen: Women, Law School, and Institutional Change*.

3. Further research is needed with regards to violence perpetrated both on and off the field. In addition to additional research on violence against women, interested scholars could look at other forms of violence off the field, including assault and murder. Furthermore, there is a need for further research of violence *on the field*; for example, the role of the "enforcer" in ice hockey.

4. Sport has rarely been used to investigate the utility of the race, class, and gender paradigm. Other areas of examination for scholars interested in race, class and gender could include race and gender differences in earnings, head coaching positions, and athletic administration.

# Additional Resources

### Theory

Baca Zinn, M., and B.T. Dill. 2005. Theorizing difference from multiracial feminism. In *Gender through the prism of difference*, ed. M. Baca Zinn, P. Hondagneu-Sotelo, and M.A. Messner, 23–28. Needham Heights, MA: Allyn & Bacon.

This volume makes a major contribution to sociological theories of difference. Systems of oppression operate independently and in the interaction with each other. These systems include racial domination, classism, patriarchy, and ageism.

Collins, P.H. 1994. Shifting the center: Race, class, and feminist theorizing about motherhood. In *Mothering: Ideology, experience, and agency*, ed. E. Glenn, G. Chang, and L. Forcey, 45–66. New York: Routledge.

Collins argues that individual identities and their social locations are often complex and interwoven. They are often subsumed under one's placement in a social order and under individual and group class and racial identifications.

### Sport Topic

Benedict, J. (2005) *Out of bounds: Inside the NBA's culture of rape, violence, and crime*. New York: Harper.

Benedict offers a major investigative journalistic account using official statistics, documents obtained through the Freedom of Information Act, and other records to document the arrests (and sometimes convictions) of professional athletes who harm their intimate partners.

Hattery, A.J. 2008. *Intimate partner violence*. Latham, MD: Rowman & Littlefield.

Using race, class, and gender theory, Hattery interrogates traditional sociological and social-psychological theories of violence—especially "family violence theory"—to understand intimate partner violence perpetuated against women who are not spouses.

Smith, E. 2007. *Race, sport and the American Dream*. Durham, NC: Carolina Academic Press.

A full chapter is devoted to incivility among athletes (collegiate and professional). Smith locates violent behavior in an uncaring and narrow culture of putting "I" or "me" first—before anyone else.

# 11 | Masculinities and the Sociology of Sport

## Issues and Ironies in the 21st Century

Bryan E. Denham, PhD

---

**Social theory:** Hegemonic masculinity

**Proponents of the theory:** R.W. Connell

**What the theory says:** Consistent with traditional gender ideals, the hegemonically masculine male is independent, powerful, emotionally unexpressive, strictly heterosexual, unflinching in the face of adversity, indifferent to pain, and unwilling to compromise his core values.

---

When it comes to constructions of masculinity, competitive sport offers an excellent foundation on which to build a conceptual discussion. Male athletes who perform at elite levels tend to be among the most celebrated individuals in American society, and the brand of masculinity to which most of these athletes subscribe—generally referred to as *hegemonic masculinity*—idealizes the male who is stoic, self-reliant, athletically rugged, strictly heterosexual, and void of complaint (Carrigan, Connell, and Lee 1987; Denham 2004). The hegemonically masculine individual sacrifices himself for the betterment of others and asks little in return; he allows his actions to tell the tale. Advertising scholars have long cited the Marlboro Man as the personification of hegemonic masculinity, given his rugged appearance, the rusticity of his environment, and his propensity to go it alone (Kolbe and Albanese 1996). In film, John Wayne played quintessentially masculine characters, defending those who could not defend themselves while fighting against corruption and injustice (Lawrence and Jewett 2002), and in a recent paper addressing the symbolic appeal of California Governor Arnold Schwarzenegger, Messner (2007) explained how Schwarzenegger had ingratiated himself to mass audiences by combining tough-guy characteristics with well-timed displays of compassion (e.g., protecting women and children from those who would harm them).

In reality, models of hegemonic masculinity correspond to the lives of very few men (Connell and Messerschmidt 2005), and, as Pleck (1981) and O'Neil (1990) have observed, the pursuit of an unrealistic gender ideal can lead men to question their self-worth and live in perpetual fear of failing to meet the expectations both of women and of other men. This chapter examines the paradoxical, strained nature of masculinity in contemporary society, examining how men who would appear to personify hegemonic masculinity—those who have played professional football and competed in the elite ranks of bodybuilding—have struggled with unrealistic expectations. The chapter begins by reviewing masculinity scholarship, then examines how traditional gender ideals manifest themselves in the lives of athletes.

## HEGEMONIC MASCULINITY

Writing about gender representations in the context of Major League Baseball, Trujillo (1991) cited pitcher Nolan Ryan as a consummate representation of hegemonic masculinity, noting that Ryan approached each outing in a stoic, workmanlike manner. Relying on his own training regimen, Ryan stayed in excellent physical condition during his career and held himself to the highest standards. In this vein, Hatty (2000) has suggested that independence and self-reliance largely define the modern self: "Dependence, from a Western perspective, is an indicator of developmental immaturity or emotional deficiency. It is also closely associated with femininity and the normalized status of womanhood" (11). Writing about gender construction in the context of bodybuilding, Klein (1993) noted similarly that "the view of men as pressure-treated, as strong, dominant, independent, and unemotional, tacitly assumes that women are weak, subservient, dependent, and emotional" (238).

In competitive sport, male athletes who appear to lack aggressiveness and "intestinal fortitude" may find themselves labeled a "pansy" or a "queer" by their coaches and teammates. A man, after all, is inherently aggressive yet cool under pressure, leads others by example, and is strictly heterosexual. Hatty (2000) has noted that sport offers a vehicle for reproducing dominant conceptions of masculinity by alleviating fears of feminization among middle-class men, and for their part the mass media foster this process by providing visual cues to audience members—the kinds of cues that Messner, Dunbar, and Hunt (2000) cited as part of the "televised sports manhood formula."

"Homophobia is crucial to the definition of masculinity," Leach (1994) suggested, "as it rules out men as potential objects of emotional or sexual attachment. Consequently, homophobia operates to reinforce oppressive heterosexual themes, such as male competition for legitimate sex objects (women)" (37). In recent decades, as women have become more independent, heterosexual men have become increasingly focused on physical appearance (Hoberman 2005). Hatty (2000), in fact, has described how male body ideals—broad shoulders, muscular chest and arms, and a narrow waist—lead to an achievement-oriented approach to masculinity. It takes work to build such a body, and the men who do so often view muscular development as a way to define themselves and prove their worth (Kimmel 1996). As Luciano (2001) argued, with a steady increase of women in the workplace during the latter half of the 20th century, heterosexual men realized they could no longer rely on the "breadwinner ethic" to attract a spouse. Consequently, large numbers of men built large, muscular bodies and became somewhat hyper-masculine around women. In short, what men lost in the workplace, they looked to regain through their musculature.

Capraro (2000) shed light on the problems that can arise when daily life becomes too much of a performance. Citing work by scholars such as Pleck (1981) and O'Neil (1990), Capraro discussed "gender role strain," which refers to tension between the actual self and the gendered, idealized self. In attempting to meet the expectations of others, Capraro explained, many men perform a role steeped in hegemonic masculinity, but in performing that role they invariably experience a certain amount of strain or conflict. With strain and conflict may come feelings of inadequacy and depression, which in turn may precipitate self-destructive behavior and self-medication in the form of substance use. As Capraro pointed out, "manly" activities, such as drinking copious amounts of alcohol, actually offer a short-term sense of power to men who otherwise lack it.

For purposes of the current chapter, then, it is essential to note that idealized forms of masculinity do not necessarily lead to satisfaction in life (Connell 1995; Connell and Messerschmidt 2005); indeed, in many cases, the pursuit of the perfect body or persona may detract from happiness and satisfaction. As Messner (1987) explained in the context of sport, the majority of men will never succeed to the extent that they believe they need to, and thus a socially constructed definition of success, especially one grounded in athletic excellence and physical perfection, can generate feelings of failure and lower self-image. Similarly, Connell (1995) stated, "The constitution of masculinity through bodily performance means that gender is vulnerable when the performance cannot be sustained—for instance, as a result of physical disability" (54).

This chapter examines that assertion from Connell (1995)—first, through a discussion of the physical and psychological challenges confronting athletes upon retirement, when adulation and generous salaries come to an abrupt halt and struggles with identity intensify. In 2007, news reports addressed the limited pensions received by former—and physically ailing—players from the National Football League (NFL). The collision of hegemonic masculinity with the basic commodification of athletes has often resulted in an ugly crash site. As Connell and Messerschmidt (2005) concluded, "Without treating privileged men as objects of pity, we should recognize that hegemonic masculinity does not necessarily translate into a satisfying experience in life" (852). That assertion may prove especially accurate in the case of professional football.

## CONSTRUCTIONS OF MASCULINITY IN PROFESSIONAL FOOTBALL

In many ways, professional football players personify hegemonic masculinity. In addition to speed and strength, football requires an ability to tolerate physical pain and psychological stress, make sacrifices for the betterment of an entity greater than oneself, and avoid showing weakness in the face of adversity; in other words, it calls on players to be machine-like in their efforts (Connell 1995; Messner 1987; Trujillo 2001). When injuries occur—and they invariably do in a sport as violent as football is—players are expected to stay mum and stoic, "sucking it up" and "taking one for the team." Players who violate these implicit rules may find themselves belittled in front of their teammates or compared unfavorably to the tougher, less egocentric players of yesteryear, "when men were men."

Indeed, nostalgia plays a significant role in constructions of hegemonic masculinity, especially in the context of competitive sport. Coaches and announcers alike posit athletes of the past as a standard for those of the present, praising, for example, the hard-hitting nonconformists who formed the Oakland Raiders of the 1970s and the stone-faced linemen who formed the "Steel Curtain" in Pittsburgh. Helping professional football come of age were heroic figures such as Dick "Night Train" Lane, "Mean" Joe Greene, and Jack "The Assassin" Tatum. Dick Butkus revolutionized the linebacker position with his fierce tackles; running back Larry Csonka sustained more broken noses than most boxers could fathom; and Tom Dempsey, a kicker with the New Orleans Saints, booted a record 63-yard (58-meter) field goal with only half of a foot on his kicking leg. Such players overcame adversity, declined to draw attention to themselves, and took pride in representing cities whose blue-collar fans withstood zero-degree temperatures to watch their teams play.

To some degree, hyperbolic stories of yesteryear really are inspiring, as players did not have access to the advanced sports medicine and scientifically engineered equipment of today. Game films from past years reveal shoulder pads, helmets, and other pieces of equipment that, in the 21st century, would not suffice in most high schools. From playing injured to playing for too many years, these athletes appeared to participate more for the love of the game than for its monetary rewards. But as heroic as the athletes of yesteryear may have been on Sunday afternoons, many have paid a steep price both physically and psychologically since retiring from football. Scholars such as Eitzen (2006, 182–184) and Coakley (2004, 355–356) have discussed the problems that athletes sometimes face when their playing days end, and journalist Dan O'Neill of the *St. Louis Post Dispatch* has described the long-term health problems encountered by members of the St. Louis Cardinals football team from the 1970s.

The group of retired athletes featured in the O'Neill (2007) report included Dan Dierdorf, Conrad Dobler, and Tom Banks, and among the problems experienced by these former NFL athletes were arthritis, failing knees and ankles, hip and back pain, severe headaches, dizziness, and memory loss. In the opening paragraph of his article, O'Neill painted a portrait that bore little resemblance to hegemonically masculine athletes:

> *Thirty years ago, Tom Banks was an All-Pro center, the axis of a football Cardinals offensive line that was among the best in the game. Today, Banks is unable to work and survives on Social Security disability. Thirty years ago, Mel Gray was among the most dangerous deep threats in the NFL and one of the fastest humans alive. Today, Gray is unable to ascend a flight of stairs and walks with a pronounced limp (D1).*

With these physical limitations come psychological pressures, some of which may involve anxieties about financial security as well as depressive episodes related to leaving the limelight and becoming a "regular person" (Messner 1992). As Messner (1987) explained, athletes generally retire at an age when the majority of men are just beginning to find professional success. Additionally, the majority of men have not sustained the kinds of repeated head trauma that many football players experience, nor have they been commodified in the same manner; the playing days of professional athletes last precisely as long as they can help a team realize success. After that, the athletes must learn a new trade, and while many are able to find positions in coaching or broadcasting, others may be qualified for very few positions outside the world of athletics. Consequently, when their playing days end, many athletes may suffer from what Messner (1987) termed a "crisis of identity" (202), in addition to chronic pain, as O'Neill (2007) indicated:

> *The 6-foot-3 Dobler brought 260 pounds with him when he pulled on a halfback sweep in '77. His post-NFL health problems have shrunk him to as low as 225 pounds. A staph infection nearly killed him last year.*

*He has had three replacements and six operations on his left knee, two replacements and seven operations on his right knee. . . . Dierdorf also has paid a severe price for his 13 Hall of Fame seasons. The tab includes two hip replacements, two knee replacements and a serious staph infection. He has to use a cane to walk more than a few steps (D1).*

Writing about football players and concussions in the *New York Times*, Alan Schwarz (2007) noted, "Football's play-with-pain mentality discourages players, from high school to the pros, from revealing their virtually imperceptible injury to coaches or trainers, often causing more serious harm" (A1). Several players for the New York Jets, the team about which Schwarz wrote, had suffered memory loss and bouts of depression due to head injuries sustained while competing in the NFL, and Schwarz cited research that has identified correlations between the number of concussions sustained and a series of psychological and physiological problems, including depression and early-onset dementia (see, for example, Guskiewicz et al. 2003; Guskiewicz et al. 2005; Rabadi and Jordan 2001). Still, league officials and team representatives continue to discount the severity of head trauma, essentially suggesting that no one is forcing people to play football for a living.

Few cases illustrate the physical and psychological demise of an esteemed athlete more dramatically than that of Mike Webster, a retired Pittsburgh Steeler who died in 2002 at just 50 years of age. Called "Iron Mike" by his teammates and generally considered the strongest player on a team that played in four Super Bowls during the 1970s, Webster suffered numerous concussions during his 17 years in the NFL. As Greg Garber (2005) reported for ESPN, "His brain showed signs of dementia. His head throbbed constantly. He suffered from significant hearing loss. Three lumbar vertebrae and two cervical vertebrae ached from frayed and herniated discs. A chronically damaged right heel caused him to walk with a limp." Webster had been homeless at various points in retirement, sleeping in his vehicle and at the Amtrak station in downtown Pittsburgh. He relied on numerous drugs to numb the pain, but the drugs only made his condition worse, leading to addiction. As Garber noted, when his Steeler teammates attempted to help, he refused their efforts, going it alone in accordance with dominant conceptions of masculinity.

Webster certainly was not the first to struggle after retiring from football. In 1991, former defensive end Lyle Alzado appeared on the cover of *Sports Illustrated* looking haggard and gaunt; an inoperable brain lymphoma had debilitated the former Denver Bronco and Oakland Raider (Denham 1999). Inside the magazine, Alzado attributed the lymphoma to prolonged abuse of anabolic steroids, and, though scientific causality was never established, his death in 1992 came to symbolize not only the dangers of steroids and other drugs of abuse, but also how the personification of hegemonic masculinity could be reduced to a terminally ill individual whose primary goal had shifted from tackling opponents to simply living another day. Alzado had nowhere to turn when his health began to fail, for while he had given professional football his best efforts, the NFL wanted little to do with someone who could prove disastrous from the standpoint of public relations. Indeed, the "don't ask, don't tell" system appeared in professional sports long before it became a politicized military issue during presidential election campaigns, as athletic officials sought to know as little as possible about certain practices.

The mass media report just a fraction of the hardships experienced by athletes of yesteryear, giving the impression that most of these individuals have ridden heroically into the sunset. Rarely, however, do such scenes occur, and professional football players, in particular, take with them all of the injuries they have sustained, and sometimes very little else. Some have memories of participating in the playoffs or even the Super Bowl, but for the most part, football players, like all professional athletes, are commodities: When their bodies no longer generate results, their careers generally come to a close. To an extent, then, one might surmise that the more "manly" a sport is, the less "manly" its participants stand to become when they retire and shift to a life without adulation and without highly skilled professionals attending to their every need. They may become just another face in the crowd.

# CONSTRUCTIONS OF MASCULINITY IN HARD-CORE BODYBUILDING

As an athletic pastime, bodybuilding perhaps contains more irony and contradiction than any other sport. This assumes, of course, that bodybuilding can be considered a sport at all; some might consider it less an athletic competition than a beauty pageant for muscular men and women. Its athletic component takes place primarily in bodybuilding gyms and health clubs—not on the posing dais—and the physical effort put forth by competitors varies considerably. Some bodybuilders enjoy the training process and approach it methodically; they monitor bodyweight, training poundage, caloric intake, and other aspects of contest preparation. Others appear less interested in the training dimensions of bodybuilding and more concerned with the applause and (perceived) admiration of contest spectators.

In terms of gender construction, while men who reach the elite ranks of bodybuilding may appear hypermasculine or Herculean from the standpoint of muscle mass, their impressive physiques sometimes serve as protective shells for emotional insecurities (Klein 1993). In building their bodies to extreme levels, these individuals have chosen to become part of a subculture that embraces a level of muscle development that can be achieved only through consistent training and large quantities of chemical substances, most commonly anabolic steroids. The quantities of steroids, human growth hormone, diuretics, and other substances used by bodybuilders go far beyond the levels consumed by other athletes (Denham 2008), and in studying constructions of masculinity in the bodybuilding community it is important to consider *why* otherwise healthy individuals would take significant risks with their short- and long-term health. What drives them to not only compromise their physical well-being but also consistently break the law by using steroids and other drugs of abuse? Anabolic steroids are classified as a Schedule III controlled substance in the United States (Denham 1997), and those caught using these substances without a prescription from a licensed physician may face time in federal prison and significant fines. Klein (1993) observed:

> *Here we have a subculture preoccupied with attaining hegemonic masculinity, but individuals within it who, because of the psychological baggage they carry with them, are only partially successful in accomplishing their goals. Their sense of masculinity and self, often on unstable footing that*

*fuels the hypermasculinity characteristic of bodybuilding subculture, works in certain respects to overcome low self-esteem and build social bonds and sense of community—but it also remains perilously superficial (240–241).*

Part of this insecurity comes from the realization that a no-holds-barred pursuit of hegemonic masculinity often involves actions that idealized males would never take. As an example, Klein (1993) wrote of "hustling" in the bodybuilding subculture of Southern California, describing how men who were homophobic, hypermasculine bodybuilders in the gym often supported their lifestyles by offering sexual favors to wealthy gay men. Most of these bodybuilders considered themselves neither gay nor bisexual, and, as Klein explained, they reinforced their beliefs by allowing just one sex act to be performed: for a gay male to perform oral sex on the bodybuilder, who rationalized involvement as passive and impersonal. Few bodybuilders admitted to hustling, but many of those Klein interviewed had little trouble identifying others who had taken part. Thus, from the standpoint of sexuality, bodybuilders who participated in hustling led at least two lives—one as a straight, homophobic, hypermasculinized male and the other as a sexually ambiguous escort.

Another contributor to insecurity among bodybuilders in the elite ranks involves the very personal nature of physique competitions. In football, the blocking skills of offensive linemen can affect the number of yards a running back gains with each carry. In baseball, a pitcher with an excellent earned run average might conclude a season with a mediocre win-loss record because the team for which he pitches scores relatively few runs. Those who do not participate in team sports can suffer injuries during competition, thus detracting from their overall performance. But in competitive bodybuilding, each scantily clad contestant walks on stage and is judged based on the appearance of his physique (with a few points set aside for posing skills). Competition is utterly personal, and when a contestant observes another bodybuilder with slightly better development, he sometimes takes irrational steps, such as increasing his use of muscle-building drugs or even having cosmetic surgery performed. As an example, in recent years, bodybuilding judges have had to learn how to spot calf implants, as some competitors have been willing to spend thousands of dollars to increase the size and improve the shape of their gastrocnemius and soleus muscles.

In fact, several aspects of the physique are beyond the control of any given bodybuilder. Competitors cannot control whether their abdominal muscles line up perfectly, creating the coveted "six-pack" look, nor can they control shoulder-to-waist differentials beyond a certain point. Some bodybuilders must contend with appearing somewhat blocky when standing next to a competitor with a superlatively tapered physique, and very few bodybuilders will ever develop peaks on their biceps that resemble those attained by Arnold Schwarzenegger in his Mr. Olympia days. Still, a portion of physique competitors will not accept their relative shortcomings, and, in pursuing the perfect body, they sometimes exacerbate the emotional insecurities that led them to bodybuilding in the first place. Those who have built their bodies solely to impress others often appear somewhat desperate, compensating for perceived flaws and a certain amount of self-loathing. Despite what some might believe, then, magic pills do not exist in bodybuilding subculture, and, in many cases, the more these athletes develop their bodies, the less comfortable they become within them.

## CONCLUSION

This chapter has focused on constructions of masculinity in the contexts of football and hard-core bodybuilding. Applying the construct of hegemonic masculinity to these pastimes, the chapter has identified ironies and contradictions associated with hypermasculine activities, observing that while elite athletes tend to be celebrated and idealized, their time in the spotlight is most certainly finite. At a certain point, even the strongest and most independent of athletes—like men in general—must face their limitations. Football players face a host of physical and psychological problems upon leaving their chosen sport, and men who reach the upper echelons of bodybuilding often arrive with significant baggage in tow.

Competitive athletics provides a useful backdrop for identifying the fluid nature of hegemonic masculinity, for, as Messner (2007) explained, subordinate groups continually affect dominant conceptions of what it means to be a man in American society:

> Hegemonic masculinity is hegemonic to the extent that it succeeds, at least temporarily, in serving as a symbolic nexus around which a significant level of public consent coalesces. But as with all moments of hegemony, this consent is situational, always potentially unstable, existing in a dynamic tension with opposition (462).

In the middle of the 20th century, supporting a family empowered men in Western society, but as women, men from racial-minority groups, and men living alternative lifestyles began to challenge the assumptions of white male hegemony, new challenges emerged for the traditional, somewhat complacent, male. Men who had enjoyed a certain amount of privilege could no longer assume that providing for a family monetarily would suffice, and as a consequence they began to take more interest in their physical appearance (Luciano 2001). Many sought physical perfection by building large, muscular bodies or seeking to reach the highest ranks of sport, but the nearly impossible odds against realizing these goals undercut self-confidence and satisfaction (Connell and Messerschmidt 2005; Messner 1987). For their part, competitive athletes also faced continued challenges, for while they had been idealized and celebrated on the gridiron and the bodybuilding stage, they nevertheless had to face the realities of retirement and the dissipation of admirers. Many continue to experience physical and psychological difficulties, leading to even more challenges away from sport.

## Suggested Research

1. While those who follow competitive sports often celebrate the accomplishments of high-profile athletes, some accomplishments likely would not have been realized without the use of performance-enhancing drugs. Sport researchers might apply the backdrop of hegemonic masculinity, with its ideals of honesty and integrity, to the somewhat tarnished records that some athletes have set in recent years, identifying the inconsistencies

between gender ideals and the realities of competitive sport played at the elite levels.

2. Playing through pain and "sucking it up" for the team have been characterized as heroic, selfless acts on the part of athletes. But where do athletes turn when the applause has stopped and the central reminder of the glory days is an aching, debilitated body? What processes leave some of the most admired athletes destitute and in search of direction after their careers have ended?

# Additional Resources

**Theory**

Connell, R.W. 1995. *Masculinities*. Berkeley: University of California Press.

This important and informative text addresses the development of hegemonic masculinity as an academic construct.

Kimmel, M. 1996. *Manhood in America: A cultural history*. New York: Free Press.

This book provides a historical overview of masculinities in the United States.

Pleck, J.H. 1981. *The myth of masculinity*. Cambridge, MA: MIT Press.

Pleck discusses the strain induced by strict adherence to standards of hegemonic masculinity.

**Sport Topic**

Courson, S., and L.R. Schreiber. 1991. *False glory: The Steve Courson story*. Stamford, CT: Longmeadow Press.

The late Steve Courson discusses the paradoxes he observed as a professional football player. The book is an excellent source of information about performance-enhancing drugs.

Klein, A.M. 1993. *Little big men: Bodybuilding subculture and gender construction*. Albany: State University of New York Press.

This definitive source on the bodybuilding subculture in Southern California addresses the paradoxical nature of elite male bodybuilding.

Messner, M.A. 1992. *Power at play: Sports and the problem of masculinity*. Boston: Beacon Press.

Messner effectively bridges the gap between academic discussion of masculinity and the experiences of retired professional athletes who must come to terms with leaving the spotlight.

Courtesy of Girls in the Game

# 12 | Getting Girls in the Game

## Negotiations of Structure and Agency in a Girls' Recreational Sport Program

*Cheryl Cooky, PhD*

---

**Social theory:** Structuration theory

**Proponents of the theory:** Anthony Giddens, Alan Ingham, John Sugden, and Alan Tomlinson

**What the theory says:** Structuration theory argues that social structure is always both constraining and enabling. *Structure* refers to the "rules and resources, or sets of transformative relations, that are organized as properties of social systems" (Giddens, 1984, 25), as well as the "institutionalized features of social systems, stretching across time and space" (185). Structure shapes the production and reproduction of social interactions, and through social interactions social structure is reproduced. This is what Giddens refers to as the "duality of social structure."

---

Applying the theoretical frameworks of Giddens (1984), this chapter demonstrates that girls' experiences in sport are shaped by the interactional dynamics between broader social structures and agency (whether collective or individual). I apply a trilevel conceptual framework (Messner 2002) examining structure, culture, and agency in order to explore the ways in which one after-school sports program in Chicago addressed the social problems that girls face in their everyday lives to empower "at-risk" youth. Part of a larger project (see Cooky 2006; Cooky 2009) this chapter focuses on how the formal structure of a sports program, as constructed within the context of cultural discourses on "at-risk" youth and girls in sport, was translated into the informal structure and everyday practices by the individual and collective agency of the adult organizers and girl participants. Specifically, I discuss the ways in which adult organizers and girl participants, through their everyday interactions, negotiated the tensions that surfaced between the program's primary objective to empower girls and the girls' resistance to the program.

When sociologists use qualitative approaches—such as observational fieldwork, interviews, and focus groups—to study sport, they are conducting inductive research. In this type of research, the researcher gathers data, then selects or develops an appropriate theory to explain the empirical findings. Inductive approaches differ from deductive approaches in that inductive research theories are not tested; rather, theoretical explanations are developed through the process of analyzing data. Most qualitative researchers do not always develop entirely new theories; decisions about which theory to use are based on the empirical findings. Given that social theories are "tools" that researchers use to explain social phenomenon, researchers select which theoretical framework is best suited to explain, analyze and interpret the empirical data. I chose to use Giddens' theories of structuration, as well as other theoretical concepts, including Bourdieu's (1979/1984) notion of cultural capital, because they best explain the empirical findings of the research.

## OVERVIEW OF THEORIES OF STRUCTURATION

The foundations of classic and contemporary sociological theory were built on the relationship between structure and agency (for a review, see Hays 1994). For example, Karl Marx's theories (also referred to as conflict theory) explain the ways in which structural forms of oppression and domination operate in capitalist societies. Marx conceptualized power as the ability to control scarce resources in a society. In capitalism, the capitalist owners control the means of production, of both material goods and of ideas. Members of the working class, who lack these scarce resources, must sell their labor to the capitalists for a wage. Because capitalist owners also control the means of knowledge production, they are able to sustain a false consciousness among the proletariat (working class). According to Marx, resistance to capitalist oppression occurs when the working class achieves class consciousness.

One limitation of classic structural theories is their potential to conceptualize the relationship between structure and agency from a top-down, determinist perspective. In other words, structure is given primary causal weight (Sideman 1998). Conversely, contemporary social theories such as structuration theory (Giddens 1984) allow one to see the ways in which agency, whether individual or collective, is enabled and constrained by social structure. Moreover, they allow one to see how social structure and institutions are constituted through individual and collective agency. Giddens' concept of "the duality of structure" states that social structures simultaneously serve the context wherein social action is possible and are reproduced through social action. In other words, according to structuration theory, social structure does not exist outside of human interaction, nor do individuals act outside of structural forces and social institutions (Giddens). As such, social structure is constituted through ongoing collective social action, while the experiences of social actors are shaped by structures of opportunity and constraint.

Giddens' theory of structuration recognizes that power is integral in understanding the relationship between structure and agency. Unlike Marx, Giddens argued that power is not necessarily linked to conflict nor is not inherently oppressive. Instead, "power is the ability to achieve outcomes" (Giddens 1984, 257). Power is "generated in and through the reproduction of structures" (258). Giddens argued that a "dialectic of control" exists wherein all individuals have some degree of power to transform or change the circumstances in which they find themselves (Sugden and Tomlinson 2002). For example, the social movements (collective agency) of the 1960s and 1970s in the United States lead to changes in the circumstances of racial, gender and sexual minorities; and lead to transformations in the culture and the social structure. Even subordinate groups have some degree of agency with which to counter dominant groups (Giddens 1984; Messner 2002). Through recognition of the dynamic interaction between social structure and agency, and the conceptualization of power as distributed in varying degrees among powerful and subordinate groups, structuration theory can address the limitation of classic structural theories as discussed above: the potential to conceptualize social relations in a deterministic fashion.

On the surface, structuration theory may appear to suggest that agency is transformative or resistant of social structures. Indeed, some cultural studies scholars conceptualize agency primarily as empowerment or as resistance to oppressive or dominating social structures. Yet as Hays (1994) argues, agency is not always resistant of social structures; it can also be reproductive of them.

She writes that "agency explains the creation, recreation and transformation of social structures; [that] agency is made possible by the enabling features of social structures at the same time as it is limited within the bounds of structural constraints; and [that] the capacity of agents to affect social structures varies with the accessibility of power and durability of the structure in question (62). Perhaps, then, it is useful to think of agency as existing on a continuum from reproductive to resistant to transformative:

Reproductive → Resistant → Transformative

Individual and collective agency can range anywhere along this continuum. Reproductive agency is when individuals' social action leads to the reproduction of the existing social structures. Resistant agency involves individuals who resist social structures (institutional rules and regulations) without necessarily transforming them. Transformative agency operates to transform social structures, changing their forms and contents.

This notion of a continuum of agency directly challenges classic theories on socialization and social reproduction in the sense that certain groups may have a vested interest in reproductive practices, while others may engage in collective agency to create resistant or transformative practices that are not reproductive of existing social structures. However, social theorists must be careful not to romanticize these resistant practices, as they are often met by what Connell (1987) refers to as "crisis tendencies." For example, the resistant and transformative collective agency exercised by women in the 1960s and 1970s challenged the gender order in social institutions such as work, family, and sport. While expanding the structures of opportunity for women, these challenges resulted in crisis tendencies in the gender order, as manifested in the backlash to feminism and the rise of conservative political ideologies in the 1980s (Faludi 1991). Thus, the resistant agency, while transformative of the social structure in some ways, can also lead to the rearticulation of ideologies that reaffirm oppressive elements within those structures.

Although structuration theories have contributed to the knowledge in the discipline of sociology and the sub-discipline of the sociology of sport, they are subject to several limitations. For one, they fail to address what social processes, interactions, or dynamics lead to reproductive or resistant social practices. Moreover, interpretations and applications of the theory often assume that resistant practices lead to social change. Conceptualizing agency as transformative while neglecting the potential for agency to be reproductive may discount the potential for the reappropriation of counterhegemonic movements or discourses by those in power (see Connell 1987; Giddens 1984; Gramsci 1971; Messner 2002). Rather, structuration theorists view agency as an integral part of structure where counterhegemonic processes are often contradictory and subject to reincorporation into the "center" of the structure of power (Messner 2002). Another limitation of structuration theory is that it does not adequately account for the role of cultural and symbolic production in the constitution and maintenance of the gender order and broader structures of power (Hays 1994, 2004). In an attempt to address this limitation, scholars are incorporating cultural analyses in their applications of structuration theory.

## CULTURE

Hays (1994) argues both for a theoretical conceptualization of structure that considers more than the material forms of structure which serve to constrain human agency and for a theoretical conceptualization of agency that acknowledges action as not simply unstructured and "free" but as productive of social structure. A key part of this "reconceptualization" of structure and agency involves the conceptualization of culture as a part of the social structure. For Hays and for Messner (2002), social structures are shaped by and through cultural processes and dynamics. Culture is a part of social structure, thereby shaping and constraining social interactions and the everyday practices of social agents.

Individuals come to understand themselves and to construct their identities partly through an engagement with cultural meanings and images. Many feminist scholars in cultural studies would argue that an individual's identity in a postmodern, capitalist society is constructed primarily through consumption of popular culture products, images, and meanings (Sturken and Cartwright 2001). Feminist cultural studies provides a theoretical perspective for understanding how girls and women derive pleasure in consuming popular culture, despite the fact that their consumption might be reproductive of larger social structures and structural dynamics that serve to keep girls and women in subordinate positions.

Michael Messner (2002) has developed a theoretical and empirical framework for examining gender and sport. In this framework, Messner examines how *social structure* (defined as the structured rules and hierarchies of sport institutions), *culture* (defined as the dominant symbols and belief systems transmitted by the sports media), and *social interactions* (defined as the routine day-to-day practices of sport participants) construct the "center of sport" despite the many challenges of women, gays, and lesbians. The "center of sport" refers to the "most highly celebrated, rewarded and institutionalized bodily practices that are defined largely by physical power, aggression and violence" (xviii). Although Messner studied gender and sport to elucidate sport's center, I utilize his conceptual framework of examining sport through a trilevel approach (structure, culture, and agency) to examine the "margins" of sport, specifically an all-girls' recreational sports program. In this study, *structure* is defined as the structured rules, regulations, and organizational practices of the Girls in the Game program that enable and constrain the actions of the girl participants. *Culture* is defined as the dominant symbols and belief systems transmitted through "common sense" knowledge, the media, and popular culture. Specifically, I examine how research on "at-risk" youth produces "common sense" discourses that inform and shape the structure of the program. For the girls, mainstream hip-hop culture (e.g., music, music videos, dance) informs *social interactions* among many of the girls and is a primary way in which some girls in the program construct their identities.

## GIRLS IN THE GAME

Girls in the Game (GIG) is a nonprofit organization founded in 1995 in Chicago through grassroots efforts by a group of men and women seeking to provide and promote fitness and health opportunities for girls. The program's goals are to enhance girls' physical well-being, self-esteem, leadership, and team-building skills, as well as to promote academic excellence, goal setting, and conflict resolution. According to its Web site, GIG is one of several not-for-profit organizations in the country dedicated to the overall health and well-being of girls through their healthy participation in sport and fitness activities, health education, and leadership development. Its twofold purpose is to ensure that high-quality fitness, health, and leadership programming is made available to girls and to reduce the barriers that young girls face in accessing such programs. GIG's mission addresses two trends from the research on girls and sport: the known benefits of girls' participation in sport and the lack of social support for girls' involvement in sport.[1]

GIG programs are offered in approximately 13 elementary schools, middle schools and high schools in Chicago, as well as Chicago Park District sites. Believing that girls deserve the chance to participate in and receive the benefits associated with sport and fitness opportunities, GIG has no geographical or economic requirements, although the vast majority of girls reside in disadvantaged or underserved communities. The population of girls is racially, economically, and socially diverse: 35 percent are African American, 31 percent Latina, 25 percent Caucasian, 5 percent Asian, and 4 percent "Middle Eastern" (categories were determined by GIG through "intake forms" that must be completed during registration). Roughly 60 percent of the girls are between 7 and 12 years old, and about 40 percent are between 12 and 16 years old. Approximately 85 percent of the girls come from families who live below the poverty line. Most of the girls who participated at the GIG program site I observed for this study are girls of color (African American) who reside in households that survive at or below the poverty line. In 2004 (the year the girls I observed had registered for the program), the poverty line for a family of four was US$18,725, and 39 percent of households headed by a black female lived in poverty (United States Census Bureau 2004). Several of the girls in the GIG program I observed lived in households that received welfare or other government subsidies. Other girls lived in households where both parents worked and had a slightly higher household income or lived with extended family members such as grandmothers and aunts.

I conducted fieldwork regarding the Girls in the Game after-school program from January 2005 through July 2005 (summer camp). Programming at the site was offered four times a week for 4 hours per day (totaling 16 hours per week) during the school year. In addition to its after-school programs, GIG also offered a summer camp and Game Days (similar to the "play days" offered for college women during the early part of the 20th century). I also conducted observations at these events and conducted semi-structured interviews with 25 girls and informal interviews with 3 adult organizers. Fieldwork and interviews were collected and analyzed using qualitative research methodology. Qualitative research methodology includes a type of method, contemporary ethnographies, that understand social understandings, experiences, and structures as socially constructed (Denzin and Lincoln 2003).

---

[1] For a thorough summary of research on girls, sport, and physical activity, see Sabo, Miller, Melnick, and Heywood (2004).

## CULTURAL ANALYSIS: DISCURSIVE CONSTRUCTIONS OF SPORT AND THE "AT-RISK" GIRL

Youth and children from low-income communities are often viewed as both the cause and the victims of social problems. Constructed in social and public policy discourse as being "at-risk," economically underprivileged and minority youth are frequently the subject of concern for educators, community groups, policy makers, and activists. These groups hope to improve not only the lives of at-risk youth but also the overall social health of the community in which they reside. The notion that after-school programs benefit "at-risk" youth and serve to alleviate social problems in low-income communities currently constitutes conventional wisdom for many organizations and institutions that work with youth. Research has found that youth who participate in highly structured leisure activities are less likely to engage in "antisocial" behavior including criminality, aggressive behavior, alcohol or drug use, delinquency, and dropping out of school (Mahoney and Stattin 2000); at the same time, they are *more* likely to develop social capital (Jarrett, Sullivan, and Watkins, 2005).

The term *at-risk* originated among educators referring to children who were at risk for academic failure (Placier 1993). The groups considered to be "at risk" in contemporary society include children from disadvantaged circumstances. The focus on children "at-risk" emerges from a "generic concern with poor and minority children" (Lubeck and Garrett 1990, 328). Moreover, the construction of the term *at-risk* serves to define the social problem itself and its subsequent solutions. The "at-risk" child is believed to be in danger of falling prey to a range of social problems, including academic failure, involvement in gangs and crime, teen pregnancy, drug and alcohol abuse, and violence. With the problem so defined, solutions depend on changing the individual attributes of the child through intervention, often in the form of after-school programs, sports, or other pro-social activities. The belief that participation in structured activities such as sport will reduce the risk factors in children's lives suggests that the solution to social problems resides in helping children become more resilient in order to avoid the dangers for which they are at risk. Based on dominant cultural discourses, the solution does not involve changing the social, political, economic, or educational institutions (Lubeck and Garrett). Rather, it is believed that positive social change can be achieved by instilling social and cultural capital in young people, fostering self-esteem, encouraging academic performance, or empowering young people, especially girls, through the provision of spaces where girls' voices are valued and heard (Denner, Meyer, and Bean 2005).

While there is a significant body of research that demonstrates a relationship between girls' participation in sport and pro-social benefits—such as decreased teen pregnancy, decreased sexual activity, improved academic performance, and higher levels of self-esteem (McHale et al. 2005; Miller et al. 1998; Pedersen and Seidman 2004)—some have questioned whether this statistical relationship is a direct result of sport participation or whether other variables contribute to the relationship (Tracy and Erkut 2002; Videon 2002). For example, Tracy and Erkut (2002) found that it is difficult to predict the effects of sport participation on the self-esteem of African American girls, because their self-esteem is often derived from different sources than that of white or Latina girls. Moreover, while research suggests that Latina girls who play sports may experience increased academic benefits compared with nonathletic peers, African American girls are sometimes negatively affected by their participation in sport (Sabo et al. 2004). Other researchers argue that there is something unique about sport—a self-selection factor—that attracts girls who are less likely to have unprotected and unsafe sex, more likely to do well in school, and more likely to interact with peers who do not drink and smoke (McHale et al. 2005; Miller et al. 2005; Videon 2002). Despite this debate, many organizations, sports programs, women's groups, and researchers strategically cite research that demonstrates a positive relationship between sport and girls' overall well-being in order to support their efforts to obtain increased funding for girls' sports programs and leagues, provide increased access and opportunity for girls to participate in sports, and advocate on the part of girl and woman athletes. The now-accepted cultural understanding that girls' participation in sport is good for them and can help improve their lives is powerful in shaping the landscape of girls' and women's sports (Cooky 2009).

## HELPING GIRLS "AT RISK": THE STRUCTURE OF GIRLS IN THE GAME

Girls in the Game differed from other after-school sports programs for girls. The organizers did not assume that providing girls with opportunities to play sports would necessarily produce all the benefits strongly correlated with sport participation. Girls in the Game went beyond teaching sports skills and providing opportunities to play sports (although it did that as well) by offering educational programs where girls could take advantage of homework tutors, nutrition and cooking classes, exercise programs, and self-esteem seminars. Girls in the Game also differentiated itself from most after-school and recreational sports programs by rejecting the philosophy that programs should be designed primarily to keep kids out of trouble and that activities should revolve solely around sports programming (Worland 2003), which have a tendency to attract boys. For example, in their research on youth in an urban recreation center, Wilson, White, and Fisher (2001) found that female youth were marginalized in the center and were active mostly as spectators to male participation. Girls in the Game addressed this issue by restricting its programming to girls.

GIG organizers also recognized the structural barriers and constraints to girls' participation in sport, and in their lives more generally, and looked for ways to help girls overcome these barriers. Since many of the children and youth in the community were from low-income families, they were eligible for free or reduced-lunch programs. Knowing that children need healthy snacks and meals in order to concentrate on schoolwork and to have the energy to be active and play sports, GIG provided an after-school snack and a healthy meal at dinnertime (called the Kids' Cafe). Another constraint to girls' participation is transportation. The girls from the surrounding schools were not able to participate without the transportation GIG provided; the schools were far away and not located in safe neighborhoods, and many girls had parents who worked during the day and could not pick them up from school and drive them to the park. GIG applied for and received grant funding to rent a school bus and hire a bus driver to transport girls from the surrounding schools.

The organizers of GIG were aware that sport has the potential to serve as a positive force in the lives of girls, and sport was an important element in the program, but it was not the sole focus. In my observations during the school year, sport was one activity among a diverse programmatic structure that included homework tutoring, healthy cooking, learning self-esteem, and dance as well as other activities. At summer camp girls participated in a variety of sport activities, including swimming, that were not available during the winter months. In the middle schools and high schools where the GIG program was implemented there was more diversity in sports activities, since the GIG staff had access to the school's sports facilities and equipment. The GIG program I observed was implemented at a park district site and shared the facilities and equipment with other groups. In addition to its programming, GIG used sport in strategic ways: to encourage girls' participation in the GIG program; to draw on the resources of sports-oriented funding agencies such as the Women's Sport Foundation; and to address the psycho-social needs of the girls. As discussed earlier, research demonstrates that girls who participate in sport have higher self-esteem and better academic achievement. However, sports organizers often assume that sport participation alone produces these benefits. GIG differed from many girls' sports programs, recognizing that sport and physical activity is only but one component of many that are needed in order to improve "at-risk" girls' lives. GIG also worked with girls specifically on self-esteem, academic achievement, body image, nutrition, and other issues as part of its programming. Through the formal structure of the program, GIG enabled girls' transformative agency by empowering them physically, psychologically, and socially. By empowering "at-risk" youth through the formal and informal aspects of its program, GIG constructed a social space that was transformative of broader social structures in which girls experienced race- and class-based forms of inequality.

## "DOING WHATEVER WE WANT": REPRODUCTIVE AGENCY AT GIG

*Today during self-esteem class we are watching "Odd Girl Out," a Lifetime movie based on a book by the same title. The movie deals with the current "social problem" among girls: relational aggression. Ja'netta and Tracy [all names used for the girls in this chapter are pseudonyms] ask what we are scheduled to do today. Once they find out, Ja'netta complains that she does not want to watch the movie. She says, "We're going to go on strike." Ja'netta, and Tracy following directly behind her, walk around the auditorium in a circle and shout, "Strike! Strike! Strike!" while punching their fists in the air. Coach Betty, projecting her voice in order to be heard over the shouting, says, "Everyone must participate in the self-esteem class whether they want to or not!"*

This excerpt from my field notes illustrates a central theme in my observations: the tensions between the values espoused by adult organizers through the informal structure of the GIG program and the reproductive agency of the girl participants, many of whom resisted participation and exercised agency to do what they wanted. For some girls, "doing what we want" involved jumping rope and socializing; for others it meant completing homework. While part of the recreational program's mission is to empower girls, this empowerment was complicated by tension between program expectations that the girls make the "right" choices and the girls' own desires to choose other options, some of which were not endorsed by the program.

In the interviews, I asked the girls whether they participated in other after-school programs or camps, and if so, how those were similar to or different from Girls in the Game. While some girls appreciated the relative freedom they had at other after-school programs—a freedom that resulted from the lack of structure and the girls' perception of the apathetic attitude of the coaches—most of the girls liked GIG better because "the coaches play with us", "the coaches are nice and show they care," "we get to do a lot of activities and try a lot of sports." The girls overwhelmingly liked GIG because the "coaches don't just sit there and do nothing." Despite the preference for the coaches' organization of activities, girls enjoyed moments during programming when they could, in their words, "do what we want." In answer to the question, "What suggestions do you have for the coaches?" a few girls responded that GIG should change its rules to allow girls to drink pop and eat candy and chips during programming.

Although girls were prohibited from eating unhealthy food or snacks during programming, they did experience moments where they could "do what they wanted." For example, during homework time, about half the girls who came to programming never had homework assignments to complete. During my orientation to the program, I was told that if girls did not have homework, then they were to read quietly to themselves or work on arts and crafts projects such as braiding string or making thank-you cards for volunteers. Girls frequently claimed that they did not have homework. Of course, it is possible that some of the girls did have homework but lied to coaches so that they could play instead. Regardless of the veracity of their claims, GIG purchased string for girls to braid into key chains or bracelets and also provided other arts and crafts activities that girls could work on during homework time. Only once did I observe a girl reading a book that was not assigned for school. Instead, girls would use homework time to socialize with one another, sometimes talking about a boy one of them liked, a girl who got into a fight at school, and other topics typically of concern to preadolescent girls. Other girls brought in jump ropes and, with the coaches' permission, jumped rope inside the auditorium. Given all the talking and jumping, the girls who did have homework did not have a quiet environment to work in and were often distracted.

Many girls actively expressed resistance to the program. Several of the public school girls did not want to participate in homework time or in the GIG classes. In contrast, many of the private school girls, who came to the program directly from their schools, and still wearing their school uniforms, did not want to participate in the GIG classes but wanted to work on homework the entire time they were there. Thus, though their reasons differed, both groups of girls resisted the schedule and structure of the GIG program. At times, coaches would reinforce the notion that the girls must participate along with everyone else. At other times, coaches would allow the girls to have "free play." This occurred more frequently toward the end of the school year when the weather was warm and teachers began assigning less homework. In deviating from the formal structure of the program, the coordinator reasoned that "the girls have had a lot of structured programming (during the school year); they need a break."

## NEGOTIATING AGENCY AND CONSTRAINT IN EVERYDAY SOCIAL INTERACTIONS: THE ROLE OF CULTURE IN SCHOOL-SANCTIONED VERSUS HIP-HOP FEMININITIES

The private school girls and a few of the public school girls who were motivated to get their homework completed were performing what Bettie (2003) refers to as "school-sanctioned femininity." According to Bettie's research, girls who perform this version of femininity prefer preppy or unisex clothing that is not overly tight or revealing, wear makeup that is "natural" (e.g., clear lip gloss), and are involved in academics and extracurricular activities. While the girls in GIG did not wear makeup and did wear the required school uniforms, even during programming, the girls enacted this "school-sanctioned" femininity in other ways. The girls who performed school-sanctioned femininity typically adhered to the institutional rules of both school and Girls in the Game, were self-motivated to complete their homework, and actively participated in the "classes" at GIG. The girls from the private school were also less likely to be disruptive during programming. They also raised their hands during programming classes (e.g., cooking); diligently completed worksheets during classes, despite knowing they would not be graded on their work; listened quietly during programming classes; followed the rules and instructions of the coaches; and took turns during class.

For example, during the cooking and nutrition class, the volunteer instructor would ask questions about the food pyramid and healthy eating. The private school girls actively participated, raised their hands (begging to be called on), and filled in the correct answers on the handouts. During one cooking class, the girls were instructed to color in the food groups of the pyramid by using crayons of certain colors. Jodi, Yeasa, and Jessica all worked on their sheets and asked other girls to pass the colors required to complete the assignment. They colored within the lines and spoke quietly to each other or were silent. At another table, Silence, Johnita, and Tracy sat around talking and were not coloring or completing their assignment. Coach Kelly warned the girls that if they did not complete their handouts they would not be able to help prepare the class snack.

Many of the girls from the public schools were more likely to perform a "hip-hop" femininity although "doing" either hip-hop femininity or school-sanctioned femininity was not universal among either group. In other words, not all public school girls enacted hip-hop femininity nor did all private school girls enact school-sanctioned femininity. There were a few public school girls who enacted school-sanctioned femininity and a few private school girls who performed hip-hop femininity, therefore the performances were not consistent among the groups. Hip-hop femininity is a version of femininity focused on strength, self-defense by means of emotional or physical aggression or violence, street smarts, and enacting a feminine "cool pose." The girls from the public schools demonstrated knowledge of hip-hop and urban culture, as this type of knowledge held more cultural currency among their peers. Moreover, knowledge of hip-hop culture shaped much of their interaction with one another, which might involve debating who was cuter (Bow Wow or Romeo, both of whom are young, black, male rap artists), singing lyrics from popular hip-hop and R & B songs, and performing the choreographed dance moves from music videos by Destiny's Child and Ciara.

For example, during one "homework time," some of the girls were in the game room playing air hockey. As they were waiting their turn, Jenny (age 12) taught Crystal (age 7) how to "pop" her back—a suggestive dance move that is common in hip-hop videos. Silence, Jenny, and Johnita often danced and sang during programming; Silence was constantly moving, dancing, and singing. She often sang songs with explicit lyrics, including a song called "Peaches & Cream," which is about the male singer's desire to perform oral sex on women. Silence also performed hip-hop dance moves. During a dance class in which the girls learned traditional African dance moves, Silence resisted instruction and chose to perform hip-hop dance moves. When the music played, instead of performing the choreographed traditional African dance that the girls had learned from the volunteer instructor, Silence continued her hip-hop routine.

Girls who performed hip-hop femininity were less likely to adhere to the rules of the program and more likely to "do what they wanted." During cooking and nutrition class, the girls ignored the coaches, talked among themselves, or looked out the window; they wanted to participate only when it came time to prepare the food. During one cooking class, Tracy sat on the windowsill looking out the window (the rest of the girls were sitting in their chairs at the tables facing the cooking instructors). She did not color in or answer the questions on the food pyramid worksheet.

Here, I wish to stress that the performance of school-sanctioned femininity or hip-hop femininity was not universal for either the private school or the public school girls. Nor did school-sanctioned femininity necessarily coincide with a complete adherence to educational goals and objectives. One might assume that the private school girls would have aspirations to go to college and build a professional career while the public school girls would aspire to careers in entertainment or music. While this was true for some girls, it was not so for all members of the groups. For example, Tanya attended the private school, and in my observations she was always diligently working on her assignments during homework time. One day, as I helped her with her math homework, she lamented how difficult school was. I asked her what she wanted to be when she grew up. Her response was "an actor in funny movies." At the same time, some girls who performed hip-hop femininity had aspirations for white-collar work. During another "homework time," Johnita, Tracy, and I were setting up a game of Monopoly. Johnita, whom I never observed working on her homework, and who attended public school and frequently performed hip-hop femininity, said she wanted to be the banker. She explained her reason: "Because I want to be a banker when I grow up, I never play Monopoly. I am always the banker."

For the girls in Bettie's (2003) research, the performances of femininity were class-based and not simply shaped by race. However, the impact of class may not have been an important variable in whether the girls in GIG performed a hip-hop or school-sanctioned femininity. While attending a private school is usually strongly correlated with high family income, the girls of GIG who attended the private school were from a similar class background as the girls of GIG who attended the public school. Many of the girls who attended the private school were there on financially based scholarships. Therefore, class differences may not have been a determining factor in whether the girls performed school-sanctioned femininity or hip-hop femininity.

The adherence to GIG's rules and behavioral expectations by the private school girls may have resulted in part from the social and cultural capital they gained as students of the private school. For Bourdieu (1979/1984), there are different forms of capital, which includes the resources, knowledge, and connections that an individual has. *Capital* refers not only to economic wealth but also to knowledge about particular forms of culture valued by dominant groups in society, (cultural capital) as well as social ties and connections (social capital). The cultural capital that the private school girls had was the type of capital recognized and valued by other institutional contexts such as GIG (Lareau 2003). The private school that the girls attended was persistent in reminding students of the rules, and it reinforced those rules on many occasions. Students who violated the rules repeatedly or were found guilty of extreme violations, such as fighting or skipping class, could be dismissed from the school. Teachers taught the girls the importance of obeying rules and authority figures and this was reinforced among the parents of the private school girls in the GIG program. Parents wanted to ensure the girls behaved and were not suspended or expelled because admission to the school was selective and tuition was expensive (although 40 percent of students enrolled were eligible for financial aid from the school). The cultural capital acquired in the educational context shaped the gendered performances of the private school girls who enacted "school-sanctioned femininity." Girls who attended the public school and lacked access to institutional forms of cultural capital did have access to other forms of cultural capital acquired from popular culture and the world of hip-hop. However, this form of capital is not typically valued or recognized in educational institutions, or in the GIG program.

## CONCLUSION

Analyzing girls' experiences through a trilevel framework (structure, culture, and social interactions) illustrate the state of play *between* large-scale institutions and the *internal* state of play within those institutions (Cooky 2006; Messner 2002). In the 1990s, the "social problem" in girls' lives centered on self-esteem and the "self-esteem gap." Research demonstrated how girls' self-esteem dramatically declined during adolescence and was significantly lower than that of boys (American Association of University Women 1992/1995; Orenstein 1996; Pipher 1994). These research findings led to the creation of programs and organizations to address this social problem, and sport was positioned as a means by which girls could be empowered.

Social structure often constrains the extent to which an after-school program such as Girls in the Game is able to alleviate social problems among "at-risk" youth. This is not to say that the girls did not benefit tremendously from the program or that the program was not successful. However, "Girls in the Game" is only one facet in the girls' lives; it is only one source of information, one "teacher" among many. Girls have to negotiate the philosophies embedded in the structure of the program to the messages they receive from their parents, peers, teachers, and popular or hip-hop culture. For some girls, particularly many of the girls who attended the private school, the messages they received at home and at school were in alignment with the philosophy and objectives of GIG. For other girls, the philosophy of GIG often contradicted the messages they received from parents, siblings, and peers. In addressing social problems among youth, then, sport programs must be cognizant of the structural and wider ideological barriers to girls' participation in sport, and in girls' lives more generally, as well as how peers and popular culture can serve as barriers to improving and enhancing the lives of young girls.

Girls in the Game required and encouraged girls to enact what Bettie (2003) has termed "school-sanctioned femininity," which differs from the ways some girls in the program "do gender" (West and Zimmerman 1987). When some girls at GIG resisted school-sanctioned femininity and the objectives of the GIG programming—by socializing instead of reading or doing homework, by not participating in the educational aspects of programming (e.g., cooking class), and by choosing instead to perform hip-hop femininity—they engaged in what Hays (1994) and Dworkin and Messner (1999) refer to as "reproductive agency." Similar to "the lads" in Paul Willis' (1977) ethnography on the impact of working-class culture in reproducing future members of the working class, the hip-hop girls are engaging in resistance by insisting on "doing what they want." Yet this resistance does not produce transformations of the existing social structure or of wider social institutions; thus it is a form of reproductive, rather than transformative, agency. This form of agency may be empowering in the sense that the girls are able to resist the adult organizers' structure of the program and thus alter the everyday social interactions in the program (e.g., jumping rope instead of doing homework). However, by disengaging with the educational system and after-school programming through resistance to its rules and requirements, the hip-hop girls may lose out on educational opportunities and could end up either underemployed or unemployed, and in this sense they are not truly empowered through their resistance. The "choice" to disengage from the educational aspects of GIG or to disengage from school itself is one that is enabled within a particular culture that in some ways celebrates and values this resistance (although that is not, of course, the sole cause of disengagement).

Girls in the Game addressed the social problems in girls' lives through the structure of the program. However, the girls exercised reproductive agency and at times resisted the adult organizers' attempts to teach them. Girls at the site who performed hip-hop femininity often resisted the "concerted cultivation" (Lareau 2003) of the program. Tension emerged as a result of the contrast between the program's structured philosophy to empower young girls and the hip-hop girls' desire to "do what we want." The structure of the program and the adult organizers who gave life to that structure empowered girls through teaching that girls have choices. GIG never demanded that girls participate or behave in a certain way. Instead, girls were taught that they have choices and options. The options that a girl chooses have consequences; if she makes a choice, she must also be willing to accept the consequences. For example, a girl could choose not to participate in cooking class. However, if she did not participate in the educational portion of the cooking class, where girls learn about health, then she would not be able to eat the snack made during the class. In this way, girls were empowered to make their own choices. However, this agency is reproductive, in that a choice to resist the programming does not lead to any changes in the rules, regulations, or organizational philosophy (structure) of the program.

Girls were able to exercise agency that was transformative, not reproductive, during homework time. Coaches often permitted girls to socialize, play air hockey, draw, make plastic bracelets, jump rope, and play outside if they reported that they did not have homework. It was easier for the coaches to allow girls to play than to have to deal with their acts of resistance. In avoiding confrontation of girls' resistance, the coaches were able to focus their attention on the girls who made the choice to complete their homework during homework time. The coaches explained the leniency by blaming outside institutions, specifically schools, for not providing girls with opportunities for physical education and play. Coaches reframed girls' resistance (jumping rope and playing outside) as "healthy," because they were getting exercise that they were not able to get during school hours.

Through the structure of its programming, as informed by broader cultural discourses on sport and "at-risk" girls, GIG is attempting to empower girls to make choices and to understand that their choices have consequences. Girls are able to exercise agency within the context of GIG to make their own choices, and while this freedom is empowering for girls within the informal structure of the program, this agency may ultimately be reproductive of wider social institutions.

## Suggested Research

1. Students can use this theoretical approach in their studies on the experiences of individuals within sport organizations.

2. Examine the ways in which the social interactions of participants, coaches, and administrators in a sport organization (team, league, or program) produce, or give "life" to, the social organization while simultaneously examining the ways in which the sport organization is produced through the interactional agency of the participants within it.

3. Examine the role of culture in informing the structure of sport organizations, as well as shaping the everyday practices within those very organizations.

## Additional Resources

### Theory

Giddens, A. 1984. *The constitution of society: Outline of the theory of structuration*. Berkeley: University of California Press.

Rejecting Marxist notions of power based on conflict and oppression, as well as Marxist notions of agency as determined by the economic base of societies, Giddens proposes a theory of structure as both constraining and enabling human agency. Power is not necessarily linked to conflict, nor is it inherently oppressive. Similar to Michel Foucault who argued that power can be "productive" (Foucault 1981), Giddens suggests that power is the "ability to achieve outcomes" and that, as such, "power is not the obstacle to freedom but is its very medium." Giddens argues that social structure is shaped by agency and that through agency social structure is constituted.

---

Hays, S. 1994. Structure and agency and the sticky problem of culture. *Sociological Theory* 12 (1): 57–72.

Hays argues for the inclusion of analytical considerations of culture in the sociological concept of social structure. For Hays, structure is more than the external constraints social actors encounter; structure also encompasses and is shaped by and through culture. Hays expands sociological understandings of agency as not simply constrained by social structure but also enabled by it. Some forms of agency are reproductive of social structure; others are resistant or transformative of it.

---

Ingham, A., and S. Hardy. 1984. Sport, structuration, subjection and hegemony. *Theory, Culture and Society* 2 (2): 85–103.

This article addresses the relevance of connections between Giddens' theory of structuration and Gramsci's theory of hegemony to an understanding of sport. Students who wish to learn more about Giddens' theory of structuration as it applies to sport will find this article of use.

---

Sugden, J., and A. Tomlinson. 2002. Theory and method for a critical sociology of sport. In *Power games: A critical sociology of sport*, ed. J. Sugden & A. Tomlinson, 3–22. London: Routledge.

Part of a larger collection on power in sport, this chapter defines the way power has been theorized in classic and contemporary social theories and outlines the distinctions between various theoretical conceptualizations of power, including Giddens' concept of structuration. Students interested in various ways in which social theorists (Giddens, Michel Foucault, Michel de Certeau, and others) understand power will find this chapter useful.

### Sport Topic

Cooky, C. (2009). Girls just aren't interested in sport: The social construction of interest in girls' sport. *Sociological Perspectives* 52 (2).

From the abstract: "Using qualitative methodologies and the sociology of accounts, I examine a recreational sports program for low-income minority girls in the metropolitan Los Angeles area. Through application of Giddens' theory of structuration to emergent themes from participant observation and interviews, the findings illustrate how structures, as they are embodied through the everyday interactions of participants, simultaneously constrain certain forms of agency while enabling other forms. This study advances sociology's disciplinary understanding of social construction by illustrating how social structure and cultural discourses interact in shaping everyday social interactions." This article will allow students to consider the theoretical framework discussed in this chapter as it is applied to a different recreational program.

---

Messner, M.A. 2002. *Taking the field: Women, men and sports*. Minneapolis: University of Minnesota Press.

Michael Messner (2002) has developed a theoretical and empirical framework for examining gender and sport. In this framework, Messner examines how *social structure*, *culture*, and *social interactions* construct the "center of sport" despite the many challenges of women, gays, and lesbians. The "center of sport" refers to the "most highly celebrated, rewarded and institutionalized bodily practices that are defined largely by physical power, aggression and violence" (xviii). This book will be useful for students who wish to learn more on the complexity of gender relations in sport, the theories utilized in this chapter and how they may be applied to sporting contexts.

Wilson, B., P. White, K. Fisher. 2001. Multiple identities in a marginalized culture: Female youth in an "inner-city" recreation/drop-in center. *Journal of Sport and Social Issues* 25 (3): 301–323.

Utilizing Chicago School symbolic interactionist theory and cultural studies theories about subcultures, the authors examine the social processes of an inner-city recreational center. Students who wish to learn more about minority or low-income girls' recreational sport may find this article of interest.

# PART

# IV

# Microlevel Theories

The chapters included in part IV use microlevel theories (or elements taken from macrolevel theories) to explicate individual concerns about power, personality, citizenship, and dominance in sport.

## Reversal Theory

In "The Mundanity of Excellence: Tiger Woods and Excellence in Golf," I locate the dominance of Woods' golf game within the context of the "reversal theory" popularized by psychologist Michael Apter. I argue that Woods' greatest asset is his ability to be consistently unintimidated by the "big stage." In fact, it seems that he loves the big stage and performs well when standing on it. Using the many records achieved by Woods in his relatively short professional career as a point of departure, I delve beneath the surface to uncover what exactly makes Woods such a dominant golfer among men who are, by all accord, very good golfers themselves.

## Symbolic Interactionism and Dramaturgy

In "Making it Big: Visible Symbols of Success, Physical Appearance, and Sport Figures," Bonnie Berry writes in the tradition of Erving Goffman, Harold Garfinkel, and George Herbert Mead. Each of these thinkers, in some way, tunes us into outward manifestations of human society such as clothing, body type, home size, and automobiles in an attempt to assess the level or range of power and success possessed by individuals. Berry analyzes the social messages transmitted by sport figures to a social audience via their physical appearance.

## Figurational (Social Process) Theory

In "Sport and Multiple Identities in Postwar Trinidad: The Case of McDonald Bailey," Caribbean sociologist Roy McCree argues that by using the microlevel elements provided by "figurational theory" we can better understand the multiple-identity crisis affecting British subjects like the sprinter McDonald Bailey, who was torn between sport allegiances to Great Britain and to Trinidad. The analysis helps explain the significance of Bailey's representation of Britain in international athletic competition for the issue of identity formation.

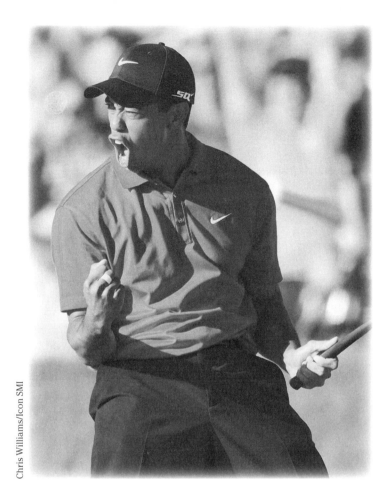

Chris Williams/Icon SMI

# 13 | The Mundanity of Excellence

## Tiger Woods and Excellence in Golf

*Earl Smith, PhD*

---

**Social theory:** Reversal theory

**Proponents of the theory:** Michael Apter (psychologist)

**What the theory says:** Reversal theory is a psychological theory addressing the flexibility and changeability of individuals. The theory specifically focuses on individuals' motivation and capacity to change, depending on circumstances.

---

As it applies to sport, the phrase that provides the first part of this chapter's title, "The Mundanity of Excellence,"[1] is about taking one's athletic abilities to levels that far surpass all others engaged in similar sporting activity (Chambliss 1989). Such extraordinary performances also take place in other areas of life—in, for example, business, academics, and the arts. Yet we have few answers as to why, in a group of similarly situated athletes who possess good skills, great athletic talent, a strong work ethic, and high levels of motivation, some go on to excel above and beyond others who remain well regarded as athletes but do not become superstars. This chapter looks at the achievements of one such athlete—Eldrick "Tiger" Woods. Tiger's father, Earl, sets the stage for our understanding of his phenomenal son:

> *Please forgive me, but sometimes I get very emotional when I talk about my son. My heart fills with so much joy when I realize that this young man is going to be able to help so many people. He will transcend this game and bring to the world a humanitarianism which has never been known before. The world will be a better place to live in by virtue of his existence and his presence. I acknowledge only a small part in that in that I know that I was personally selected by God himself to nurture this young man and bring him to the point where he can make his contribution to humanity. This is my treasure. Please accept it and use it wisely. Thank you (qtd. in Smith 1996).*

Woods arrived on the sporting scene at an early age. In all his years of playing golf, he has been described as a "phenomenon" (Billings 2003; Cole and Andrews 2000; Dawkins 2004; Hall 2001). But what brought Tiger to the larger public, beyond the elite world of golf, was his insistence that, even though his father was an African American man with clearly African American features, he would describe himself differently. His mother, Kultida, is Thai, and Tiger stirred controversy when he insisted that he would define himself as a composite of the various contributions to his racial heritage: African American, Asian American, Caucasian American, and Native American. The term he arrived at was "Cablinasian," a portmanteau word denoting his entire ancestral heritage. Having demolished the stirrings (at times hyperbolic) about his ethnicity or race, Tiger set about to be the best golfer he could, regardless of insistence that he identify himself as African American.

---

[1] The first part of this title is adapted from Daniel F. Chambliss (1989).

# TIGER THE GOLFER

Tiger Woods began his ascent to the top of the golf world early in his career. His father taught him the game of golf and coached him carefully. Tiger strove for excellence and built excellence into his daily training, and he carries this goal with him daily (Peters and Austin 1989). What makes Woods' dominance all the more remarkable is that, unlike the pioneering Jackie Robinson, whose name is connected for all time with professional baseball mainly because he integrated the game, Woods' name is attached to golf because of the excellence he brings to his golf game. Even in those tournaments that he does not win, Woods has amassed a record in his 12-years on the Professional Golfers' Association (PGA) tour that includes 23 second-place and 17 third-place finishes.

To be where Woods is in the world of professional golf is doubly remarkable in that golf, more than any other sport, was and remains virtually off-limits for underrepresented minority group members, especially African Americans. Of all registered professional golfers, 84 percent are white (Hack 2008; Pells 2005).

Furthermore, much like Martina Navratilova, one of the greatest female tennis players of all time, Tiger Woods has transformed the game of men's golf. Each in their own way, both Navratilova (who brought power to the sport of women's tennis) and Woods (who introduced physical fitness, weight lifting, and running to professional golf) remade their respective sports into games of power. Instead of "throwing one down" in the clubhouse before a match—and after it—Woods takes a "systems" approach to his training (Johnson 2007), implementing the kind of regimen that has long been a part of other professional sports such as football and basketball. He says that he was a talented high school athlete, running the 400 m and cross country events (Johnson 2007), and decided to approach golf in similar fashion:

> *[I] decided long ago to treat golf as a sport. I let other people treat it like a hobby. It would be asinine for someone not to work out and go play football. It doesn't make sense for golf, either.*

So the question that interests me is this: How do we *explain* the person, Tiger Woods, who treks around the golf course weekend to weekend, tournament to tournament, dominating like no other golfer, against the very best golfers in the world?

# THEORY OF DOMINANCE IN SPORT

To understand the career achievements of Tiger Woods—how he can continually demolish the best golfers in the world—requires a theoretical perspective not embedded within some unexplainable characteristic to which good performance in sport is attributed, such as race, speed, gender, or height (Smith 2007; Mulkay and Gilbert 1981). While important, these do not help us *explain* sport dominance.

When persons who are knowledgeable about the game of golf (including golf announcers) tell us what to expect from Tiger Woods, they often talk in terms of dominance (Feinstein 1999, 2008; Wilbon 2005). Week after week, by the time Sunday comes around, the announcers make comments suggesting that Tiger

Woods doesn't play to win by 1 stroke—he plays to win by 10. In examining his record, they note that he plays to beat the tournament records of greats like Arnold Palmer and Jack Nicklaus not by 1 victory but by 10. Thus, knowledgeable experts insist that Woods' motivation involves a desire to perform not simply well enough to win but well enough to become totally dominant—to bury his opponents—and that he is not content simply to have a good day at the golf course (Feinstein 2008). The data presented in tables 13.1 and 13.2 seem to support the claim that Woods intends not only to win but to dominate, as few other players have dominated the world of competitive golf in the manner that Woods has.

My observations in following Woods' career lead to a similar perspective about how far he outdistances other professional golfers, many others share this view. Golf analyst John Feinstein (2008) made the following argument:

> Maybe they should make Tiger Woods start playing with one hand tied behind his back. After all, he proved that he's better than everyone else in the world playing on one leg. Maybe the next step is to make him prove he can win playing with one hand. A few years ago, when the PGA Tour came out with the slogan, "These Guys Are Good," a number of players suggested it be rewritten to say, "These Guys Are Pretty Good, But This One Guy Is Great."

In this vein, two announcers for the Golf Channel, Kelly Tilghman and Nick Faldo, provided some on-air "advice" for golf's elites, whose combined performances are rarely enough to beat Woods. Faldo (a golfer himself) said that the upcoming play-

**Table 13.1** Tiger Woods' Performance in the Majors 1997–2008

| Major championship | Times won | Years won | Finishes in top 5 (when not winning) |
|---|---|---|---|
| Masters | 4 | 1997, 2001, 2002, 2005 | 4 |
| U.S. Open | 3 | 2000, 2002, 2008 | 3 |
| PGA Championship | 4 | 1999, 2000, 2006, 2007 | 2 |
| The Open Championship | 3 | 2000, 2005, 2006 | 2 |
| Total | 14 | | 11 |

**Table 13.2** Summary of Tiger Woods' Performance in the Majors 1997–2008

| | |
|---|---|
| Total Major tournaments played | 46 |
| Total Major victories | 14 |
| Total Major finishes in top 5 | 25 |
| Percentage of wins in major tournaments | 30 |
| Percentage of top 5 finishes in major tournaments | 54 |

ers should "gang up" on Woods to beat him at his game. Tilghman then advised PGA Tour players that the only way to prevent Woods from winning virtually every tournament would be for the players to "lynch him in a back alley" (Sirak 2008).

It is of little importance at the individual level whether Tilghman's remark was intended as racist by her or interpreted as such by him. Enough has been said about this already, including Wood's own statement that he did not take her comment as racist and that he did not think there was any ill intent (Associated Press 2008). Regardless, such a remark is offensive within the larger African American civil society in that there is a 200-year history of racial lynching against mainly African American men for any number of "reasons," including (most often) any indication of their interest in or relationships with white women (Johnston 1970). Extending the analysis further, scholars of lynching note that it was primarily a tool of social control, a way to remind all African Americans of their subordinate place in the social, political economy of the United States (Davis 1983; Patterson 1998; Hattery and Smith 2007). Lynching was a mechanism for controlling "uppity Negroes" who threatened the social order. In this context, the exchange between Tilghman and Faldo is illustrative of the sheer dominance of Woods' play and the threat of his dominance to the social order of golf, a sport that remains dominated by white men with upper class privilege.

My attempt at explaining Tiger Wood's dominance in golf uses reversal theory, which is most often referenced to the work of Michael Apter (1989). According to Apter's work, reversal theory explains individual behavior; it is framed in three states:

Telic-Paratelic

Conformist-Negativist

Mastery-Sympathy

Figure 13.1 provides further illustration of reversal theory and its three states.

In Apter's work, we find that the core of the theory involves individual motivation and the structure of mental life. For Woods, this means—and it has been corroborated—that mentally, he, more than other golfers, can focus on the task at hand, letting nothing bother or upset his concentration. Another aspect of this theory of the structure of mental life is the ability to craft a deep desire from a basic social-psychological standpoint to (over)value winning. This desire is connected to the emotions (some of which we see in Woods when his opponents get too close), and, finally, to the way in which Woods views the world—that is, seeing the world in his own particular way. I would frame this as a positive myopia.

From this perspective, it is state 3, the mastery-sympathy stage, that is most applicable. Woods has the ability to believe that what he is doing is all-encompassing—a task bigger than himself. He wants power, he wants to win, and he is not going to ease up or become sympathetic to opponents whom he beats week after week, year after year. Woods has the ability to ignore others' world views and not let them infiltrate his view of himself. This applies especially to public figures like Al Sharpton, who is not satisfied with Woods' acceptance of the Tilghman apology. Sharpton put it thus (McLaughlin 2008):

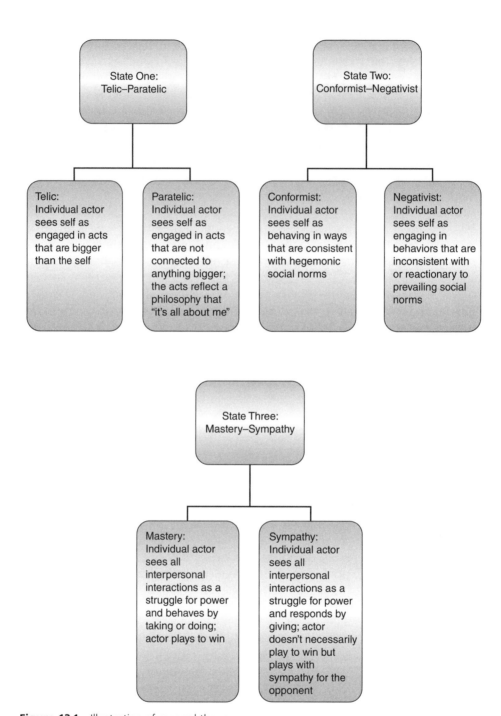

**Figure 13.1** Illustration of reversal theory.

*Lynching is not murder in general. It is not assault in general. It is a specific racial term that this woman should be held accountable for. What she said is racist. Whether she's a racist—whether she runs around at night making racist statements—is immaterial.*

Woods also has the ability to "close ranks" around himself and not let the "talking heads" remind him (or constrain him based on the idea) that he is just a black guy who is golfing. Woods will say, when confronted with this message, that he doesn't want to be the best black golfer but that he strives to be the best golfer in the world—who just happens to be black (Smith 2007). In observing Woods, it is clear that he does not let journalists, TV commentators, or anyone else shape his world view. Another example, in addition to his refusal to let the "lynch" remark distract him from play, involves comments made by golfer Fuzzy Zoeller when Woods won his first Masters Tournament in 1997:

*That little boy [Tiger Woods] is driving it well and he's putting well. He's doing everything it takes to win. So, you know what you guys do when he gets in here? You pat him on the back and say "congratulations" and "enjoy it" and tell him not to serve fried chicken next year. Got it? [Turns to walk away, then adds another comment.] Or collard greens, or whatever the hell they serve ("Golfer says" 1997).*

Woods passed both incidents off as "nothing" and refused to be deterred from getting the job done on the golf course. Though once again scholars of race and sport (and others) analyzed Zoeller's comments as "racist," Woods did not allow these comments to infiltrate his world view or his view of himself; he refused to be distracted and has gone on to win three more Masters titles (for a total of four), thus tying the number of wins by golf great Arnold Palmer; he is now second only to the record of six wins amassed by Jack Nicklaus. This Masters Tournament record alone proves that Woods belongs among the elites of golf, and he is only 33 years old.

It is by following the dictates of reversal theory that Woods' reaction, which can be characterized as an apparent lack of reaction, is best explained. The theory allows us to recognize Woods' focus. What the theory does not account for are experiential factors such as racism, sexism, and religious bigotry. The explanatory power of the theory is enhanced when we add these considerations to the model. In the context of "country club" sports in the United States (e.g., golf, tennis), Woods has been very myopic in staying the course, even though from the very beginning roadblocks were thrown in his way as he progressed (Wilbon 2005). Woods had to address racism at every turn: his participation in tournaments was blocked, his father's coaching practices were questioned, he endured the hurling of racial epitaphs because not only was he frequently the *only* African American teenager participating in the tournaments held at country clubs, but more so because he was *dominating* the competition. No other successful golfer (including greats such as Arnold Palmer, Jack Nicklaus, and Phil Mickelson) has had to negotiate these distractions.

When Woods wins, he wins big. When he won the 1997 Masters, his 12-stroke margin of victory was the largest in Masters history, and this is unexceptional for

Woods, who often wins by a striking margin. When Woods won the 2000 U.S. Open by a margin of 15 strokes Clifton Brown (2000) of the *New York Times* wrote:

> *Tiger Woods looked natural making unforgettable shots, he looked natural making history, and it seemed natural that Woods, the world's best player, won the 100th United States Open today in record-setting fashion. Woods was making a dramatic statement that his skills have never been in more perfect harmony. On a picture-perfect day at Pebble Beach, one of golf's most sacred locations, Woods finished with a 12-under-par total of 272 to win the Open by a record-setting 15 strokes over Ernie Els of South Africa and Miguel Angel Jimenez of Spain, who tied for second place at 3 over par. It was the largest victory margin in a major championship, surpassing the 13-stroke margin by Old Tom Morris at the 1862 British Open. The winning margin also broke the United States Open record that had stood for 101 years, surpassing the 11-stroke victory by Willie Smith in 1899.*

On average, across his 14 career victories in Majors, Woods has won by a margin of 4.69 strokes. These feats, according to reversal theory, allow us to underscore the fact that Woods has not only mastered the mechanics of the game of golf but also is in full control of his emotions—that his "game face," so often commented on, is in fact an outward expression of complete control and concentration. He can see holes that are in front of him, read his opponents' mistakes, and wield mastery at not only choosing the right club but also understanding the relevant forces of nature (e.g., wind, temperature, slope, grass height).

Owen (2000) points to a technical part of Woods' game that speaks directly to how he is able to incorporate technical flawlessness into his play in pursuit of dominance. In speaking with editors of *Golf Digest*, Owen reports the following:

> *The camera recorded fifteen driver swings from five different angles. When the prints came back from the lab, the magazine's editors discovered that only five frames among the hundreds taken during the shoot had captured Woods's swing at the approximate moment his club head came into contact with the ball—a problem they had never encountered before. "With other tour players, we almost always get a picture of impact with every swing," Roger Schiffman, the executive editor, told me. When Woods makes his normal swing, the head of his driver moves at about a hundred and twenty miles an hour—a good fifteen miles an hour faster than the club head of a typical touring pro, and about thirty miles an hour faster than the club head of an average amateur. Between one Hulcher frame and the next, Woods' driver travelled through roughly two hundred degrees of arc, which means that a ball sitting unthreatened on the tee in one frame would be long gone by the next.*

As the data in tables 13.1 and 13.2 show, Woods has been consistent in his short professional career, and even though this chapter does not document his amateur career, he was a consistent winner there as well. The data in table 13.3 show Woods' world ranking in PGA tournaments and his percentage lead compared to the other top golfers worldwide.

**Table 13.3**  World Rankings Through December 2008

| Rank | Name | Points* | Majors | Percentage lead** |
|------|------|---------|--------|-------------------|
| 1 | Tiger Woods | 13.79 | 14 | ----- |
| 2 | Sergio García | 8.59 | 0 | 38% |
| 3 | Phil Mickelson | 7.95 | 3 | 42% |
| 4 | Padraig Harrington | 7.51 | 3 | 45% |
| 5 | Vijay Singh | 7.44 | 3 | 46% |

* The World Ranking Points for each player are accumulated over a 2-year "rolling" period with the points awarded for each event maintained for a 13-week period to place additional emphasis on recent performances—ranking points will then be reduced in equal decrements for the remaining 91 weeks of the 2-year ranking period. Each player is then ranked according to his average points per tournament, which is determined by dividing his total number of points by the tournaments he has played over that 2-year period. There is a minimum divisor of 40 tournaments over the 2-year ranking period. The winners of the Masters Tournament, the U.S. Open, the Open Championship, and the PGA Championship are awarded 100 points (60 points for 2nd place, 40 for 3rd, 30 for 4th, down to 1.50 points for a player completing the final round), and the winner of the Players Championship is awarded 80 points (points are awarded down to 1.20 points for 60th place and ties). The PGA Championship has a minimum 64 points for the winner (points to 56th place). Minimum points levels for the winners of official Tour events have been set at 6 points for the Canadian Tour (points to 6th place), 12 points for the European Challenge Tour (points to 14th place), 14 points for the Asian, Sunshine and Nationwide Tours (points to 17th place), 16 points for Australasian and Japanese Tours (points to 19th place), and 24 points for European and the United States Tours (points to 27th place). In addition, the Open Championships of Australia, Japan and South Africa have a minimum of 32 points for the winner (points to 37th place), and the Flagship events on the Asian and Nationwide Tours have a minimum of 20 points for the winner (points to 22nd place). In the cases of co-sanctioned Tour events, the minimum point levels are determined using the "average" of the minimum Tour ranking points from each Tour (rounded up to nearest whole number).

** The percentage of points Woods has over his competition. In other words, Garcia would have to gain 38% more points in order to catch Woods.

Woods is a complete golfer. In changing from his longtime instructor and trainer Butch Harmon to Hank Haney in 2004, Woods made a move that many thought he should have made years earlier. Woods' own assessment was, Why change if I am winning? But in overcoming what Jaime Diaz calls "the fear of change," Woods moved to another level in golf. Though he was in no way slumping, he switched to Haney specifically to get help that he needed in order to change his swing, which contributed to his sheer dominance: he has won six Major Tournaments since making this change (Diaz 2007).

Reversal theory helps explain that Woods, at this juncture of his career could look in on his game, see that changes were needed, and overcome his fear of change. Apter's work demonstrates that reversals are a significant part of one's psychological makeup and that they occur when we move between motivational states. At state 3, mastery, Woods looks up and knows that winning will require change. He overcomes his fear and switches to Hank Haney, and his victories accumulate.

This did not go unnoticed by golfer Adam Scott, who sums up the theoretical approach that helps us explain Tiger Woods' excellence (qtd. in Campbell 2008):

*I'm blown away by the motivation that he has, and I just think it's a pure desire to succeed that helps him win all the time. You would think he might get tired of it, but I guess not. He's certainly pushing everyone else harder.*

## DISCUSSION

*Golf Digest* writer Tim Rosaforte (2007) has commented that "the scary thing [about Tiger] is, this is just the opening act." Today, with the extension of what Veblen (1899/2008) described as the "leisure class," golfers are growing exponentially. The meaning of all this is the power of Tiger Woods. The advertising revenue he brings to networks like CBS and NBC is astonishing. What this means is that even "moderate" players, who are well back on the leaderboard, can earn more than a decent living.[2]

Here is a fuller excerpt of Rosaforte's (2007) assessment of Woods:

*The only thing I could offer was a graphic that flashed up on a screen at the Golf Channel after Tiger won the Bridgestone Invitational the week before, showing the staggering comparison between where Woods was with his 58th career victory, and the career victories of Johnny Miller, Greg Norman, and the like. It wasn't even close. Tiger was already beyond double of all the greats who played through the Nicklaus era. About the only salient point I could muster upon seeing all those numbers was: "And he's not even in his prime yet."*

There is some data to support this contention. Writing in the *Observer*, Kevin Mitchell notes the following (2008):

*Look at the PGA Tour money leaders for 2008 so far. Eighteen players have already earned a million dollars or more. Woods sits at the top with [US]$3,615,000 (£1.8m). Behind him are Phil Mickelson ([US]$2.16m) and Vijay Singh ([US]$1.96m). It goes on through a familiar cast of names, all millioned-up and thankful to The Man: Choi, Ogilvy, Leonard, Cink, down to Trahan and Els . . . then on through to golfers who would be obscure battlers in any other sport but are wealthy athletes in golf. Thanks to one man. Who, for instance, is Boo Weekley? Boo is from Florida, two years older than Woods at 35, and made his pro debut shortly after Tiger shook up the world. Boo has lived a comfortable, largely anonymous life on the tour, earning [US]$3.9m in 11 unspectacular seasons. In 10 tournaments this year he has missed two cuts, finished in the top 10 three times, won nothing and earned [US]$694,685. He has much to be grateful for to Woods, as do those farther down the list. The player in 50th place on the US Tour earned nearly [US]$1.7m in 2007: in 1995 it was [US]$350,000.*

---

[2] We often forget that the kind of money these professional golfers make is far and away superior to what ordinary working Americans earn. Recent data provided by the U.S. Department of Education show that the average annual wage for working Americans is US$40,405.48. The median wage for those with a BA or BS degree is US$48,400 for men and US$39,500 for women (U.S. Department of Education, table 20-1).

Woods not only wins golf championships, he earns a lot of money for being the number one golfer in the world. As of 2007, Woods has won over an estimated US$100 million from both his winnings and endorsements. He has won 14 professional major golf championships, second highest of any male player, and 64 PGA Tour events, tied for third all time. He has more career Major wins and career PGA Tour wins than any other active golfer. Finally, Woods is the youngest player to achieve the career Grand Slam. To be sure, this level of achievement amounts to dominance.

It is important to note here that Woods is so dominant that even though the world's second-best golfers are an excellent group of professionals—including golfers we would all recognize, such as Phil Mickelson and Vijay Singh—the field behind Woods is so dispersed that no single golfer ever gets close. Woods' opponents simply cannot make up the distance he has put between himself and the rest of the field.

In Daniel F. Chambliss' (1989) research essay, "The Mundanity of Excellence," we learn that

> *Olympic sports, and competitive swimming in particular, provide an unusually clear opportunity for studying the nature of excellence. In other fields, it may be less clear who are the outstanding performers: the best painter or pianist, the best businessperson, the finest waitress or the best father. But in sport (and this is one of its attractions) success is defined more exactly, by success in competition. There are medals and ribbons and plaques for first place, second, and third; competitions are arranged for the head-to-head meeting of the best competitors in the world; in swimming and track, times are electronically recorded to the hundredth of a second; there are statistics published and rankings announced, every month or every week. By the end of the Olympic Games every four years, it is completely clear who won and who lost, who made the finals, who participated in the Games, and who never participated in the sport at all.*

Athletes can only be understood in terms of the changing relationships they form with each other. This requires a historical perspective and an emphasis on important relational aspects such as power and dependency (Smith 2007; Dunning 1999). For Tiger Woods, it is about his relationship to the field of professional male golfers.

Clearly, this applies to our understanding of Tiger Woods in the larger context of his dominant place in international golf. For example, the definition of excellence used in this chapter is adapted from the essay by Chambliss (1989, 72). The term is meant to refer to a consistent level of high performance, and, as Chambliss puts it, "the excellent athlete regularly, even routinely, performs better than his or her competitors. Consistency of superior performances tells us that one athlete is indeed better than another, and that the difference between them is not merely the product of chance." Tiger Woods is dominant because he is the best. In his book *Superclass: The Global Power Elite and the World They Are Making*, Rothkopf pays special attention to the issue of dominance (2008, 29–30). He theorizes one of the best cases for Woods' dominance. He puts it this way:

*As uncommon as—by definition—they are, we are all familiar with the extraordinary among us. In almost every human pursuit, levels of talent and accomplishments seldom ascend in smooth, small increments. In sports, for example, the levels of proficiency are more like the quantum levels of an atom, representing substantial, geometrical leaps in capability. The gap between the average amateurs and the top amateurs—between the weekend tennis hacker and the ranked college player, for example—is enormous. The gap between top amateurs and average professionals and those who can play at the top level of their sports year in and year out is yet again exponentially greater. And, finally, most strikingly, there is the chasm that separates the top ten or twenty in any sport, and the once-in-a-generation best of the best who appear in ones and twos sprinkled through history. Among millions of dedicated, talented, and enthusiastic athletes, an amazingly gifted few set themselves apart: the Michael Jordans and Pelés of the world. The pattern persists from sport to other human pursuits, from art to literature, to politics to business: Tolstoy and Dickens, Rothschild and Rockefeller, Mao and Mandela. These are the few who define the direction of their professions and their eras. They are emulated, become beacons, and very often, there are clusters of such individuals atop their fields—some well-known, some invisible—who dominate the worlds around them. . . . [W]hen you consider that these athletes are drawn from a pool of talent encompassing hundreds of millions, each one of these top cadres is literally one in a million, perhaps even more elite than that.*

In closing, this chapter on Eldrick "Tiger" Woods and his dominance in the sport of professional golf, let me restate the original argument: reversal theory offers a framework for understanding Woods' dominance in a sport that has traditionally been open only to white men.[3]

## CONCLUSION

Tiger Woods has not been the subject of scholarly debate in the sociology of sport. What little research has appeared on Woods has focused primarily on his race as an African American[4] male playing in the predominantly white sport of professional golf (Billings 2003; Cole and Andrews 2000; Dawkins 2004; Hall 2001). Many of the books about Woods that appear in digital lists such as WorldCat and or the various bibliographies found on Amazon.com are intended for children—unauthorized biographies and journalistic books often consisting of previously published interviews.

This chapter steps outside this narrow "racial box" and analyzes what it is that Woods does on the golf course. No one that I know of has attempted to explain theoretically why Woods is a consistent winner who so dominates the difficult

---

[3] Note, though this is not the topic of this chapter, women and Jews have also been categorically denied access to the sport of golf.

[4] I remind the reader that Woods has spoken publicly about his decision to define his own racial identity as Cablinasian (for a lengthier discussion, see Smith 2007).

game of professional golf (see table 13.3). To explain this phenomenon, I have chosen reversal theory above other theories in the sociology of sport (see the chart on pp. xviii-xxi in the book's introduction) because it points specifically to how individuals focus on tasks at hand and how they remain flexible enough to make needed changes, overcoming any fear of change, which is common among the highly superstitious population of professional athletes.

Eldrick "Tiger" Woods has been a master of both motivation and flexibility, taken together to indicate here what Malcolm Gladwell calls an "outlier." In view of Gladwell's theory, as laid out in *Outliers: The Story of Success*, Woods' story is not that of someone who overcame tremendous disadvantages but that of someone who took advantage of the "gifts" that came with being the son of Earl Woods and Kultida Woods. There is no question that Woods was born with tremendous gifts—natural ability—but there may be others born with similar talents who never achieve his level of dominance. Why? Because, as reversal theory suggests and as Gladwell points out, it is not enough to inherit "gifts"; one must have the ambition and work ethic to turn them into dominance (285):

> It is not the brightest who succeed. Nor is success simply the sum of the decisions and efforts we make on our own behalf. It is, rather, a gift. Outliers are those who have been given opportunities—and who have had the strength and presence of mind to seize them.

And, it is clear, Tiger Woods not only dominates the world of professional golf: He has changed the game forever.

## Suggested Research

1. Reversal theory is well suited to explain not only dominance in sport but also how superstar athletes make critical, career-extending changes as they near the peak of their career. One example is Muhammad Ali, who evolved from the brash, trash-talking, circling and dancing boxer to the stand-in-one-spot-and-be-hit (thus inventing the rope-a-dope) fighter. Reversal theory is primed to help us explain Ali who late in his career continued to win heavyweight boxing world championships because he was willing to change his boxing style (Dailey 1999).

2. Reversal theory can also help us explore both motivations and emotions as they affect certain decision that athletes make. For example, one might consider basketball legend Michael Jordan's decision to play professional baseball, or the bizarre plot by figure skater Tonya Harding to have her rival Nancy Kerrigan attacked physically.

3. Using reversal theory, but looking outside of SportsWorld, sociologists could explore the monumental research output of the late Robert K. Merton in comparison with that of other famous sociologists. Merton and his motivation, work ethic, and goals could be analyzed in comparison with those of his mentor, Talcott Parsons, and other sociologists such as James Coleman, William J. Wilson, Alice Rossi, Harriet Zuckerman, and Arlene Kaplan Daniels to see just what differentiates his output from theirs. Merton remains by far the most productive sociologist ever.

## Additional Resources

### Theory

Kerr, J.H. 1999. *Motivation and emotion in sport: Reversal theory.* New York: Psychology Press.

Reversal theory's systematic conceptual framework offers a unique perspective for interpreting behavior in sport contexts.

---

Annesi, J. 1997. Three-dimensional state anxiety recall: Implications for individual zone of optimal functioning research and application. *The Sport Psychologist* 11:43–52.

Annesi's article provides experimental data to illustrate the importance of focus for athletes in overcoming anxiety.

### Sport Topic

Owen, D. 2000. The chosen one. *New Yorker*, August 21, 106.

This noted journalistic account of Woods' excellence gives some insight into his swing and how technically different it is from those of other top golfers.

---

Wooden, J. 1997. *Wooden: A lifetime of observations and reflections on and off the court.* New York: McGraw-Hill.

We learn about basketball and life from legendary college basketball coach John Wooden.

---

Woods, E. 1997. *Training a tiger: A father's guide to raising a winner in both golf and life.* New York: Collins Living Books.

Tiger Woods' father, Earl Woods, has been both credited with shaping Tiger's career and career goals and criticized for putting immense pressure on him early in his life. The book offers an inside look at Earl Woods' philosophy of golf and life.

---

# 14 | Making it Big

## Visible Symbols of Success, Physical Appearance, and Sport Figures

*Bonnie Berry, PhD*

---

**Social theory:** Symbolic interactionism and dramaturgy

**Proponents of the theory:** George Herbert Mead, Harold Garfinkel, Erving Goffman

**What the theory says:** Through the use of outward and visible social symbols, we influence our society in hopes of being viewed in a favorable light. These symbols, such as clothing and body size, hold symbolic meaning (e.g., power, success). Through our interaction with other societal members, we create an image, if not a reality, of ourselves and our place in society. This process is often thought of as impression management. We can think of this process as playing a part in a play (hence, *dramaturgy*).

---

This chapter addresses the intended social messages transmitted by sport figures via their physical appearance to a social audience. To say "sport figures" is to use the term generously, since I describe not only sport figures as we popularly know them (i.e., professional and celebrity sports participants) but also those who want to physically resemble these sport figures. Of the latter, people who are fitness conscious—nonprofessional fitness-oriented sports participants who alter their bodies to appear physically powerful and who align themselves with physical evidence of financial success and criminality—may imagine themselves as pro sport figures with similar evidence of success (e.g., physical, sexual, and economic power). Secondarily, I examine physical alterations disguised as health issues, as we see in media and advertisement advice to appear lean and muscular. Not unexpectedly, gender and race play important parts in this analysis of social messages sent by physical appearance.

The findings of this analysis are interpreted through sociological theory—mainly, symbolic interaction, and, more specifically, impression management and dramaturgy. All members of society attempt to present themselves in a particularly favorable way in order to amass admiration and various kinds of opportunity (e.g., economic, romantic). Symbolic interactionism, as discussed later in more detail, refers to the social meaning of symbols, as when large body size represents power. These symbols are experienced through social interaction, as in the obvious example of visually observing a large person and thinking "power." The visible symbols of sport figures' physical construction (e.g., their bodies, hairstyles, tattoos), their accoutrements (e.g., jewelry, cars, spouses, and lovers), and the verbiages used to describe fitness and social power as found in the media all have social meaning and social consequences.

## THE NULL HYPOTHESIS AND METHODOLOGY

A conjectural null hypothesis might state that sport figures physically resemble people in general; have ordinary-looking partners; and dress, groom, and accessorize in status quo fashion. Unsurprisingly, the findings do not support such conjecture. To get ahead of myself, sport figures hope to portray themselves to the social audience as extraordinarily physically, economically, and socially powerful.

Their impression management is not unique to them, since most if not all members of society engage in impression management; however, the manner in which sport figures engage in impression management is distinct.

The methodology involves observations of fitness and sports magazines, relying on a sampling of such magazines published in late 2007 and early 2008. The magazines were selected randomly, with the one stricture that they address health (e.g., *Women's Health*) or sport (e.g., *Sports Illustrated*). I perused newsstands, pharmacies, and bookstores and selected 15 magazines. The observations were designed to note a number of traits about sport figures, including purely physical features (height, weight, musculature, skin color, hairstyle, race, gender, age). Other traits examined include accoutrements designed to manage the social impression of the sport figure and of the sport itself. These accoutrements may be purposely attached by the sport figures to themselves, such as luxury items used to denote financial success, or they may be more subtle behavior by advertisers who hope to pair a particular sport with a particular lifestyle—for example, linking golf with expensive liquors, watches, and resorts.

The methodology is based on the principles of visual sociology and relies on visual inspection of magazine images. Significantly, these images include words as well as photos, computer graphics (CG), and cartoon images. These images are symbolic of what the sport figures, the advertisers, and the magazine publishers are hoping to convey to the readership.

In examining sport, fitness, and health magazines, one must remember the salience of physical appearance. To wit, "health" has little to do with the reason for images conveyed in sport, fitness, and (even) health magazines. As this chapter shows, health magazines are geared toward advising the reader on how to improve one's appearance, largely through weight loss and supplement use, rather than on health.

Bear in mind also that sport, fitness, and health magazines are motivated by advertising, which, in turn, is geared to promote fantasy in the viewer. If all goes well in the advertising world, the magazine viewer will think, for example, "If I engage in these sports activities, wearing these athletic clothes, and taking these supplements, I'll be hugely muscular, win prizes, and be surrounded by gorgeous and adoring women. I'll be considered dangerous and not to be messed with by my peers. And I will accumulate wealth beyond my wildest imagination." That is but one scenario, and variances manifest on the basis of gender (e.g., women believing they will lose weight if they follow low-fat recipes and go for walks) and sport (e.g., golfers being more influenced by association with symbols of wealth than by intimidating physiques). Let us now consider the many intriguing observations of sport, fitness, and health magazines.

## OBSERVATIONS OF SPORT, FITNESS, AND "HEALTH" MAGAZINE IMAGES

The following is a description of the imageries (similar to the one you saw on page 187 at the start of this chapter) found in sports and fitness magazines. These images involve a diversity of concerns, including financial success, physical power wielded through physical strength, grooming, body size, sexual opportunity, primitiveness, race, age, gender, and beauty (per societal beauty standards). Health is presented as an issue but is rarely treated as a true issue.

As Susan Alexander has already pointed out in her comprehensive review of stories, advertisements, and advice columns in *Men's Health* magazine, the male viewers and readers are primarily encouraged to consume (2003). The items they should consume—cars, clothes, jewelry—are supposed to reflect a masculine and, more significant, financially successful lifestyle. In this sense, *Men's Health* magazine serves as a guide for what men should buy in order to *appear* to be successful members of society. Of course, there are also offerings of advice for men's health and fitness. The stories and the ads in this magazine center on clothes, tools, plastic surgery, baldness cures, cars, sex, sports and fitness (equipment, food, drugs, exercise programs, sport figures), success images and advice (how to become financially successful), gadgets (phones, office and stereo equipment), cosmetics, grooming equipment (body shavers), diet and health tips, jewelry, and perfume. Clearly, this is a mainstream catalog of what men should want and the items with which they should surround themselves in order to send the social message of "success." There is a slight edginess insofar as we may see the occasional sport figures festooned with tattoos. One also finds (though far less so than in the fitness magazines cited below) war imagery, as though fighting fat and building one's body are akin to waging a battle. Mostly, however, the magazine addresses consumer purchases and sex, judging from both the visual images and the words. If men have the right bodies, grooming, clothes, cars, stereos, watches, cologne, and sexual technique, they will be engulfed in beautiful women desirous of sexual activity with them. On the whole, *Men's Health* magazine offers much sex advice (dos and don'ts), products promising to advance sexual prowess, and stories about what women want sexually.

In comparison, *Women's Health* magazine shows a much greater focus on relationships than do *Men's Health* and other men's magazines. There is a small but still significant focus on sex, but for the most part the magazine places a great deal of emphasis on diet and exercise as the means by which to achieve "health" (read: weight loss).

*Hers*, a "muscle and fitness" magazine for women, focuses primarily on weight loss, diet, and exercise, and it includes a number of drug ads (for weight loss). One such ad utilizes sex and violence imagery ("removes fat like a blow torch!") and a promise to "wildly enhance sex while burning fat." The advertisements for weight-loss drugs and the sexual references are nowhere nearly as prominent as they are in men's fitness magazines (discussed later). Instead, women's fitness magazines place much more emphasis on dieting and recipes.

Although not specified in the title, *Health* magazine is womancentric. Nonetheless, on the cover of one issue, only two of the eight callouts have to do with health (in this case, cancer and headaches). The other six address beauty, and four of them involve weight loss. The cover model, as is the case for the other women's fitness and health magazines, is a pretty, young, white woman. There are almost no non-white women in this magazine. Indeed, in women's health and fitness magazines, nearly all of the models, as well as the "real" people, are young, attractive, and white. The "health" addresses are thinly disguised; looks and consumer purchases are what this magazine is about.

*Eating Light* (a *Woman's Day* special interest publication) is another woman-centric diet magazine. It includes few pictures of people, and those it does include depict young white women. One wonders about the absence of nonwhite women in diet magazines. In times past, it was commonly accepted that nonwhite women were unconcerned about their weight, but that is no longer the case, as has been clearly identified in studies showing that, as African Americans became more middle class, they adopted the same white worries about physical appearance, particularly pertaining to diet and body size (Etcoff 1999; Bordo 1995). Again, though, pictures of women do not constitute the bulk of photographs in this magazine; most pictures here show food, along with the recipes that instruct readers on how to prepare diet food. Similarly, *Diet* magazine (a *Better Homes and Gardens* special interest publication) offers recipes and hints for dieting. It is womancentric (depicting only a few men) and, as with the other diet magazines, the women are almost entirely white.

*Maximum Fitness* is a men's magazine. It says so, unmistakably, in bold and all-capital letters, on the front cover, reminding me very much of the warning "No Girls Allowed" on little boys' clubhouse doors. The cover of one issue includes an unaccounted-for magazine feature for "hot sex," showing two beautiful women (one white and one black). Inside the magazine, we find displayed numerous ads for muscle-building supplements; a great number of images in the vein of battle, fight, and war (e.g., "gear up for battle," "Fight Pain, Fight Fatigue, Fight through a few more reps"); and a CG picture of a man-tank hybrid roaring forward presumably because he takes a drug called "XPAND"). Violent imagery is notable, such as the supplement ad promising to give the user "bone-crushing" strength, as though that would be a positive trait to have and an ability that would be put to use, and the words *huge* and *big* feature prominently in muscle-building supplement ads. There is a lot of sex—for instance, an advice piece suggesting an "awesome threesome" and plentiful photos of women in suggestive poses. Advertisements for sexual aids offer devices and drugs to make penises larger, thicker, and longer and to make sex last longer.

In addition to the stories and advertisements for sex, there is sexism. One advice column states categorically and without nuance that "women want a man that they feel is in control" and "being too nice hurts your chances with the ladies." Interestingly, ads in the back of the magazine offer sexual opportunities for homosexual encounters as well as heterosexual ones, which suggests that the readers of the magazine may not be heterosexual and may be gay and therefore uninterested in their "chances with the ladies."

*Fitness Rx* is another men's magazine. Lest there be any confusion (and more dramatically than the specification displayed on the *Maximum Fitness* cover), the *Fitness Rx* cover states that it is "FOR MEN!" As with *Maximum Fitness,* there is no shortage of sexual innuendo, sexual performance advertisements (such as sex-aid drugs), or advice about how to attract sexual partners. There is a great deal of war and assault imagery—one steroid ad uses the word "wrath" and violent pictorial imagery—and these violence images are sometimes combined with sex imagery. For instance, drugs for muscle building also promise sex, with photos of beautiful women clinging to muscle-bound hulks, and making use of words such as *huge.* One ad for a fitness supplement shows an unrealistically muscled man scooping up a small, beautiful woman by her tiny waist with one gigantic arm while the other gigantic "arm," which is CG-generated and composed of metal strips, reaches toward an unseen enemy. The background is a hodgepodge of burning buildings, ruins, and assorted wreckage. The woman looks up at our hero, beseechingly, apparently grateful that he is there to protect her. There is much mixing of sex with supplement ads; one such ad for a testosterone drug promises to give the reader "the muscle . . . the strength . . . the sex drive," raising the question of why they do not have adequate sex drive. Words like *explode* and *explosion* are common and may refer to violence or sex. An interesting twist that this magazine offers is the primitive imagery: we find an advice story on "Want better sex? Get in touch with your inner cave man" and one on the "Paleolithic Diet" ("So easy a cave man could do it!").

There is also an element of intolerance and social superficiality in *Fitness Rx*. For instance, we find a small story encouraging fat stigma by advising strong men (presumably representing the readers) to "get rid of your fat friends!" In addition, sexism abounds. There is, for example, an article on the correctness of women doing housework, and the conclusion is this: "Women wanted suffrage, so suffer." Along these lines, the piece mentioned earlier on "Neanderthal" sex suggests that rape is not out of the question as a form of "rough sex"; there is, according to the author, a "fine line . . . between date rape, sexual abuse, and rough sex. What you might consider unbridled passion, she might call sexual assault" (Loughlin 2008, 147).

Much of the imagery is unrealistic, such as the one admonishing men to avoid smoking tobacco because it can cause impotence. An appeal to avoid smoking is reasonable and even laudable, but the visual manner in which it is made in this men's fitness magazine uses a greatly exaggerated feature to make the point. A cartoon man is standing next to a bed upon which lies a beautiful albeit disappointed woman. He is freakishly muscled, as are most of the real and not-real (CG and cartoon-drawn) men in the magazine. But this cartoon man is designed to show what can happen to sexual organs if men smoke. He has a huge, knee-length, limp cigarette for a penis. He has a normal, true-proportion cigarette in his mouth, so we are to assume that his penis is alleged to be enormous, even in its limp state. The message: Fitness-conscious men have very, very large sexual organs.

In men's fitness magazines, the majority of the men—real, computer graphic, and cartoon—are white. The majority are nearly naked except for workout trunks. One extremely muscled cartoon man is naked except for a kitchen apron, showing the proper way to cook a steak.

Moving vastly away from fitness magazines, we turn to *Golf Digest*. This magazine advertises expensive consumer goods (e.g., pricey watches, alcoholic beverages, cars, golf equipment) and elite resorts. There is a pairing of money (financial success) and luxury and golf throughout. Commonly, golf sport figures are older, out-of-shape white men; at times, white men who are really quite fat are shown as models of golf figures. Incongruously, one ad shows an obese white male golfer called "the Beast," with an intimidating scowl on his face, as though we should be frightened by such a man. This is not to say that people of size are less intimidating than the muscular men in the fitness magazines. It is to point out that, *regardless* of physical condition (hypermuscular or flabby), sports and fitness figures are alleged to be frightening.

Sadly, sexism permeates the golfing world, as it does the rest of the sports world. The very few women golf figures displayed in *Golf Digest* and elsewhere (e.g., on television) are small and pretty. The contrast between male golfers and female golfers is stark, illustrating that even in the game of golf, women are pressured to adhere to unrealistic social dictates to be thin, young, and pretty, while men are not subject to such standards.

*Sports Illustrated* (specifically, the NBA Preview issue) displays a lot of tall, thin black men with tattoos and shaved heads. A very few basketball players have corn rows, and a few white players have long hair. *Sports Illustrated* attends to all manner of sports, and thus we can find photographic portrayals of a wide array of sport figures. Figure skaters are thin, white, young, and often very attractive. When performing in competitions, their work requires the wearing of formfitting and beautiful (glamorous and sparkly) clothes that show off their bodies and their skating skills. Baseball players can be somewhat largish, though most are in excellent physical condition. Some have long hair (e.g., Manny Ramirez and, formerly, Johnny Damon), which sets them apart from other baseball players. Some football players are very, very large and in questionable physical condition. True, they must be strong and able to run relatively fast. But it is not unheard of to see football players with huge abdomens. They, like baseball players, sometimes sport unusual hair styles, such as exceptionally long hair or unnaturally colored hair.

To a far lesser extent than the fitness magazines, *Sports Illustrated* makes use of intimidating language. For example, in one story, a football player remarked that his coach told the players to "BE A NIGHTMARE." Language used to describe football players can include words like *warrior*. Similarly, a story about a hockey player shows a "bad," assaultive, and intimidating image (describing him as "When he is BAD..."), and being "bad" (violent to other hockey players) is touted as a good trait to have. An ad for athletic shoes shows a large, fierce-looking black man, advising the viewer that with such shoes, one can "maul" one's opponents.

Aside from threatening messages, we also find language describing a team of football players as "the new elite." As proof of elite status, and as better understood in analyses by Benedict and Yeager (1998) and Benedict (1998), we are reminded that successful black sport figures are presented as enormously wealthy, displaying their wealth by means of their clothes, their furs, their jewelry, and, significantly, the women with whom they associate. In sports magazines and elsewhere, sport figures are connected with gorgeous women, often sexily dressed and often of unclear race. The women whom sport figures date and marry are generally much better looking than the sport figures themselves. This is also true outside of sports and fitness culture insofar as wealthy, but not necessarily attractive, men are associated with beautiful, young women (Berry 2007).

## INTERPRETATIONS:
## SOME FEATURES ON WHICH TO FOCUS

The findings from the magazine observations point to a number of features upon which to focus in order to develop a symbolic interactionist interpretation of sport figures' personal appearance. Not unexpectedly, gender is a major factor and is most notable in the near-total exclusion of women in discussion and visual portrayals of sport. Race has long been an integral factor in addresses of sport, with the assumption that African American men in particular are represented, if not represented well. This would be especially true of contact sports such as football and basketball that require brute strength and an affinity for violence, both indicating racism as leveled against African American men. Dangerousness is an oft-ignored feature but an important one when considering the sociology of sport. Not all sports involve dangerousness or a dangerous image; think, for example, of rowing and gymnastics. However, a goodly proportion of sports, especially male contact sports, require or are at least enhanced by an image of dangerousness and a willingness to do violence. Size is not unrelated to the latter remarks, with large size symbolizing physical prowess and the ability to do violence. Conversely, female sport figures, like all females, are socially rewarded for being small. Finally, a sporty appearance refers specifically to the physical appearance image, as it can be transferred to society via size, hairdressing, clothing, and jewelry. All are designed to reflect well in the social mirror, to make our images acceptable and admirable.

## Gender and Sexism

Sexism is common and ordinary in and outside of the context of sport. The mere fact of the proportionality of men's to women's sports and fitness magazines is telling, with men's sports and fitness magazines outnumbering women's. Note also, as I have illustrated above, the difference in content. Women's fitness magazines focus almost exclusively on weight and offer plentiful advice on how to lose it. The women in these magazines are young, white, and pretty, as are the women in men's sports and fitness magazines, even if the men are not attractive. Recall, more specifically, that the few women as seen in *Golf Digest* and in other media are small and cute, whereas the male golfers are not infrequently out of shape, older, and unattractive. Recall also the blatant sexist comments in the advertisements and in the advice columns in the fitness magazines.

The height of sexism in the sports world, combined with racism, was experienced in 2007 when a sports commentator (Don Imus) referred to members of the Rutgers University women's basketball team as "nappy-headed hos." In this one phrase, we have an unmistakable example of the social punishment of sport figures due to their physical appearance, their gender, and their race (appearance-related traits). It is also notable that the sports commentator was not seriously punished for his remark. After a brief stint of unemployment, he is again serving as a radio commentator. His relative lack of punishment and the punishing effects of racism, sexism, and lookism as visited upon the women's basketball team are not restricted to the sports world, of course. They merely constitute another instance of these "isms" being more or less socially acceptable.

## Race

Observations of media portrayals of sport figures point to the variance of race across sports. That is, some sports attract or allow certain races, while other sports are (whether intentionally or not) more exclusionary. As described in Berry and Smith (2000), the sports world has long experienced racial prejudice in terms of who, racially, is involved in what type of sport and, more particularly, what roles they may play. For instance, the rise of black pitchers in baseball is a relatively new phenomenon; previously, black baseball players had been relegated to outfield positions. As seen in the magazines discussed above and in many other venues, it is clear that whites gravitate to sports geared traditionally toward the wealthier classes, such as golf, while contact sports such as basketball and football are the purview of minority sport figures. Some sports, such as baseball and bodybuilding, are more inclusive, allowing for whites, blacks, and Hispanics in more equal proportions.

## Dangerousness

As with sports figures—and for the same reasons—rap and R&B celebrities, both male and female, have been using steroids, which has "struck a chord about the increasing pressure on these performers to maintain perfect, even super-human physiques as part of their overall image and brand" (Sisario 2008, B1). The editor of a book about hip-hip history, Jeff Chang (2006), finds that there is a "battle aesthetic" operating with these performers, propelling them to demonstrate that they are "badder" than everybody else. This image of badness, Chang goes on to say, is part of the hip-hop swagger. Both hip-hop performers and sport figures are leaning heavily on a Schwarzeneggerian body as part of their public image. They can gain this powerful-looking body through use of anabolic steroids and human growth hormone, which have immediately visible effects through decreasing fat tissue and increasing muscle.

Besides the powerful-appearing bodies, rappers also put forward an imagery of "success" and wealth, very much as sport figures do, with their jewelry, cars, and beautiful romantic partners. Jeff Chang concludes that the marketing of the images is key to so many different bottom lines. It is not just the music industry but the whole range of consumer products endorsed by these celebrities—again, not unlike sport figures' endorsements of consumer products. The ripped body of a sports or rap figure is part of a "brand," or, as we would say in the social sciences, an *image* or a *symbol*, that speaks to machismo and braggadocio.

Another crossover of the images put forward by rappers and some sport figures is criminality as a form of powerfulness. In other words, the criminality and dangerousness image overlaps sports and hip-hop, and, as shown in the observations described in this chapter, size is a strong indicator of alleged dangerousness and readiness for criminality. In some segments of society, illegal behavior carries little stigma; indeed, it can enhance one's image of powerfulness among rappers and some sport figures. Troubles with the law, or the perception of willingness to be in legal trouble, can assist in establishing the all-important celebrity story line.

## Size

Moving away from demographics and toward sheer appearance descriptors, young consider size. Body size has received enormous media and scholarly attention of late in connection with the related health concern about the "obesity epidemic," and there has long been a concern about female obsession with thinness and its attendant health concerns. Typically, societies consider height a positive trait, especially in men. And typically, body mass is limited in its appeal, such that muscularity is a positive trait, especially in men, but fat is not a positive trait for either men or women. However, large size, even if it includes fat, can be a good thing in many (but not all) sports. Here we find a reversal of our usual social constraints on body size in that size signifies power.

Depending on the sport, sport figures often want to be big as a way of seeming physically powerful or as a way of deterring injury. Sumo wrestlers, basketball players, football players, and other contact sport figures, as well as bodybuilders, are larger than average (obese, tall, bulky, and extraordinarily muscular, respectively). The exceptions, such as short basketball players, are so unusual that they are remarked upon in media depictions. By contrast, swimmers, tennis players, skaters, gymnasts, and rowers are not particularly large. They set themselves apart from average members of society in terms of low body fat, good musculature, and attractive aesthetics.

It bears noting that some sport figures, in terms of body size alone, might be considered freakishly different. Yet, at the same time, some aspire to be freakishly different in this regard, perhaps because such extreme size (for instance, muscularity) speaks to power. There is a certain amount of fantasy involved in these aspirations toward physical difference, not only as portrayed in bodybuilding magazines but also in our toys. "GI Joe" has evolved over the generations from a normal-looking, well-proportioned doll in 1982 to a larger version in 1992 and then to the absurd version of the mid-1990s that does not resemble a normal human in any way (Kolata et al. 2002; see also Alexander 2003 on the GI Joe doll's unrealistic proportions).

## A Sporty Appearance

As mentioned earlier, women's and men's health and fitness magazines are really geared toward *looking* good. *Appearance* is tantamount to health issues, as has been well documented in my and others' work on the topic of physical appearance. But there is something disingenuous about media presentations of health and fitness issues when the real issue is physical appeal. This disingenuousness is more disturbing when we are encouraged to ingest questionable substances, such as growth hormones or diet pills, in order to achieve appearance perfection. High school boys who want to look good and be attractive to high school girls are ingesting steroids. They don't want to *be* athletic or necessarily successful in sports. They just want to *look* athletic (Egan 2002).

## SYMBOLIC INTERACTION, DRAMATURGY, AND IMAGE MAKING

Having explored an array of sociological theories in previous analyses of social reaction to physical appearance (Berry 2008a), I've discovered that the best-fit model is symbolic interactionism, particularly the dramaturgy and impression management perspectives. Through these explanations, we can hope to understand the various "images" put forward by sport figures. These images send messages of social power derived from or representing sexual, economic, and physical prowess.

Interactionism is a microsociology, emphasizing interpersonal relations. Though micro in focus, interactionism is, as is true of all sociology, relevant on a societal scale. Symbolic interactionism, advanced by George Herbert Mead (1974), concentrates on the manner in which people develop their own identities and their understanding of how society operates. Besides focusing on face-to-face interaction rather than on broad-scale social systems, microsociology focuses on *meanings*, as in Mead's interest in the role of verbal and nonverbal symbols; hence the term *symbolic interactionism*. These two focuses (face-to-face interaction and nonverbal symbols) are pertinent to the study of social aesthetics, since the *visual* is paramount. Our very identity is determined by how we are reflected in society (in the social mirror, per Mead's terminology)—by how others see us. Through social experience, such as winning an intimidating encounter or gaining adoration from sports fans, we come to know our place in society.

To take it a step further, and as Herbert Blumer (1969) puts it, meanings (which are derived from interpersonal interaction) that we attach to all we observe (e.g., facial features, attire, tattoos) are managed and transformed through interpretation (attributing positive and negative values to people based on their features) and self-reflection. If we want to look "bad," based on what we think society will think of us, we may get tattoos or ingest steroids.

According to Goffman's (1959) dramaturgy approach, social behavior can be thought of as a staged performance in which the actors intentionally convey specific impressions to others. Dramaturgy is behavior through which we communicate information about ourselves to others, thereby managing others' impressions of us. We do what we can to enhance the images we emit to others, thus justifying our claims to power. We discretely hide, alter, or slant our self-presentations when doing so is appropriate or advantageous. We do this with our clothes, jewelry, cars, human companions, animal companions, tattoos, body alterations (e.g., bodybuilding, steroid ingestion, dieting, plastic surgery, skin lightening), facial expressions, dialogue, and so on. We can think of these many contrivances as costumes and props. We hope that what we wear and who we associate with speaks volumes to the social audience. This can happen in commonplace ways, as when we associate ourselves with attractive people, hoping to be seen as someone worthy of attractive partners. It can also happen in surprising ways, as when we surround ourselves with dangerous or exotic nonhuman animals, who serve as props for sending a signal to the social audience that we are dangerous and exotic ourselves (Berry 2008b). If we attach to ourselves attractive mates, unusual nonhuman animals, or expensive items, we are presenting ourselves as worthy, powerful, and special. This is the reason that many of us, sport figures included, own and prominently display designer goods as signs of our economic power (Thomas 2007).

The types of images that sport figures hope to transmit reflect the social messages of sexual attractiveness, physical prowess, dangerousness, and wealth. Physical appearance features can be capitalized upon and altered as a means of setting oneself apart and thereby seeming "special," as is done with tattoos, extreme musculature, and signs of wealth (expensive designer clothing, fur coats, massive jewelry, trophy partners and trophy animals, and expensive cars). All of these accoutrements are intended as "signs of success."

For example, male sport figures (more than female sport figures), especially those in contact sports and in bodybuilding, hope to appear as large and muscular as possible as a means of visible physical intimidation. In addition to sheer body size and shape, sexual power can be socially transmitted by the attachment of attractive sexual partners. This is the case for male sport figures, who are not uncommonly married to or romantically linked with women who are younger, sometimes whiter, and more attractive than they are. It is also the case for many men in their fantasies, as we find in men's fitness magazines illustrating unrealistically beautiful women adoring unrealistically muscled men. The muscles, in these cases, are part of the impression management.

Some sport figures hope to seem dangerous, edgy, violent, and even prone to criminality. As with rappers and hip-hop artists, body size and tattoos may serve as the props indicating dangerousness. Displays of dangerousness are also evident in their facial expressions, their stances, and, more obviously, the words attached to advertisements and stories about them. This is not true across the board, and it is particularly untrue of golfers, which is the sports purview of middle-class white men. Yet golfers are not immune to using props to establish a certain image. Golfers' images are composed of financially secure, white, older males who frequent country clubs and resorts, drink expensive liquors, and wear expensive but tasteful (not gaudy) watches.

As couched in terms of social exchange theory, one way to set ourselves apart in a society and to be viewed favorably is to be attached to favorably viewed people, such as physically beautiful people. Since most of us are not especially attractive, we do not have much luck in attracting beautiful people as our partners. If, however, we have something to offer beautiful people, such as fame, money, or power, then they may agree to be associated with us (Katz 1995). In this way, sport figures (and other financially endowed and celebritorious people) can gain social prestige. By being associated with a person who is beautiful as defined by society (e.g., young, thin, and white or white-appearing), we gain a halo effect. It is assumed that we have something to offer (likely wealth or social prestige), since otherwise these beautiful people presumably would not be with us. Recall the magazine advertisements and stories showing sport figures with physically desirable partners.

## CONCLUSION

This chapter has shown that, as viewed in ordinary health and sports magazines, sport figures (as loosely defined) hope to present themselves to society in a visually favorable light. They attempt to manage their outward impression as athletic, powerful, attractive (thin, in the case of women), sexually magnetic, and dangerous. This study reinforces what is known about symbolic interaction as we commonly understand it in sociology (as impression management, social mirror, and involving symbolic meanings of visual symbols). Yet this study provides a slight contrast to the way we usually apply symbolic interactionism in the sense that we ordinarily do not think of these particular symbols as positive signs transmitted to the broader society. That is, in the context of sports imagery, the "positive" symbols of power are generated oftentimes as fantastic (read: involving fantasy) and unrealistic images of human bodies. Unrealism is also made verifiable in the message put forward in these magazines that, if we take steroids (for example), we will instantly become hugely muscled and exhibit sexual stamina that is actually beyond the possible for most of us.

Recall the image of the cartoon man with the knee-length but limp penis. The cartoon exhorted the reader to avoid smoking (in itself a good public service message) because it would cause impotence. The underlying message is that this man, toned and muscled beyond belief, had a nontumescent penis of gigantic proportion. We are led to believe that, in a tumescent state, the penis would have been much, much larger. Overall, and to get away from sexual organs as the focus (although sex was a primary concentration in these magazines), sport figures, like all of us, hope to present themselves in a socially favorable light, in this case within the subcontext of sports and fitness. They do so through attachments and accoutrements (e.g., jewelry, clothing, human and nonhuman companions) and through physical alterations (e.g., steroid use and exercise).

Through these devices, sport figures may hope to set themselves apart from ordinary society. They may engage in body modifications and may attach to themselves power-granting props as a means of signaling to the social audience that they are indeed special. The specialness they hope to be granted has largely to do with sexual, economic, and physical power.

## Suggested Research

1. Examine a woman's place in sport—specifically, the role of a woman's physical appearance as it helps and hinders women's role in sports. We are seeing more women involved in contact sports such as boxing, and it would be useful to consider the contrast between the usual small-is-better approach to women in sports and the large-and-powerful-is-good approach when thinking of women (e.g., boxers) in sports.

2. Question the utility of the power-size-dangerousness element in male sports. Is there a way to reduce this dimension so that men and boys no longer feel the need to be physically powerful to the point of being frightening? If that were possible, and I believe it is, we might be able to alleviate the pressure that men and boys feel to be physically powerful, thereby reducing power displays, including violence, as perpetrated by male sport figures.

## Additional Resources

**Theory**

Garfinkel, H. 1967. *Studies in ethnomethodology.* Englewood Cliffs, NJ: Prentice Hall; and Goffman, E. 1974. *Frame analysis.* Cambridge, MA: Harvard University Press.

These texts provide useful and more detailed addresses of symbolic interactionism. Ethnomethodology is also referred to as the sociology of everyday life, and here we find reference to the many everyday things we do to represent ourselves in a positive light to our fellow members of society. Frame analysis is more a constructionist viewpoint showing how we, as members of society, frame or construct our surroundings and our interpretations of social events in ways that make sense to us.

**Sport Topic**

Macus, J. 2008. Given reprieve, N.F.L. star's dogs find kindness. *New York Times*, February 2, A1, A7.

> This news account of Michael Vick's dogs, whom he held captive and used for dogfights, illustrates the horrors of animal abuse as practiced by a prominent sport figure. Not only were the dogs mistreated in ways one would expect in dogfighting circles (suffering, for example, purposely cropped ears and tails), they also suffered the effects of the fights themselves (including death). One especially heartbreaking story involved a female dog used for breeding. Her teeth had been removed so that she could not fight back while being raped. This sad story illustrates, as I've mentioned in the text, that some people use nonhuman animals to represent themselves as dangerous, unusual, powerful.

Associated Press

# 15 | Sport and Multiple Identities in Postwar Trinidad

## The Case of McDonald Bailey

*Roy D. McCree, PhD*

Social theory: Figurational (process sociology) theory

Proponents of the theory: Norbert Elias, Eric Dunning, Joseph Maguire

What the theory says: In his attempt to explain the nature of identity, German sociologist Norbert Elias (1996) noted that individuals and nations may display multiple identities which are indissolubly connected and shaped by particular asymmetrical relations of power. This approach to explaining the nature of identity formation has also been adopted by one of Elias' major followers, Joseph Maguire (1999, 2005).

One issue that has gained increasing prominence in contemporary sport is that of dual, or in some cases triple, national loyalties of participants in international sports competition due to the particularities of their birth, parentage, migration, or to the political history of their countries. Across a range of sports—whether soccer, tennis, cricket, rugby, hockey, or track and field—and a range of countries, the issue has been a subject of media, public, and scholarly attention which in itself has been fueled by the study of globalization processes (Bale and Maguire 1994; Maguire 1999, 2005). Examples abound, some of them in controversial circumstances, and several well-known international cases are those of Martina Navratilova (Czech American tennis player), Greg Rusedski (Canadian-born British tennis player), Freddy Adu (Ghanian-born American soccer player), and Zinedine Zidane (Algerian-born soccer captain of France). Track and field has also had a growing list of such persons, including Zola Budd (South African–born British runner); Bernard Lagat (Kenyan-born, American middle-distance runner); Francis Obikwelu (Nigerian-born Portuguese sprinter); Linford Christie (Jamaican-born British sprinter); Ben Johnson and Donovan Bailey (both Jamaican-born Canadian runners); and Ato Boldon (Trinidadian-born sprinter with U.S. citizenship).[1] These developments have helped direct more attention to the whole question of multiple identities and their contested political nature both generally and within sport (Smith and Porter 2004; Burdsey 2006; Carrington 2007).

However, while the issue of dual nationality or multiple identities in sport has intensified in recent times, it is not entirely new. This chapter examines the issue as it played itself out in track and field within the period of British colonialism in the English-speaking Caribbean from 1945 to 1953; specifically, it focuses on the experiences of the black British sprint champion McDonald Bailey. In discussing the increasing ethnic diversity of postwar Britain linked to its imperial history, and this diversity's implications for sport representation as well as notions of English identity, Smith and Porter (2004, 17) make reference to the early Asian and black athletes "such as the cricketer Kumar Shri Ranjitsinhji ('Ranji') and the Great Britain Olympic sprinters Jack London and MacDonald Bailey, [who] competed at representative level" for Britain.[2] However, what the authors ignored or perhaps do not know is

---

[1] For a list of relevant soccer players, type the phrase "List of football players with dual nationality" into the Answers.com search box at www.answers.com/topic/list. See also Kabukuru (2005) and, for more on Obikwelu, www.squidoo.com/FrancisObikwelu.

that Bailey's representation of Britain had implications not only for the notion of English identity but also for the nascent identity of then-colonial Trinidad, as well as for that of Bailey, which is the major focus of this chapter. Against this backdrop, the chapter is organized into three major parts: (1) theoretical considerations surrounding the issue of identity formation, in particular relation to national identity; (2) the methodology of the study; and (3) the significance of Bailey's representation of Britain in international athletic competition for the issue of identity formation.

## THEORETICAL CONSIDERATIONS

In examining the issue of identity formation in particular relation to the development of nationalism in 19th- and 20th-century Europe—and within the broader context of "state formation" during this period—Elias (1996) attempted to show how notions of the individual and the nation are two sides of the same coin and not as discrete as they are normally presented as being. "The image of a nation experienced by an individual who forms part of that nation . . . is also a constituent of that person's self image. The virtue, the value, the meaningfulness of the nation are also his or her own" (Elias 1996, 151-152). Or, as Maguire (1999, 184) puts it, "The 'image' of the nation is also constitutive of a person's self image" or personal identity. Furthermore, the image(s) of the nation, or the sense of what constitutes its national identity or national character, are bound up in the emotions and "habitus codes" of the individual, which Bourdieu conceived basically as the values and behavioral predispositions of the individual and which are shaped by their particular social class, and educational background (Maguire 1999, 185) or "conditions of existence" (Bourdieu 1986, 169–225).[3] The related notions of habitus and identity, however, are neither monolithic nor singular but are multilayered, as they may exist at the individual, group, and national levels and are also subject to challenge and change. For instance, in the language of Elias, the individual may have a particular "I-We" identity or habitus code; the first-person singular pronoun serves to represent the sense of individuality or "individual self" and the first-person plural pronoun serves to represent the collective identity, be it as a member of a group or of a nation (Maguire 1999, 186–187; Elias 1996, 151–153). Relatedly, individuals may display multiple identities along "local, regional, national, and global"

---

[2] Jack London was born in Guyana (formerly British Guiana) of a white Scottish mother and a black father but was taken to Britain when only 3 months old (*Daily Express*, March 23, 1948). London was a leading British sprinter (100 m) between 1925 and 1931 and won silver (100 m) for Britain at the 1925 Amsterdam Olympics (*Daily Express*, March 23, 1948). Bailey was born in Trinidad in 1920 but moved to Great Britain in 1944 to join the Royal Air Force. He ran for Britain from 1945 until his retirement in 1953 and represented England at both the 1948 and 1952 Olympic Games, winning the 100 meter bronze in the latter. Bailey set numerous sprint records in Britain and Europe. He was also the first man to win 14 British national sprint titles over the 100 meter and 200 meter distances between 1946 and 1953, and he equaled the world 100 meter record, then held by the American Jesse Owens, of 10.2 seconds in 1951 (Lagerstrom 2000; Linley 2000). Due to Bailey's athletic exploits, British journalist David Miller noted as recently as 2000 that he was "to become a byword in Britain's sporting culture," and British athletic historian Mel Watman (1968) saw him as part of "'the Holy Trinity' of post-war British athletics," together with the Englishman Roger Bannister and the Jamaican Arthur Wint (cited in Polley 1998, 146).

[3] It has been noted that Elias was the first to use the term "habitus," but its "popularization" has been attributed to Bourdieu (Dunning and Mennell 1996; Dunning, Goudsblom, and Mennell 2000).

lines (Elias 1996, 153, cited in Maguire 1999, 185-186). Writing of the pluralized or multilayered nature of identity and the habitus Elias said:

> *[T]he social habitus . . . in more complex societies . . . has many layers. Someone may, for example, have the peculiarities of a Liverpool-English or a Black Forest–German European. It depends on the number of interlocking planes in his (sic) society how many layers are interwoven in the social habitus of the person (Elias 1987/1991, 183, cited in Maguire 1999, 186).*

Following on Elias, Maguire wrote that

> *people in complex nation-states . . . have multiple identities that are many-layered—local, regional, national, global. These layers form a flexible lattice work of the habitus of a person (Elias 1996, 153, cited in Maguire 1999, 185–186).*

The related notions of nation, nationalism, and national identity are founded, therefore, on a particular collective identity or "we-image," to which the individual's identity or "I-image" is indissolubly connected. The notion of nationalism, as it emerged, was based on the valorization of this collective identity or collectivity, called "nation," above all else. Defining nationalism and the political context in which in which it emerged in 19th- and 20th-century Europe, Elias wrote:

> *It is simply intended to refer to one aspect of an overall transformation which specific state-societies in conjunction with the balance of power within a specific figuration of interdependent societies underwent during a specific period of time. It refers to a social belief system which, latently or acutely, raises the state-society, the sovereign collectivity to which its members belong, to the position of a supreme value to which all other values can and sometimes must be subordinated (Elias 1996, 153–154).*

Elias' multidimensional approach to understanding identity formation, derived more fundamentally from his figurational conception of society in which society was conceived as a network or figuration of interdependent human beings although power inequalities existed. In this figuration, there was no rigid demarcation between society and individual, individual and nation or micro and macro dimensions of social relations since they all referred to "inseparable aspects of the same human being" (Elias 1978; 1939/2000, 455).

However, notwithstanding the indissoluble connection between collective and individual identity, or the supposed normative supremacy of the nation ("sovereign collectivity"), Elias at the same time recognized that conflicts and tensions could arise between the interests of the nation (e.g., fighting or dying for country) and the value placed on the "individual human being" (e.g., sanctity of human life). Describing the dilemma posed by these "contradictory codes," Elias wrote:

> *In nineteenth- and twentieth-century state-societies, people are . . . brought up with dispositions to act in accordance with at least two major codes of norms which are in some respects incompatible with each other. The preservation, integrity and interests of the state-society, of their own sovereign collectivity and all it stands for, are assimilated by each individual*

*as part of his or her habitus, as a guiding principle of action which in certain situations can and must override all others. At the same time, however, they are brought up with a humanist, egalitarian or moral code, whose supreme value overriding all others is the individual human being as such (1996, 157–158).*

He noted further that these codes "may be activated in different situations and at different times" but that "many situations activate both at the same time" (Elias 1996, 158).

There is, however, no single theory or approach to the study of nationalism in general or to the link between sport, nationalism, and national identity in particular. Some of the other approaches include the related notions of globalization, imperialism (more so cultural imperialism), and Anderson's notion of the nation as an "imagined community." Globalization has been generally conceived as the process by which the peoples and nations of the world have become more and more interconnected and interdependent in a process powered by the communications revolution and economic liberalization, although imbalances in power and material resources still persist across the world (Held and McGrew 2004; Maguire 1999). There are competing interpretations, however, as to the character and consequences of this process, particularly as it relates to issues of nationalism and national identity. One view holds that globalization has led to the erosion of the traditional nation-state and, invariably, of notions of national identity, while another view posits that it has led to the reinforcement or reassertion of the nation-state and of notions of national identity as people resist the intrusion or dominance of foreign cultural forms both outside of (Held and McGrew 2004) and within sport (Maguire 1999; Hargreaves 2002). From a sociological standpoint, globalization, including the globalization of sport, has been associated with three major processes: homogenization (through Americanization, or Westernization), pluralization (existence of different national cultures and influences side by side), and hybridization (formation of new cultural practices through the mixing or amalgamation of various cultures) (Houlihan 1994, 2003). In this respect, particular focus has been given to the global spread of American sport forms such as basketball, of media entities such as ESPN, of American sporting goods, and of the American commercial approach to sport organization (Kidd 1991; Klein 1991; Mandle 1994).

However, although globalization does engage the issue of identity and provides tugs and tensions for received notions of the nation and of national identity, it has three major limitations as it relates to this study: (1) It tends to be anchored more at the global level of analysis, though attention has also been paid to the links between the local and the global dimensions of international relations. (2) Although globalization has been an unfolding historical process, the present discourse is anchored more in the present period of American hegemony, whereas the period of my study (1945–1953) is anchored in the period of British hegemony, albeit on the wane at the time. (3) As used, it is very much a today-centered construct, and the modern-day context in which it is used is quite different from the context of the 1940s and 1950s in which my study is situated. In terms of its level of analysis (world), its time focus (post 1980s), and the context (communications revolution, Internet, economic liberalization) in which it is used, it was not seen as appropriate or particularly useful for the object of my study. In terms of contemporary sport migration, however, it should assume more relevance. Given the colonial period of the study (1940s and 1950s), and Britain's imperial position as the "mother country," the old concept of imperialism, which described the direct or indirect control or domination of one country over another—politically, economically, and culturally—with or without the use of force, might also seem relevant (Tomlinson 1991; Cain and Harrison 2001). However, apart from its presentation of people as passive subjects and the failure to capture how subordinate groups can also influence dominant groups, the concept is also unable to capture the plural, shifting, dynamic nature of colonial identity at the time as expressed in sport and generally.

The notion of cultural imperialism, however, has been particularly used in the study of the global diffusion of modern sport (Guttmann 1993). Within recent times, Anderson's conception of a nation as an "imagined community" has become a popular approach to the study of nationalism and national identity. For him, a nation is a collective entity that exists largely in the imagination or minds of those who identify with it, "because the members . . . will never know most of their fellow-members, meet them, or even hear of them, yet in the minds of each lives the image of their communion" (Anderson 1983, 6). However, because of its focus on what Smith (1998, 137) calls "individual cognition—imagination," which is "the key to the rise and spread of nationalism," this is seen as deflecting "attention away from collective attachment and sentiment" (see Hargreaves [2002] for a critique of this notion in the context of sport). In other words, the "individualist and voluntarist" notion of the nation fails to capture its collective character and invariably the links between individual and collective identity. Consequently, this approach cannot really help to deal with the plural nature of identity and the tensions which may exist along its multiple or various axes—which is the object of this study—since its central focus is the supposed imaginative or individualistic character of the entity called "nation" and its historical emergence.

However, while several theories may exist to study any social phenomena, one's choice of theory (or theories) is very much conditioned by the extent to which a theory is deemed relevant to or effective in explaining the particular phenomena or problematic that forms the object of one's study; what is appropriate for one situation may not be appropriate for another. In the instance at hand, the approach of Elias seemed more helpful in capturing the identity dilemmas faced by McDonald Bailey; the connection to the plural, shifting, and contradictory nature of identities that characterized colonial society and metropole–colony relations as a whole; and the way in which burgeoning changes in the balance of power between Britain and its colonies after World War II helped, through the rise of nationalist sentiments, to define the sociopolitical function of sport and the identity of the athlete. This approach avoided the global and today-centered focus of globalization, the individualistic focus of the notion of "imagined communities," and the passive conception of people presented by notions of imperialism. The choice of Elias' approach was made in recognition, as well, of his pioneering contribution to the development of the sociology of sport, which was largely shunned by other leading sociologists and social theorists of the day.

Guided by this discussion of identity formation particularly in relation to national identity, nationalism, and the relations of power in which or through which it may emerge and even be conditioned, the main objective of this essay is to examine the experiences of former black Trinidadian, West Indian, and British champion sprinter Emmanuel McDonald Bailey and the insights they afford into this process of identity formation during the immediate postwar period spanning the years 1945 to 1953. Although Trinidad was still a colony of Britain and not yet a "sovereign collectivity" as described by Elias, nationalist feelings or a particular "we-image" still existed on the island and became the ideological basis for political independence, which was granted in 1962.

## METHODOLOGY

The study was based on the life history method (LHM). This approach to social inquiry involves examining the experiences of particular individuals, groups, or organizations, based on their interpretations of those experiences, through the use of interviews and various secondary sources of information that may include documents of various kinds, as well as documentaries. This study was based on two major sources of data generation: (1) interviews with the actor and with surviving athletes and officials who knew of Bailey and (2) documents, consisting mainly of accounts from the major newspapers of the day, both in Britain and in Trinidad and Tobago. For Britain, these included the *Daily Express*, the *Daily Mail*, and the *Times*; for Trinidad and Tobago, they included the *Trinidad Guardian* and the *Port of Spain Gazette*.

## ATHLETIC REPRESENTATION AND MULTIPLE IDENTITIES: TRINIDADIAN OR BRITISH

Bailey was first called to represent Britain in international athletic competition in 1945, after the end of the war (*Port of Spain Gazette*, August 13, 1945). What did representing Britain mean to Bailey? He helps provide the answer. For instance, writing in his then-weekly column for the *Daily Express* in 1952, Bailey expressed the delight and "honour" he felt when he was first selected to represent Britain in May 1945: "Naturally I was thrilled and delighted to have the honour of being chosen to run for this country and to have the chance of wearing my first international colours" (May 17, 1952). Bailey's reaction was shared by some in Trinidad. Here, for instance, the local daily newspaper, the *Port of Spain Gazette*, reacts to the development:

> *Cabled advice received yesterday by Mr. MacDonald Bailey*[4] *reveals that Trinidad has had the signal honour conferred on it of having MacDonald Bailey selected to represent Great Britain in an athletic meeting to be held in Paris. . . . Travelling to Scotland to represent the AAA [British Amateur Athletic Association] he more than held his own and had the further honour of dining with the Lord and Lady Provost (August 13, 1945).*

---

[4] The reference made here is to Bailey's father.

And, in relation to representing Britain at the 1948 Olympic Games, Bailey reportedly stated, "If Britain wants me I shall be honoured and delighted" at the prospect, although he did say, "I want to make it quite clear that I am still prepared to run for my country" (*Trinidad Guardian*, January 27, 1948). To Bailey, then, and to some in Trinidad, representing Britain was seen as an honor and, presumably, a source of personal pride and prestige, though there were some who resented his decision (*Trinidad Guardian*, January 20, 1948). Consistent with our guiding analytical framework relating to the indissoluble link between individual and collective identity, it is suggested that this feeling of being honored on the part of Bailey and some within the colony can be seen as an expression of how the image of a collectivity (in this case, imperial Britain) can shape not just the self-image of the individual but that of another collectivity (here, the colony of Trinidad). All of this was taking place in the context of a metropole–colony figuration—relations of power in which the former was ascendant and valorized more than the latter, which was dependent and generally viewed as backward by people within both Britain and the colonies (Braithwaite 1953; Lewis 1938/1977; Williams 1942). In other words, in order to understand how representing Britain was seen as a mark of honor by Bailey and some in the then-colony of Trinidad, we have to approach it not just in terms of a simple imperial framework of dominant and subordinate but relatedly, in terms of the differential valorization and construction of both: Britain was advanced, dominant, and superior, while Trinidad, its colony, was backward, dependent, and inferior. In this context, being selected to represent Britain enhanced one's self-worth regardless of the exploitation associated with its imperialist "we-image."

However, unlike his selection to represent Britain in 1945, Bailey's selection to represent Britain at the 1948 Olympic Games was received with mixed reaction in his native Trinidad, as there were expressions of "disappointment" (*Port of Spain Gazette*, July 18, 1948) as well as support (*Port of Spain Gazette*, July 18 and 29, 1948; *Trinidad Guardian*, January 20, 1948). One headline summed it up thus: "Opinions are Divided On Bailey's Decision To Run For Great Britain" (*Port of Spain Gazette*, July 18, 1948), and one of the dissenting voices stated clearly, "It is quite time that Bailey should realize that he is not an Englishman." Echoing these sentiments over 50 years later, one of the surviving athletes from the 1948 Trinidad Olympic team stated in a 2003 interview that people were disappointed because "they felt he had betrayed the country by going to run for England" (interview with author, April 8, 2003).

Moreover, a former president of the Trinidad Athletic Association has noted that "there was a hard core feeling that this man had let us down. He had betrayed us and there was a sort of resistance to him coming into the Association" (interview with author, January 26, 2004). The nationalist backlash against Bailey's selection persisted well beyond 1948 and was expressed in several ways. First, he was not nominated for the inaugural Trinidad Sportsman of the Year award in 1951 or even included among the top 10 athletes of that year as selected by local sports journalists (*Trinidad Guardian*, January 13, 1952). This is all the more remarkable in light of the fact that in 1951 Bailey had equaled the world 100 meter record in

Belgrade, capital of the former Yugoslavia (*The Times*, August 27, 1951) and that it was also the same year in which he had won the sprint double (100 and 200 meters) for the fifth time at the annual British championships (*Daily Express*, June 4, 1951). Second, Bailey revealed in interview that he was never commended by the Trinidad Athletic Association after equaling the 100 meter world record in 1951. Third, he was never nominated to receive a Coronation Medal from the governor to commemorate the coronation of Queen Elizabeth II in 1953; such medals were awarded to 390 local persons for outstanding achievement in their particular field (*Trinidad Guardian*, June 3, 1953).

Clearly, then, Bailey's representation of Britain at the 1948 Olympics—the first since Berlin in 1936, and the first in which the colony had ever participated—had offended nascent nationalist sentiments on the island, whose independence from Britain, "granted" in 1962, was still some 14 years away. Prior to the 1940s, the entire British West Indies was shaken by what has been called the 1930s labor revolts, which fueled strong anti-imperialist, pro-independence, and nationalist sentiment in the islands. Such was the impact that a special British Royal Commission, headed by Lord Moyne, was appointed to investigate the causes of the revolts and make the necessary prescriptive solutions (Thomas 1987). While the political momentum created by the labor revolts, as well as the development of nationalist sentiment, would have been interrupted from 1939 to 1945 by World War II, the postwar period served to create the stable conditions for its resurgence. And it was within this context of a growing nationalism that the 1948 Olympic Games were held and Bailey was selected to represent Britain. In Eliasian terms, his representation was tantamount to a failure to recognize the supremacy of the interests of the Trinidad collectivity, "to which all other values," including the honor of representing Britain, should have been "subordinated."

It is interesting to note, however, that while on the one hand Bailey's action was seen to smack of betrayal of Trinidadian nationalist sentiments, there also existed, within the same society and at the same time, a significant element of loyalty toward Britain and its monarchy. This can be illustrated, for instance, in the financial contribution made to the war effort through the existence of several war funds on the island: the Red Cross Fund, the Bomber Fund, the Win the War Fund, the Win the War Association Welfare Fund, and the Red Cross Invasion Fund (*Trinidad Guardian*, April 22, 1941, and March 22, 1942; *Port of Spain Gazette*, September 1, 1945). In addition, many sports clubs and organizations throughout the island donated the proceeds from their sporting events to the war effort (*Trinidad Guardian*, February 18, 1941, and May 4, 1944). For the British West Indies as a whole, Scobie (1972, 190) has noted that "by the middle of 1944, the British West Indies had also contributed over £750,000 to the United Kingdom for general war purposes, nearly £400,000 for war charities and more than £425,000 for the purchase of aircraft for the Royal Air Force. Their governments and peoples had lent the United Kingdom over £1,400,000 free of interest."

Apart from this financial contribution, British loyalty was also revealed in the outpouring of emotion that followed the death of King George VI in 1952 (*Port of Spain Gazette*, February 7, 1952), the death of Queen Mary in 1953 (*Trinidad*

*Guardian*, March 26, 1953), and the Coronation of Queen Elizabeth II in 1953 (*Trinidad Guardian*, April 9, 1953). The celebration of the Coronation was marked by a series of events that included the granting of scholarships to worthy school children, the awarding of Coronation Medals to outstanding individuals, and the staging of massive youth rallies, a military parade, and fireworks displays which culminated in a mini carnival throughout the island (*Trinidad Guardian*, May 1–30, 1953, and June 2–10, 1953). In one newspaper (*Trinidad Guardian*, March–June 1953), the author counted no less than 15 poems dedicated to the Queen, one of which, titled "On Every Mind," read in part:

> *Her Majesty Elizabeth most dear*
> *Will soon be crowned in England's air*
> *But we of this small happy country town*
> *Will join in gala and sincere renown* (*Trinidad Guardian*, May 30, 1953).

The depth of identification with and loyalty to Britain and its monarchy was underlined further in an editorial appearing in one of the major dailies, part of which read as follows:

> *However critical our people sometimes become at the application to the Colony of British colonial policy or the interpretation of that policy by those who share responsibility for its interpretation, they treasure their British heritage. And on such royal occasions as Coronation of a Sovereign, existence of such feeling is put beyond question* (*Trinidad Guardian*, May 30, 1953).

While one can see this double loyalty as contradictory, it can also be seen as consistent with the multiple identities that were inherent in metropole–colony relations, for while on the one hand the people were British colonial subjects, on the other hand they were also West Indian, or Trinidadian, or Jamaican, depending on their island of origin. It was the peculiar or particular context, however, that determined which identity assumed or ought to have assumed prominence or salience over another.

In the context of sport—particularly international sporting competition, which serves to define more sharply the boundaries of collective and individual identities—it was the local island identity (in this case, being or feeling Trinidadian) that was "activated," while in the context of international war and the rituals of royal death, pomp, and pageant, under colonial or imperial rule, it was British identity or loyalty. In the particular case of Bailey, however, both a British identity code ("If Britain wants me I shall be honoured and delighted") and a Trinidadian identity code ("I want to make it quite clear that I am still prepared to run for my country") were simultaneously activated and came into conflict as the Trinidadian nationalist expectation required that the latter override the former.

Borrowing from Elias and Bourdieu, it can be said that in colonial Trinidad the social habitus of the individual was a multilayered one composed of several overlapping identities that included those of the island, its British heritage, the West Indies, and the particular social grouping to which the individual belonged, be it an ethnic or a class grouping. These layers of identity formed the crux of "a flexible lattice work" of the person's and colony's habitus, a flexibility evident in the varied privileging of one over the other depending on the prevailing context and the nature of the actors' perceived interests, expectations, and motives.

To illustrate this point further, we can use the West Indian cricket team, whose players are drawn from the many islands that make up the former British West Indies. Because of the team's regional character, the identity that has tended to be privileged or has assumed salience historically, at least symbolically in terms of political and literary rhetoric, has been that sense of West Indianness, though this has always existed in tension and conflict with nationalisms from the various islands (e.g., Jamaica, Barbados, St. Vincent) that constitute the West Indies. C.L.R. James (1963) also directed attention to the multiple and problematic nature of identity formation in the West Indies. While recognizing the peculiarities of language and culture that characterized it, James also noted that one of the fundamental and inescapable features of the West Indian condition was its European and, more so, British heritage, of which sport, and cricket in particular, together with the "gentlemanly" values it espoused, was the most visible and celebrated expression. The nature of Bailey's dilemma thus derived from a convergence or clash of two fundamentally separate "we-images"— one driven by a British sensibility and the other by a Trinidadian sensibility—which were both wrapped up in the social habitus.

Consequently, while some have seen Bailey's decision to represent Britain at the 1948 Olympic games as a negation of his Trinidadian identity or as antinationalist, in spite of his self-proclaimed nationalist orientation, it can also be seen as an expression of the multiple identities bequeathed in part by colonialism, as well as the tensions or conflicts they can generate. Figure 15.1 portrays the diverse and

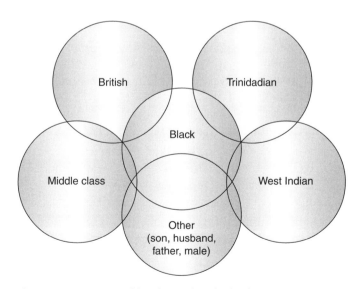

**Figure 15.1** McDonald Bailey and multiple identities.

overlapping nature of identities of a national, ethnic, race, class, gendered, and even familial (e.g., son, father) nature which may have characterized Bailey, as well as others in colonial and postcolonial Trinidad, though it is unable to capture which ones may tend to assume dominance and when.

## CONCLUSION

The historical issue of dual national allegiances and multiple identities, together with the conflicts they have spawned, has surely intensified globally over the last 20 years, both within and outside of sport, leading to a revision of traditional notions of national identity and nationalism. In the context of sport, this intensification has been aided largely by an increase in athletic migration, sporting competition, media coverage, greater professionalization, and commercialization of sport, which can be seen in a range of disciplines inclusive of track and field as well as road running. Attempts to theorize and understand these developments have also spawned several theoretical approaches, which vary in their focus, effectiveness, or utility depending on one's research objectives and the theories' intrinsic merits. By considering the experiences of former British track athlete McDonald Bailey in the context of British imperialism and colonialism after World War II, we have examined a historical antecedent to recent contemporary developments and showed the types of fissures, tensions, and contradictions that various identities can generate in the process of identity formation, particularly as they related to issues of national identity, nationalism, and the indissoluble yet problematic link between the individual (I-image) and the collectivity or nation (we-image). The study highlights the need to conduct more historical case studies across a greater range of sports so that we can better historicize, contextualize, and theorize the continuities as well as the changes in the contemporary manifestation of the phenomenon of identity formation in general and its expression in sport.

## Suggested Research

1. The development of sport in Britain's former colonies, such as those of the Caribbean, both during and after colonialism, is still very much an under researched area. The framework adopted here is relevant to historical research that explores links between nationalism, colonialism, and the way in which sport was implicated in both processes.

2. Contemporary sport has seen the proliferation of national as well as global sports stars, sports heroes, and sports icons linked to the commercialization of sport, the influence of the media, and politics. Writing the biographies of such individuals can be used as a way to examine the indissoluble links and tensions between individual and national identities.

3. The conflicts that often arise—notably in soccer, between professional players, their clubs, and the prospect of representing their country—are amenable to a framework grounded in the reality of multiple identities and the fissures which underpin them.

# Additional Resources

**Theory**

Norbert, E., and E. Dunning, eds. 1986. *Quest for excitement: Sport and leisure in the civilizing process.* Oxford, UK: Blackwell.

Elias and Dunning can be considered as founding fathers in applying figurational sociology and the related theory of civilizing processes to the study of sport. The latter involved a processual transformation in standards of etiquette, greater self-control, interdependence, increased repugnance of the incidence of violence, the strengthening of the state, and the reduction of power differentials in society. The text shows how these processes affected the role and development of sport as it became less violent, more orderly, and more democratic from the 18th century onward.

---

Dunning, E., and C. Rojek, eds. 1992. *Sport and leisure in the civilizing process: Critique and counter-critique.* London: MacMillan.

This text contains contributions from several major sport scholars who provide a constructive critical examination of the figurational approach to studying sport in the areas of violence, crowd disorder, drug use, and race and gender. It represents in large measure a response to the many criticisms of this approach which include, namely, its resemblance to functionalism and evolutionism; its inadequate treatment of power, the state, and gender in sport; and attempts to correct the misrepresentations and misunderstandings that characterize theorizing in sport, particularly in relation to this approach.

---

Dunning, E. 2002. Figurational contributions to the sociological study of sport. In *Theory, sport and society*, ed. J. Maguire and K. Young, 211-37. London: JAI.

Dunning is one of the leading exponents of the figurational approach to understanding sport. Here he surveys the literature and shows how it has been applied, particularly to explaining the development of modern sport from its informal, unruly folk origins; the historical incidence of violence, especially soccer hooliganism; and issues of globalization, race, gender, and drugs in sport. It is a very good source for examples of work from this perspective.

---

Giulianotti, R. 2004. Civilizing games: Norbert Elias and the sociology of sport. In *Sport and modern social theorists*, 145–160. London: Palgrave MacMillan.

In this article, Giulianotti provides a brief and critical assessment of Elias's contribution to sociology and to the sociology of sport through his discussion of such concepts as "figuration," to which he likened society, and his related theory of "civilizing processes." The theoretical approach has been variously described as untestable, ethnocentric, Eurocentric, even "racist," as well as counterempirical (e.g., there were 130 wars and 27 million war deaths in the second half of the 20th century, and how is this consistent with a civilizing process?), and in need of more "refinement."

---

**Sport Topic**

Bale, J. 1991. *The brawn drain: Foreign student athletes in American universities.* Champaign: University of Illinois Press.

> This pioneering text presents an in-depth examination of the contested nature of student athletic migration to the United States. It examines the benefits of this migration for U.S. colleges, for the athletes concerned, and for their countries of origin. However, it also examines the negative challenges for these athletes (racism, exploitation) and for the sender countries (dependence, underdevelopment of sport).

---

Bairner, A. 2001. *Sport, nationalism, and globalization: European and North American perspectives.* New York: State University of New York Press.

> Based on several "first-world" countries, including Northern Ireland, Scotland, the United States, Canada, and Sweden, Bairner challenges the view that globalization is weakening notions of national identity, nationalism, and their links to sport or sporting nationalism due to the emergence of a more homogenous global culture centered on Americanism.

---

Allison, L., ed. 2005. *The global politics of sport: The role of global institutions in sport.* London: Routledge.

> This edited collection focuses in large part on the way in which transnational or global sporting organizations such as FIFA and the IOC not only dominate the regulation of international sport but also have helped to erode the centrality of the state as the main axis of international relations.

---

Davies, H. 1999. *Dwight Yorke.* London: Manchester United Books.

> This book provides a rich biographical account of soccer star Dwight Yorke, from the Caribbean island of Tobago, who excelled for Manchester United in the 1990s. It provides useful insights into his identity changes and challenges as a black migrant player due to the cultural adjustments required in a new society as well as his construction as a media celebrity and sports hero.

---

Guttmann, A. 1994. *Games and empires: Modern sports and cultural imperialism.* New York: Columbia University Press.

> Guttmann takes issue with the cultural imperialist approach to explaining the global diffusion of British- and American-derived sport forms. This approach is seen as misrepresenting the dynamic nature of ludic diffusion by presenting it simply in terms of Westernization, a move which fails to capture how subordinate groups and nations can also influence the dominant as well as accept, resist, or reinterpret such Westernization for their own benefit (as happened with such sports as cricket in the British West Indies and baseball in Cuba). The Gramscian-inspired concept of cultural hegemony is seen as more useful in capturing this ludic dynamic.

---

# Epilogue

When we think about sports—all sports—depending on where we were born, our race or ethnicity, our gender, and, of course, our age, we think of different things.

I can imagine that young Native American boys might well ruminate on the folklore surrounding the victory by Billy Mills (of the Oglala Sioux Tribe) in the 10,000 meter run at the 1964 Tokyo Olympics. Born into grinding poverty on the Pine Ridge reservation in South Dakota, Mills overcame despair and hopelessness, served his country as a U.S. Marine, and moved on to become an honored American and role model for Native American youth.

Or, they may celebrate the extraordinary feats of legendary Jim Thorpe (of the Sac and Fox Nation) early in 20th-century America, when Native Americans were considered by many to be less than human. The Thorpe story is well known: After being orphaned, Thorpe attended the Carlisle Indian Industrial School in Pennsylvania, and gave a superb performance at the 1912 Summer Olympics in Stockholm, Sweden, competing in the decathlon and pentathlon and winning multiple events. Thorpe was easily the outstanding performer in Stockholm, and from there he became a household name in sports.

Mills' and Thorpe's feats underscored the fact that the less advantaged, too, including nonwhites, women, Indians, and African Americans, when given a chance, could compete with anyone. Proving their worthiness to a "majority" white American sport audience who may have accepted these feats on the fields of play, however, did not lead to their acceptance by white America outside these arenas of athletic accomplishment.

Who cares, or who cared? As long as everyone was comfortable watching events that included *some* women and *some* nonwhites (or maybe not), the old rules still applied. The sports, the country clubs, the restaurants, the institutions of higher learning all accepted the status quo. Social segregation remained a strong cultural institution not only in American society but also around the world. These are complexities that need to be examined critically.

These complexities bothered Syracuse running back Ernie Davis, who, in 1961, became the first African American to win the coveted Heisman Trophy (Smith 2007). Davis was astounded to learn that, after being recruited by a host of colleges and universities out of Elmira Free Academy in upstate New York, his chosen institution Syracuse did not allow him to live on campus or eat in the dining halls. After he won the Heisman and had a casual visit with President John F. Kennedy, he and a white teammate were refused dining services at a Maryland restaurant (Gallagher 2008).

To try to make sense of the dissonance between what Ernie Davis experienced, for example, and a sporting public that was jumping and shouting for athletes to whom they would refuse service in a restaurant—or to whom they would refuse to sell a home—and to attempt to address these athletes' lack of full access to all other institutions (occupations, public schools for their children, membership in country clubs), several women and men came together at the Mayo Memorial Auditorium on the campus of the University of Minnesota in 1978 and, after engaging debates, formed the first "sociology of sport" organizing committee. In attendance, and involved in the discussions, were a group of people often credited with starting the North American Society for the Sociology of Sport, or, as it is commonly known, NASSS.[1]

With this inaugural event, we see the beginning of the annual conferences, early publication outlets such as *Arena Review* and *Journal of Sport and Social Issues* (first editor: Jim Frey), and later the founding of the *Sociology of Sport Journal*, owned and published by Human Kinetics. In total, what this means is that an organizational, subdisciplinary web has been established for systematic research, teaching, and intellectual dissemination—publishing—about the world of sport.

This is a relatively recent and important development. In 1973, sociologist Charles H. Page, reviewing a volume titled *Sport: Readings From a Sociological Perspective* (1972; edited by our contributor Eric Dunning) in the *American Sociological Review* could note that what was missing from serious sport research was social theory. He put it thus:

> *What was long an area of shameful neglect, however, in recent years has become an active field of historical study, empirical research, conceptual refinement, and, in lesser measure, theoretical formulation (474).*

Even then, the issue was how to theoretically address this growing field of endeavor, its findings, and sociological theory?

The systematic study of sport as a social institution has come a long way since 1978, yet, as I suggested in the introduction, there is still much to be done to further integrate the sociology of sport as a subdiscipline inside of the larger field of sociology; simultaneously, there is still much that scholars who seek to study the institution of sport can learn from the theories and methods employed by sociologists and other social and behavioral sciences. It has been my intention, and the intention of each contributor, to fill that gap and further that integration. My hope, as editor, is that the reader—be he or she a sport enthusiast, a social scientist, or a sport scholar—will take something away from this book that improves his or her own understanding of the ways in which this integration can move the discourse to the next level.

---

[1] Though the origins of NASSS are not well detailed, according to the official NASSS Web site, www. nasss.org/about.html, the founding members were a small group of scholars who began meeting to discuss their research on sport. This group included Susan Greendorfer, Lee Vander Velden, Peggy Cramer, Eldon Snyder, March Krotee, and Andrew Yiannakis.

# References

## Preface

Edwards, H. 1973. *Sociology of sport.* Homewood, IL: Dorsey Press.

Loy, J., and G. Kenyon. 1969. *Sport, culture and society.* New York: Macmillan.

Merton, R.K. 1965. *On the shoulders of giants: A Shandean postscript.* Chicago: University of Chicago Press.

## Introduction

Carpenter, L.J., and R.V. Acosta. 2008. Women in intercollegiate sport: A longitudinal, national study—Thirty one year update, 1977–2008. www.acostacarpenter.org.

Dunning, E. 1999. *Sport matters: Sociological studies of sport, violence and civilization.* London: Routledge.

Edwards, H. 1973. *Sociology of sport.* Homewood, IL: Dorsey Press.

Loy, J. 1992. The dark side of agon: Men in tribal groups and the phenomenon of gang rape. Paper presented at the annual conference of the North American Society for the Sociology of Sport, Toledo (November).

Loy, J., and G. Kenyon. 1969. *Sport, culture and society.* New York: Macmillan.

Maguire, J., and K. Young, eds. 2002. *Theory, sport and society.* Oxford, UK: JAI.

Merton, R.K. 1957. *Social theory and social structure.* New York: Free Press.

———. 1968. The Matthew Effect in Science. *Science* 159:56–63.

Messner, M.A. 2002. *Taking the field: Women, men, and sports.* Minneapolis: University of Minnesota Press.

Rood, J. 2008. Citi, AIG Won't Drop Big Sports Sponsorships. ABC News.com, November 24. www.abcnews.go.com/print?id=6321691.

Smith, E. 2007. *Race, sport, and the American Dream.* Durham, NC: Carolina Academic Press. (2nd edition forthcoming in 2009.)

Zakaria, F. 2008. *The Post-American world.* New York: Norton.

## Chapter 1

Beamish, R., and I. Ritchie. 2006. *Fastest, highest, strongest: A critique of high-performance sport.* London: Routledge.

Brohm, J.M. 1978. *Sport: A prison of measured time.* Trans. I. Fraser. London: Inks Links.

Edwards, H. 1969. *Revolt of the Black athlete.* New York: Free Press.

Fainaru-Wada, M., and L. Williams. 2006. *Game of shadows: Barry Bonds, BALCO and the steroids scandal that rocked professional sports.* New York: Gotham Books.

Hoberman, J. 1992. *Mortal engines: The science of performance and the dehumanization of sport.* New York: Free Press.

Nietzsche, F. 1882/1974. The parable of the madman. In *The gay science,* ed. W. Kaufmann, 181–182. New York: Vintage Press.

Weber, M. 1946a. Science as a vocation. Trans. H.H. Gerth and C.W. Mills. In *From Max Weber: Essays in sociology,* ed. H. Gerth and C.W. Mills, 129–158. New York: Oxford University Press.

———. 1946b. Politics as a vocation. Trans. H.H. Gerth and C.W. Mills. In *From Max Weber: Essays in sociology,* ed. H. Gerth and C.W. Mills, 77–128. New York: Oxford University Press.

———. 1956. *Wirtschaft und Gesellschaft: Grundriss der verstehenden Soziologie* [Economy and society: Outlines of an interpretive sociology]. 2 vols. Tübingen: Mohr.

———. 1958a. *The Protestant ethic and the spirit of capitalism.* Trans. T. Parsons. New York: Scribner's.

———. 1958b. Politik als Beruf [Politics as a vocation]. In *Gesammelte politische Schriften* [Collected essays in politics], ed. J. Winckelmann, 396–450. Tübingen: Mohr.

———. 1968. Wissenschaft als Beruf [Science as a vocation]. In *Gesammelte Aufsätze zur Wissenschaftslehre von Max Weber* [Collected essays in the philosophy of science], ed. J. Winckelmann, 582–613. Tübingen: Mohr.

## Chapter 2

Allan, J. 1989. *Bloody casuals: Diary of a football hooligan.* Glasgow, Scotland: Famedrams.

Armstrong, G. 1998. *Football hooligans: Knowing the score.* Oxford, UK: Berg.

Benn, T., and B. Benn. 2004. After Olga: Developments in women's artistic gymnastics following the 1972 "Olga Korbut phenomenon." In *Sport histories: Figurational studies of the development of modern sports,* ed. E. Dunning, D. Malcolm, and I. Waddington, 172–190. London: Routledge.

Bloyce, D. 2004. Baseball: Myths and modernization. In *Sport histories: Figurational studies of the development of modern sports,* ed. E. Dunning, D. Malcolm, and I. Waddington, 88–103. London: Routledge.

Buford, B. 1991. *Among the thugs*. London: Secker and Warburg.

Colwell, S. 2004. The history and sociology of elite level football refereeing. PhD diss., University of Leicester.

Cooper, I. 2004. Game, set and match: Lawn tennis, from early origins to modern sport. In *Sport histories: Figurational studies of the development of modern sports*, ed. E. Dunning, D. Malcolm, and I. Waddington, 104–120. London: Routledge.

Curry, G. 2001. Football: A study in diffusion. PhD diss., University of Leicester.

Dunning, E., ed. 1971. *The sociology of sport: A selection of readings*. London: Cass.

———. 1999. *Sport matters: Sociological studies of sport, violence and civilization*. London: Routledge.

Dunning, E., and G. Curry. 2004. Public schools, status rivalry and the development of football. In *Sport histories: Figurational studies of the development of modern sports*, ed. E. Dunning, D. Malcolm, and I. Waddington, 31-52. London: Routledge.

Dunning, E., D. Malcolm, and I. Waddington, eds. 2004. *Sport histories: Figurational studies of the development of modern sports*. London: Routledge.

Dunning, E., P. Murphy, I. Waddington, and A. Astrinakis, eds. 2002. *Fighting fans: Football hooliganism as a world phenomenon*. Dublin: University College Dublin Press.

Dunning, E., P. Murphy, and J. Williams. 1988. *The roots of football hooliganism*. London: Routledge & Kegan Paul.

Dunning, E., and K. Sheard. 2005. *Barbarians, gentlemen and players: A sociological study of the development of rugby football*, 2nd ed. London: Routledge.

Elias, N. 1971. The genesis of sports as a sociological problem. In *The sociology of sport: A selection of readings*, ed. E. Dunning, 88-115. London: Cass.

———. 1978. *What is sociology?* London: Hutchinson.

———. 1994. *Reflections on a life*. Trans. E. Jephcott. Oxford: Polity Press.

———. 1996. *The Germans: Power struggles and the development of habitus in the nineteenth and twentieth centuries*. Trans. (with a preface by) E. Dunning and S. Mennell. Ed. M. Schröter. Oxford: Polity Press.

———. 2000. *The civilizing process: Sociogenetic and psychogenetic investigations* (single integrated edition). Oxford: Blackwell.

———. 2009. The quest for excitement in leisure. In *Quest for excitement: Sport and leisure in the civilizing process*, ed. N. Elias and E. Dunning, 63-90. Oxford: Polity Press.

Elias, N., and E. Dunning. 2009. *Quest for excitement: Sport and leisure in the civilizing process*. Oxford: Polity Press.

Elias, N., with J. Scotson. 1965. *The established and the outsiders: A sociological enquiry into community problems*. London: Cass.

Goudsblom, J. 1992. *Fire and civilization*. New York: Penguin.

Giulianotti, R. 1999. *Football: A sociology of the global game*. Oxford, UK: Polity Press.

Green, K. 2004. *Physical education teachers on physical education: A sociological study of philosophies and ideologies*. Chester: Chester Academic Press.

Harper, C. 1990. Football hooliganism. Lothian and Borders Police Fact Sheet 10, www.lbp.police.uk/publications/factsheetpack/10.htm.

Hughes, J. 2003. *Learning to smoke*. Chicago: University of Chicago Press.

Jarvie, G., and J. Maguire. 1994. *Sport and leisure in social thought*. London: Routledge.

Kiku, K. 2004. The development of sport in Japan: Martial arts and baseball. In *Sport histories: Figurational studies of the development of modern sports*, ed. E. Dunning, D. Malcolm, and I. Waddington, 153-171. London: Routledge..

Krüger, M. 1977. Zur Bedeutung der Prozess—und Figurationstheorie für Sport und Sportwissenschaft. *Sportwissenschaft* 27 (2): 129–142.

Leach, E. 1986. Violence. *London Review of Books* 8:1.

Liston, K. 2005. Playing the "masculine–feminine" game: A sociological analysis of the fields of sport and gender in the Republic of Ireland. PhD diss., University College Dublin.

Maguire, J. 1999. *Global sport: Identities, societies, civilizations*. Oxford, UK: Polity Press.

———. 2000. Sport and globalization. In *Handbook of sports studies*, ed. J. Coakley and E. Dunning, 356-369. London: Sage.

Malcolm, D. 1997. Stacking in cricket: A figurational-sociological reappraisal of centrality. *Sociology of Sport and Social Issues* 23:355–360.

———. 1999. Cricket spectator disorder: Myths and historical evidence. *The Sports Historian* 29 (1): 16–37.

———. 2002. Cricket and civilizing processes: A response to Stokvis. *International Review for the Sociology of Sport* 37 (1): 37–57.

———. 2004. Cricket: Civilizing and de-civilizing processes in the imperial game. In *Sport histories: Figurational studies of the development of modern sports*, ed. E. Dunning, D. Malcolm, and I. Waddington, 71-87. London: Routledge.

Mennell, S. 1987. *All manners of food: Eating and taste in England and France from the Middle Ages to the present.* Bloomington, Il.: University of Illinois Press.

Murphy, P., J. Williams, and E. Dunning. 1990. *Football on trial: Spectator violence and development in the football world.* London: Routledge.

Rigauer, B. 2000. Marxist theories. In *Handbook of sports studies*, ed. J. Coakley and E. Dunning, 28-47. London: Sage.

Roversi, A. 1994. *Soccer hooliganism.* Bristol, UK: Wright.

Sheard, K. 2004. Boxing in the Western civilizing process. In *Sport histories: Figurational studies of the development of modern sports*, ed. E. Dunning, D. Malcolm, and I. Waddington, 15–30. London: Routledge.

Smith, A., and I. Waddington. 2004. Using "sport in the community" schemes to tackle crime and drug abuse among young people: Some policy issues and problems. *European Physical Education Review* 10:279–297.

Smith, D. 1984. Norbert Elias—Established or Outsider? *Sociological Review* 32 (2): 367–389.

Smith, S. 2004. Clay shooting: Civilization in the line of fire. In *Sport histories: Figurational studies of the development of modern sports*, ed. E. Dunning, D. Malcolm, and I. Waddington, 137–152. London: Routledge.

Twitchen, A. 2004. The influence of state-formation processes on the early development of motor racing. In *Sport histories: Figurational studies of the development of modern sports*, ed. E. Dunning, D. Malcolm, and I. Waddington, 121-136. London: Routledge.

Van Bottenburg, M. 2001. *Global games.* Trans. B. Jackson. Champaign: University of Illinois Press.

Van der Brug, H. 1986. *Voetbalvandalisme.* Haarlem, Netherlands: De Vrieseborch.

Van Limbergen, K., C. Colaers, and L. Walgrave. 1987. *Research on the societal and psychosociological background of football hooliganism.* Louvain, Belgium: Catholic University.

Waddington, I., with D. Malcolm and I. Jones. 2000. The people's game? Football spectatorship and demographic change. *Soccer and Society* 1 (1): 129–143.

Waddington, I., with M. Roderick and G. Parker. 2000. Playing hurt: Managing injuries in English professional football. *International Review for the Sociology of Sport* 35 (2): 165–180.

Williams, J., E. Dunning, and P. Murphy. 1988. *Hooligans unterwegs: Englische fans in Europa.* Sandhausen: Fan Treff.

———. 1989. *Hooligans abroad: The behaviour and control of English fans in continental Europe.* London: Routledge & Kegan Paul.

## Chapter 3

Birrell, S., and M.G. McDonald, eds. 2000. *Reading sport: Critical essays on power and representation.* Boston: Northeastern Press.

Bochner, A.P., and C. Ellis, eds. 2002. *Ethnographically speaking: Autoethnography, literature, and aesthetics.* Lanham, MD: Rowman & Littlefield.

Brooks, A. 1997. *Postfeminisms: Feminism, cultural theory and cultural forms.* London: Routledge.

Cole, C.L., and D.L. Andrews. 1996. "Look—It's NBA *Showtime!*": Visions of race in the popular imaginary. *Cultural Studies: A Research Volume* 1:141–181.

Dandaneau, S.P. 2000. *Taking it big: Developing sociological consciousness in postmodern times.* Thousand Oaks, CA: Pine Forge Press.

Denzin, N.K. 1989. *Interpretive interactionism.* 2nd ed. Thousand Oaks, CA: Sage.

———. 1990. Presidential address on the sociological imagination revisited. *The Sociological Quarterly* 31:1–22.

———. 1997. *Interpretive ethnography: Ethnographic practices for the 21st century.* Thousand Oaks, CA: Sage.

———. 2003. *Performance ethnography: Critical pedagogy and the politics of culture.* Thousand Oaks, CA: Sage.

Echols, A. 1993. *Daring to be bad.* 3rd ed. Minneapolis: University of Minnesota Press.

Ellis, C. 2004. *The Ethnographic I: A methodological novel about autoethnography.* Walnut Creek, CA: Altamira Press.

Ellis, C., and A.P. Bochner. 2003. Autoethnography, personal narrative, reflexivity: Researcher as subject. In *Collecting and interpreting qualitative materials* (2nd ed.), eds. N. Denzin and Y. Lincoln, 199–258. Thousand Oaks, CA: Sage.

Feagin, J.R., and H. Vera. 1995. *White racism.* New York: Routledge.

Foucault, M. 1973. *The order of things: An archaeology of human sciences.* New York: Vintage.

Gallagher, J. 1973. Billie Jean, three years later. *Houston Post*, September 21, np.

Gitlin, T. 2000. Afterword. In *The sociological imagination: Fortieth anniversary edition*, 229–242. New York: Oxford University Press.

Hahn, L. 1998. The shots heard 'round the world. *Tennis* 34:22–25.

Hebdige, D. 1979. *Subculture: The meaning of style.* New York: Routledge.

Heywood, L., and J. Drake. 1997. Introduction. In *Third wave agenda: Being feminist, doing feminism*, 1–20. Minneapolis: University of Minnesota Press.

Jackson, S.J. 1994. Gretzky, crisis, and Canadian identity in 1988: Rearticulating the

Americanization of culture debate. *Sociology of Sport Journal* 11:428–446.

Jackson, S.J. 1998. A twist of race: Ben Johnson and the Canadian crisis of racial and national identity. *Sociology of Sport Journal* 15:21–40.

King, B.J., and F. Deford. 1982. *Billie Jean*. New York: Viking Press.

Loy, J., and D. Booth. 2004. Consciousness, craft, commitment: The sociological imagination of C. Wright Mills. In *Sport and modern social theorists*, ed. R. Giulianotti, 65–80. New York: Palgrave MacMillan.

McDonald, M.G., and S. Birrell. 1998. *Reading sport: Historical articulations of a method*. Paper presented at the annual meeting of the North American Society for the Sociology of Sport, Las Vegas.

———. 1999. Reading sport critically: A methodology for interrogating power. *Sociology of Sport Journal* 16:283–300.

Mills, C.W. 1959/2000. *The sociological imagination*. 40th anniversary ed. New York: Oxford University Press.

Richardson, L. 1997. *Fields of play: Constructing an academic life*. New Brunswick, NJ: Rutgers University Press.

———. 2003. Writing: A method of inquiry. In *Collecting and interpreting qualitative materials* (2nd ed.), ed. N. Denzin and Y. Lincoln, 499–541. Thousand Oaks, CA: Sage.

Smith, D. (2001). Williams decries fans as racist. *USA Today*, March 26, 3C.

Spencer, N.E. 1997. Once upon a subculture: Professional women's tennis and the meaning of style. *Journal of Sport & Social Issues* 21:363–378.

———. 2000. Reading between the lines: A discursive analysis of the Billie Jean King vs. Bobby Riggs "Battle of the Sexes." *Sociology of Sport Journal* 17:386–402.

———. 2004. Sister Act VI: Venus and Serena Williams at Indian Wells: "Sincere fictions" and white racism. *Journal of Sport & Social Issues* 28:115–135.

———. 2007. Presidential address: *Fifteen minutes of fame: Billie Jean King, the "Battle of the Sexes," and the politics of community*. Paper presented at the annual meeting of the North American Society of the Sociology of Sport (NASSS), Pittsburgh.

Theberge, N., and P. Donnelly, eds. 1984. *Sport and the sociological imagination*. Fort Worth: Texas Christian University Press.

## Chapter 4

Bale, J. 2004. *Roger Bannister and the four-minute mile*. London: Routledge.

Bannister, R. 1964. The meaning of athletic performance. In *International research in sport and physical education*, ed. E. Jokl and E. Simon, 71–72. Springfield, IL: Thomas.

Bascomb, N. 2004. *The perfect mile: Three athletes, one goal, and less than four minutes to achieve it*. Boston: Houghton Mifflin.

Beamish, R., and I. Ritchie. 2005. From fixed capacities to performance-enhancement: The paradigm shift in the science of "training" and the use of performance-enhancing substances. *Sport in History* 25:412–433.

———. 2006. *Fastest, highest, strongest: A critique of high-performance sport*. London: Routledge.

Bourdieu, P. 2004. *Science of science and reflexivity*. Trans. R. Nice. Cambridge: Polity Press.

Bowler, P.J., and I.R. Morus. 2005. *Making modern science: A historical survey*. Chicago: University of Chicago Press.

Dimeo, P. 2007. *A history of drug use in sport 1876–1976: Beyond good and evil*. London: Routledge.

Eriksson, L. 2007. Sociology of scientific knowledge. In *The Blackwell encyclopedia of sociology* (vol. VIII), ed. G. Ritzer, 4097–4100. Oxford, UK: Blackwell.

Hoberman, J. 1992. *Mortal engines: The science of performance and the dehumanization of sport*. Toronto: Free Press.

Holland, G. 1954. The golden age is now. *Sports Illustrated*, August 16, 46–52, 83–94.

Kidd, B. 1996. *The struggle for Canadian sport*. Toronto: University of Toronto Press.

Kuhn, T.S. 1962. Energy conservation as an example of simultaneous discovery. In *Critical problems in the history of science*, ed. M. Clagett, 321–356. Madison: University of Wisconsin Press.

———. 1970. *The structure of scientific revolutions*. 2nd ed., enlarged. Chicago: University of Chicago Press.

Latour, B., and S. Woolgar. 1979. *Laboratory life: The social construction of scientific facts*. London: Sage.

Merton, R.K. 1957. *Social theory and social structure*. Rev. and enlarged edition. Glencoe, IL: Free Press.

———. 1973. *The sociology of science: Theoretical and empirical investigations*, ed. and with an introduction by N.W. Storer. Chicago: University of Chicago Press.

Mignon, P. 2003. The Tour de France and the doping issue. In *The Tour de France 1903–2003: A century of sporting structures, meanings and values*, ed. H. Dauncey and G. Hare, 227–245. London: Cass.

O'Neil, P. 1954. Duel of the four-minute men. *Sports Illustrated*, August 16, 20–23.

Orwell, G. 2003. The sporting spirit. In *Shooting an elephant and other essays*, 195–199. London: Penguin Books.

Ritchie, I. 2008. Sociological theories of sport. In *Canadian sport sociology* (2nd ed.), ed. J. Crossman, 21–39. Toronto: Thomson/Nelson.

Russett, C.E. 1989. *Sexual science: The Victorian construction of womanhood*. Cambridge, MA: Harvard University Press.

Shapin, S. 1996. *The scientific revolution*. Chicago: University of Chicago Press.

Stanfield, R., and M. Wrenn. 2007. Thomas Kuhn and scientific paradigms. In *The Blackwell encyclopedia of sociology* (vol. V), ed. G. Ritzer, 2493–2497. Oxford, UK: Blackwell.

Storer, N.W. 1973. Introduction. In *The sociology of science: Theoretical and empirical investigations*, ed. and with an introduction by N.W. Storer, xi–xxxi. Chicago: University of Chicago Press.

Turner, S. 2007. Scientific norms/counternorms. In *The Blackwell encyclopedia of sociology* (vol. VIII), ed. G. Ritzer, 4109–4112. Oxford: Blackwell.

Waddington, I. 2005. Changing patterns of drug use in British sport from the 1960s. *Sport in History* 25:472–496.

Wagg, S., and D.L. Andrews, eds. 2007. *East plays west: Sport and the Cold War*. London: Routledge.

World Anti-Doping Agency (WADA). 2003. *World anti-doping code*. www.wada-ama.org/rtecontent/document/code_v3.pdf.

Yesalis, C.E., and M.S. Bahrke. 2002. History of doping in sport. *International Sports Studies* 24:42–76.

## Chapter 5

Adelman, M. 1986. *A sporting time: New York and the rise of modern athletics, 1820–1870*. Champaign: University of Illinois Press.

Austrian, Z., and M.S. Rosentraub. 2002. Cities, sports and economic change: A retrospective assessment. *Journal of Urban Affairs* 24 (5): 549–563.

Coakley, J. 2007. *Sports in society*. New York McGraw-Hill.

Feagin, J.R. 1988. *Free enterprise city: Houston in political-economic perspective*. New Brunswick, NJ: Rutgers University Press.

Greater Indianapolis Chamber of Commerce. 2009. About Indianapolis: Sports recreation. www.indychamber.com/sportsRec.asp.

Hardy, S. 1982. *How Boston played: Sport, recreation, and community 1865–1915*. Boston: Northeastern University Press. ———. 1997. Sport in urbanizing America: A historical review. *Journal of Urban History* 23 (6): 675–708.

Ingham, A.G., and R. Beamish. 1993. The industrialisation of the United States and the "bourgeoisification" of American sport. In *The sporting process*, ed. J. Maguire, E. Dunning, and R. Pearton, 169–206. Champaign, IL: Human Kinetics.

Jonas, A.E.G., and D. Wilson. 1999. The city as growth machine: Critical reflections two decades later. In *The urban growth machine: Critical perspectives two decades later*, ed. A.E.G. Jonas and D. Wilson, 3–18. Albany: State University of New York Press.

McCallum, K., A. Spencer, and E. Wyly. 2005. The city as an image-creation machine: A critical analysis of Vancouver's Olympic bid. *APCG Yearbook* 67:24–46.

McGovern, S. 2003. Ideology, consciousness, and inner-city redevelopment: The case of Stephen Goldsmith's Indianapolis. *Journal of Urban Affairs* 25 (1): 1–25.

Minutes of the City-County Council and Special Service District Councils of Indianapolis, Marion County, Indiana. August 2, 2004. www.indy.gov/eGov/Council/PDF/Council/Minutes/min08-02-04.pdf.

Molotch, H. 1976. The city as growth machine: Toward a political economy of space. *American Journal of Sociology* 82:309–330.

Nasaw, D. 1993. *Going out: The rise and fall of public amusements*. New York: Basic Books.

Nielsen, W.A. 1985. *The golden donors*. New York: Truman Talley.

Nevarez, L. 2005. Urban political economy. In *Encyclopedia of Sociology*, ed. G. Ritzer, 5122–5125. Cambridge, MA: Blackwell.

Peterson, P.E. (1981). *City limits*. Chicago: University of Chicago Press.

Riess, S. 1980. *Touching base: Professional baseball and American culture in the Progressive Era*. Westport, CT: Greenwood Press.

———. 1989. *City games: The evolution of American urban society and the rise of sports*. Champaign: University of Illinois Press.

Ritchie, I., and S.S. Kennedy, eds. 2001. *To market, to market: Reinventing Indianapolis*. New York: University Press of America.

Schimmel, K.S. 1995. Growth politics, urban development, and sports stadium construction in the United States: A case study. In *The stadium and the city*, ed. J. Bale and O. Moen, 111–155. Staffordshire: Keele University Press.

———. 2001. Sport matters: Urban regime theory and urban regeneration in the late-capitalist era. In *Sport in the city: The role of sport in economic and social regeneration*, ed. C. Gratton and I. Henry, 259–277. London: Routledge.

———. 2002. The political economy of place: Sport studies and urban studies perspectives.

In *Theory, sport and society*, ed. J. Maguire and K. Young, 335–351. London: Elsevier Science.

———. 2006. Deep play: Sports mega-events and urban social conditions in the USA. *Sociological Review* 54 (s2): 160–174.

———. 2007. Here we grow again! (Re)placing sport infrastructure in the (re)developed city. Paper presented at the World Congress of the International Sociology of Sport Association, Copenhagen, Denmark.

Schimmel, K.S., A.G. Ingham, and J.W. Howell. 1993. Professional team sport and the American city. In *Sport and social development: Traditions, transitions, and transformations*, ed. A.G. Ingham and J. Loy, 211–244. Champaign, IL: Human Kinetics.

Stone, C.N. 1989. *Regime politics: Governing Atlanta, 1946–1988*. Lawrence: University Press of Kansas.

Wilson, D. 1996. Metaphors, growth coalition discourses and black poverty neighborhoods in a U.S. city. *Antipode* 28 (1): 72–96.

Wilson, D., and J. Wouters. 2003. Spatiality and growth discourse: The restructuring of America's Rust Belt cities. *Journal of Urban Affairs* 25 (2): 123–138.

## Chapter 6

Bailey, W.S., and T.D. Littleton. 1991. Athletics and academe: An anatomy of abuses and a prescription for reform. New York: Macmillan.

Barley, S.R., and P.S. Tolbert. 1997. Institutionalization and structuration: Studying the links between action and institution. *Organization Studies* 18:93–117.

Baxter, V., and C. Lambert. 1991. Competing rationalities and the politics of interorganizational regulation. *Sociological Perspectives* 34 (2): 183–203.

Baxter, V., A.V. Margovio, and C. Lambert. 1996. Competition, legitimation, and the regulation of intercollegiate athletics. *Sociology of Sport Journal* 13 (1): 51–64.

Berger, P., and T. Luckman. 1967. *The social construction of reality: A treatise in the sociology of knowledge*. New York: Anchor Books.

Bignell, J. 1997. *Media semiotics: An introduction*. Manchester, UK: Manchester University Press.

Brand, M. 2006. President's message—Call for moderation is a complex message, not a mixed one. *NCAA News Online*, September 11. www.ncaa.org/wps/ncaa?ContentID=10977.

Brown, G.T. 2002. The $6 billion plan: NCAA wants TV contract to increase revenue, decrease tension between scholarly mission and commercial image. *NCAA News Online*, March 18. www.ncaa.org/wps/ncaa?ContentID=27806.

Brown, R.W. 1996. The revenues associated with relaxing admission standards at Division I-A colleges. *Applied Economics* 28 (7): 807–814.

Byers, W. 1995. *Unsportsmanlike conduct: Exploiting college athletes*. Ann Arbor: University of Michigan Press.

Case, B., H.S. Greer, and J. Brown. 1987. Academic clustering in athletics: Myth or reality? *Arena Review* 11 (2): 48–56.

Chu, D. (1989). *The character of American higher education and intercollegiate sport*. Albany: State University of New York Press.

Creswell, J.W. 1998. *Qualitative inquiry and research design: Choosing among five traditions*. Thousand Oaks, CA: Sage.

Debner, J.A., and L.L. Jacoby. 1994. Unconscious perception: Attention, awareness and control. *Journal of Experimental Psychology: Learning, Memory, and Cognition* 20:304–317.

DeBrock, L., W. Hendricks, and R. Koenker. 1996. The economics of persistence: Graduation rates of athletes as labor market choice. *Journal of Human Resources* 31 (3): 512–538.

DeVenzio, D. 1986. *Rip-Off U: The annual theft and exploitation of revenue producing major college student-athletes*. Charlotte: Fool Court Press.

DiMaggio, P.J., and W.W. Powell. 1983. The iron-cage revisited: Institutional isomorphism and collective rationality in organizational fields. *American Sociological Review* 48:147–160.

Duncan, M.C., and B. Brummett. 1991. The mediation of spectator sport. In *Television criticism: Approaches and applications*, ed. L.H. Vande Berg, and L.A. Wenner, 367–387. New York: Longman.

Eitzen, D.S. 1987. The educational experiences of intercollegiate student-athletes. *Journal of Sport and Social Issues* 11 (1–2): 15–30.

Elsbach, K.D., and R.M. Kramer. 1996. Members' responses to organizational identity threats: Encountering and countering the business week rankings. *Administrative Science Quarterly* 41:442–476.

Feldman, M.S. 2000. Organizational routines a source of continuous change. *Organization Science* 11:611–629.

Feldman, M.S., and B.T. Pentland. 2003. Reconceptualizing organizational routines as a source of flexibility and change. *Administrative Science Quarterly* 48:94–118.

Friedland, R., and R.R. Alford. 1991. Bringing society back in: Symbols, practices, and institutional contradictions. In *The new institutionalism in organizational analysis*, ed. W.W. Powell and P.J. DiMaggio, 232–262. Chicago: University of Chicago.

Funk, G.D. 1992. *Major violations: The unbalanced priorities in athletics and academics.* Champaign, IL: Leisure Press.

Gerdy, J.R. 1997. *The successful college athletic program: The new standard.* Phoenix: American Council on Education and Oryx Press.

———. 2006. *Air ball: American education's failed experiment with elite athletics.* Oxford: University Press of Mississippi.

Gough, P. 2006. Pardon the interruptions: Primetime ads increasing. *The Hollywood Reporter. com,* May 5. www.hollywoodreporter.com/hr/esearch/searchResult.jsp?keyword=Pardon+the+interruptions%3A+Primetime+ads+increasing&x=26&y=14&exposeNavigation=true&kw=&configType=&searchType=ARTICLE_SEARCH&an=thr&action=Submit&searchInterface=THRSearch&matchType=mode%2Bmatchallpartial&numOfrecordsPerPage=10.

Green, B.C., C. Costa, and M. Fitzgerald. 2003. Marketing the host city: Analyzing exposure generated by a sport event. *International Journal of Sports Marketing and Sponsorship* 4 (4): 335–354.

Gruneau, R., D. Whitson, and H. Cantelon. 1988. Methods and media: Studying the sports/television discourse. *Society and Leisure* 11:265–281.

Hofstede, G., B. Nuijen., D.D. Ohayv, and G. Sanders. 1990. Measuring organizational cultures: A qualitative and quantitative study across twenty cases. *Administrative Science Quarterly* 35:286–316.

Jepperson, R.L. 1991. Institutions, institutional effects, and institutionalism. In *The new institutionalism in organizational analysis,* ed. W.W. Powell and P.J. DiMaggio, 143–163. Chicago: University of Chicago Press.

Madden, P.A., and J.W. Grube. 1994. The frequency and nature of alcohol and tobacco advertising in televised sports 1990 through 1992. *American Journal of Public Health* 84:297–299.

Maraniss, D. 1999. *When pride still mattered: A life of Vince Lombardi.* New York: Simon & Schuster.

Meyer, J., and B. Rowan. 1977. Institutional organizations: Formal structure as myth and ceremony. *American Journal of Sociology* 83:340–363.

National Collegiate Athletic Association. 2002. CEOs don't blink on corporate tag. *NCAA News,* March 18. www.ncaa.org/wps/ncaa?ContentID=46329.

National Collegiate Athletic Association. 2006a. *2006 Division I men's basketball championship handbook.* NCAA: Indianapolis, Indiana.

National Collegiate Athletic Association. 2006b. *2006 Division I women's basketball championship handbook.* NCAA: Indianapolis, Indiana.

———. 2008a. *Our Mission.* www.ncaa.org/wps/ncaa?ContentID=1352.

———. 2008b. *The NCAA's advertising and promotional standards.* www.ncaa.org/wps/ncaa?ContentID=635.

Nelson, R.R., and S.G. Winter. 1982. *An evolutionary theory of economic change.* Cambridge, MA: Harvard University Press.

Neuendorf, K.A. 2001. *A flowchart for the typical process of content analysis research.* www.april6thshop.com/content/flowchart.html

———. 2002. *The content analysis guidebook.* Thousand Oaks, CA: Sage.

Padilla, A., and D. Baumer. 1994. Big-time college sports: Management and economic issues. *Journal of Sport and Social Issues* 18:123–143.

Patton, M.Q. 2002. *Qualitative research and evaluation methods.* 3rd ed. Thousand Oaks, CA: Sage.

Putler, D.S., and R.A. Wolfe. 1999. Perceptions of intercollegiate athletic programs: Priorities and tradeoffs. *Sociology of Sport Journal* 16:301–325.

Riffe, D., S. Lacy, and F.G. Fico. 1998. *Analyzing media messages: Using quantitative content analysis in research.* Hillsdale, NJ: Erlbaum.

Rossman, G.B., and S.F. Rallis. 1998. *Learning in the field: An introduction to qualitative research.* Thousand Oaks, CA: Sage.

Ryan, G.W., and H.R. Bernard. 2000. Data management and analysis methods. In *handbook of qualitative research* (2nd ed.), ed. N.K. Denzin and Y.S. Lincoln, 769–802. Thousand Oaks, CA: Sage.

Sack, A.L. 1987. College sport and the student-athlete. *Journal of Sport and Social Issues* 11 (1–2): 31–48.

Sack, A.L., and E.J. Staurowsky. 1998. *College athletes for hire: The evolution and legacy of the NCAA's amateur myth.* New York: Praeger Publishers.

Schwartz, P.J. 2007. *Forbes sports values: The most valuable college football teams,* November 20. www.forbes.com/sportsbusiness/2007/11/20/notre-dame-fooball-biz-sports-cx_ps_1120collegeball.html.

Schwartz, P.J. 2008. *Forbes sports values: The most valuable college basketball teams,* January 2. www.forbes.com/2007/12/27/college-basketball-valuations-biz-sports_cz_js_0102basketball.html.

Scott, W.R. 2001. *Institutions and organizations.* 2nd ed. London: Sage.

Scott, W.R., M. Ruef, P.J. Mendel, and C.A. Caronna. 2000. *Institutional change and healthcare organizations: From professional dominance to managed care.* Chicago: University of Chicago Press.

Seo, M., and W.E.D. Creed. 2002. Institutional contradictions, praxis, and institutional change: A dialectical perspective. *Academy of Management Review* 27:222–247.

Shapiro, S., D.J. MacInnis, and S.E. Heckler. 1997. The effects of incidental ad exposure on the formation of consideration sets. *Journal of Consumer Research* 24:94–104.

Silk, M.L., and J. Amis. 2000. Institutional pressures and the production of televised sport. *Journal of Sport Management* 14:267–292.

Southall, R.M., M.S. Nagel, J. Amis, and C. Southall. (2008). A method to March Madness: Institutional logics and the 2006 National Collegiate Athletic Association Division I Men's Basketball Tournament. *Journal of Sport Management* 22 (6): 677–700.

Sperber, M. 2000. *Beer and circus: How big-time college sports is crippling undergraduate education*. New York: Holt.

Strauss, A., and J. Corbin. 1990. *Basics of qualitative research: Grounded theory and techniques*. Thousand Oaks, CA: Sage.

The evolution of women's college sports. 2001. *USA Today*, September 26. www.usatoday.com/sports/college/2001-09-27-women-timeline.htm.

Thomas, B. 2006 (October 2). Letter to Dr. Myles Brand. Available from the Committee on Ways and Means, U.S House of Representatives, Washington, DC 20515.

Thornton, P.H. 2002. The rise of the corporation in a craft industry: Conflict and conformity in institutional logics. *Academy of Management Journal* 45:81–101.

Vasquez, D. 2005. Ad dollars and sense of March Madness. *MedialifeMagazine.com*, March 17. www.medialifemagazine.com/News2005/mar05/mar14/4_thurs/news4thursday.html.

Washington, M. 2004. Field approaches to institutional change: The evolution of the National Collegiate Athletic Association 1906–1995. *Organization Studies* 25:393–414.

Washington, M., and M.J. Ventresca. 2004. How organizations change: The role of institutional support mechanisms in the incorporation of higher education visibility strategies, 1874–1995. *Organization Science* 15:82–97.

Weiberg, K. 2001. Too much corporate fruit around to reduce the harvest. *NCAA News*, October 22. www.ncaa.org/wps/ncaa?ContentID=13584.

Wimmer, R.D., and J.R. Dominick. 1994. *Mass media research: An introduction*. 5th ed. Belmont, CA: Wadsworth.

Zimbalist, A.S. 1999. *Unpaid professionals: Commercialism and conflict in big-time college sports*. Princeton: Princeton University Press.

Zucker, L. 1977. The role of institutionalization and cultural persistence. *American Sociological Review* 42:726–743.

## Chapter 7

Athletes in Action. 2009. About Athletes in Action. www.aia.com/about.

Baker, W.J. 2007. *Playing with God: Religion and modern sport*. Cambridge, MA: Harvard University Press.

Bellah, R. 1964. Religious evolution. *American Sociological Review* 29:358–374.

———. 1967. Civil religion in America. *Daedalus* 96:1–21.

———. 1980. Introduction. In *Varieties of civil religion*, ed. R. Bellah and P. Hammond, vii–xv. New York: Harper & Row.

Bellah, R., R. Madsen, W. Sullivan, A. Swidler, and S. Tipton. 1985. *Habits of the heart: Individualism and commitment in American life*. Berkeley: University of California Press.

Berger, P. 1967. *The sacred canopy*. New York: Doubleday.

———. 1980. *The heretical imperative: Contemporary possibilities of religious affirmation*. New York: Anchor Books.

Berman, M. 1988. *All that is solid melts into air: The experience of modernity*. New York: Penguin Books.

Casanova, J. 1994. *Public religions in the modern world*. Chicago: University of Chicago Press.

Chaves, M. 1994. Secularization as declining religious authority. *Social Forces* 72:749–74.

Cherry, C., B. DeBerg, and A. Porterfield. 2001. *Religion on campus*. Chapel Hill: University of North Carolina Press.

Coakley, J. 2007. *Sports in society: Issues and controversies*. Boston: McGraw-Hill.

Durkheim, E. 1912/1995. *The elementary forms of religious life*. Trans. K. Fields. New York: Free Press.

Giddens, A. 1991. *Modernity and self-identity: Self and society in the late modern age*. Cambridge: Polity Press.

Guttmann, A. 1978. *From ritual to record: The nature of modern sports*. New York: Columbia University Press.

Hammond, P. 1992. *Religion and personal autonomy: The third disestablishment in America*. Columbia: University of South Carolina Press.

Hoffman, S. 1992. Evangelicalism and the revitalization of religious ritual in sport. In *Sport and religion*, ed. S.J. Hoffman, 111–125. Champaign, IL: Human Kinetics.

Jackson, S., and M. Csikszentmihalyi. 1999. *Flow in sports: The keys to optimal experiences and performances*. Champaign, IL: Human Kinetics.

Kliever, L.D. 2001. God and games in modern culture. In *From season to season: Sports as American religion*, ed. J.L. Price, 39–48. Macon, GA: Mercer University Press.

Ladd, T., and J.A. Mathisen. 1999. *Muscular Christianity: Evangelical Protestants and the development of American sport*. Grand Rapids, MI: Baker Books.

Marx, K. 1978. Manifesto of the Communist Party. In *The Marx-Engels reader*, ed. R.C. Tucker, 469–500. New York: Norton.

Mathisen, J. 2006. Sport. In *Handbook of religion and social institutions*, ed. H.R. Ebaugh, 285–303. New York: Springer.

Overman, S. 1997. *The influence of the Protestant ethic on sports and recreation*. Aldershot, UK: Averbury.

Polanyi, K. 1944. *The great transformation*. Boston: Beacon.

Price, J.L. 2001. From Sabbath proscriptions to super Sunday celebrations: Sports and religion in America. In *From season to season: Sports as American religion*, ed. J.L. Price, 15–38. Macon, GA: Mercer University Press.

———. 2005. An American apotheosis: Sports as popular religion. In *Religion and popular culture in America* (rev. ed.), ed. B.D. Forbes and J.H. Mahan, 195–212. Berkeley: University of California Press.

Putney, C. 2001. *Muscular Christianity: Manhood and sports in Protestant America 1880–1920*. Cambridge, MA: Harvard University Press.

Rousseau, J.-J. 1762/1968. *The social contract*. New York: Penguin Books.

St. John, W. 2005. *Rammer jammer yellow hammer*. New York: Crown Books.

Storch, E., J. Roberti, E. Bravata, and J. Storch. 2004. Strength of religious faith: A comparison of intercollegiate athletes and non-athletes. *Pastoral Psychology* 52:485–492.

Tschannen, O. 1991. The secularization paradigm: A systematization. *Journal for the Scientific Study of Religion* 30:395–415.

Wallis, R., and S. Bruce. 1991. Secularization: Trends, data, and theory. *Research in the Social Scientific Study of Religion* 3:1–31.

Warner, R.S. 1993. Work in progress toward a new paradigm for the sociological study of religion in the United States. *American Journal of Sociology* 98:1044–1093.

Weber, M. 1958. Science as a vocation. In *From Max Weber: Essays in sociology*, ed. H.H. Gerth and C.W. Mills, 129–156. New York: Oxford University Press.

Wilson, B. 1982. *Religion in sociological perspective*. New York: Oxford University Press.

Yamane, D. 1997. Secularization on trial: In defense of a neo-secularization paradigm. *Journal for the Scientific Study of Religion* 36:107–120.

———. 1998. Spirituality. In *Encyclopedia of religion and society*, ed. W.H. Swatos, 492. Walnut Creek, CA: AltaMira Press.

———. 2005. *The Catholic Church in state politics: Negotiating prophetic demands and political realities*. Lanham, MD: Rowman & Littlefield.

———. 2006. Civil religion. In *The Blackwell encyclopedia of sociology* (vol. II), ed. G. Ritzer, 506–507. Oxford, UK: Blackwell.

Yamane, D., and T. Blake. 2008. Sport and sacred umbrellas on campus: The religiosity and spirituality of college athletes. Unpublished manuscript, Department of Sociology, Wake Forest University, Winston-Salem, NC.

Young Men's Christian Association. 2009. History of the YMCA Movement. www.ymca.net/about_the_ymca/history_of_the_ymca.html.

## Part III

Cole, N. 2008. Syracuse University basketball player Eric Devendorf suspended for the rest of academic year. *The Post-Standard*, December 10. http://blog.syracuse.com/orangebasketball/2008/12/syracuse_university_basketball_2.html/.

Zimbalist, A. 1999. *Unpaid professionals: Commercialism and conflict in big-time college sports*. Princeton, NJ: Princeton University Press.

## Chapter 8

Acker, J. 2006. *Class questions, feminist answers*. New York: Routledge.

Andersen, M.L. 2001. Restructuring for whom? Race, class, gender, and the ideology of invisibility. *Sociological Forum* 16:181–201.

Baca Zinn, M., and B.T. Dill. 2005. Theorizing differences from multicultural feminism. In *Gender through the prism of difference*, ed. P. Hondagneu-Sotelo, M. Baca Zinn, and M.A. Messner, 23–28. New York: Oxford University Press.

Carpenter, L. J. and R.V. Acosta. 2005. *Title IX*. Champaign, IL: Human Kinetics.

Carpenter, L.J., and R.V. Acosta. 2006. Women in intercollegiate sport: A longitudinal, national study—Twenty-nine year update, 1977–2008. http://webpages.charter.net/womeninsport/

Collins, P.H. 1994. Shifting the center: Race, class, and feminist theorizing about motherhood. In *Mothering: Ideology, experience, and agency*, ed. G.A. Chang, 45–65. New York: Routledge.

———. 2004. *Black sexual politics : African Americans, gender, and the new racism*. New York: Routledge.

Crenshaw, K. 1991. Mapping the margins: Intersectionality, identity politics, and violence against women of color. *Stanford Law Review* 43:1241–1299.

Davis, A. 1983. *Women, race, and class.* New York: Vintage Books.

Engels, F., and E. Leacock. 1972. *The origin of the family, private property, and the state.* New York: International.

Epstein, C.F. 1970. *Woman's place: Options and limits in professional careers.* Berkeley: University of California Press.

———. 2007. Great divides: The cultural, cognitive, and social bases of the global subordination of women. *American Sociological Review* 72:1–22.

Esqueda, C., and L.A. Harrison. 2007. The influence of gender role stereotypes, the woman's race, and level of provocation and resistance on domestic violence culpability attributions. *Sex Roles* 53:821–834.

Goldman, E. 1911. Marriage and love. In *Anarchism and other essays*, 233–245. New York: Mother Earth.

Hattery, A.J., and E. Smith. 2007. *African American families.* Thousand Oaks, CA: Sage.

Hattery, A., E. Smith, and E. Staurowsky. 2008. They play like girls: Gender equity in NCAA sports. *The Journal for the Study of Sports and Athletes in Education* 1:249–272.

Hill, S., and J. Sprague. 1999. Parenting in black and white families: The interaction of gender with race and class. *Gender & Society* 13:480–502.

Jaggar, A. 1983. *Feminist politics and human nature.* Lanham, MD: Rowman & Allanheld.

Kane, M.J. 1996. Media coverage of the post Title IX female athlete: A feminist analysis of sport, gender, and power. *Duke Journal of Gender Law & Policy* 3 (1): 95–127.

King, D.K. 1988. Multiple jeopardy, multiple consciousness: The context of a black feminist ideology. *Signs* 14:42–72.

Kozol, J. 2001. *Ordinary resurrections: Children in the years of hope.* New York: Harper Perennial.

———. 2005. *The shame of the nation: The restoration of apartheid schooling in America.* New York: Crown.

Lorber, J. 1995. *Paradoxes of gender.* New Haven, CT: Yale University Press.

Padavic, I., and B.F. Reskin. 2002. *Women and men at work.* Thousand Oaks, CA: Pine Forge Press.

Smith, Earl. 2007. *Race, Sport and the American Dream.* Durham, NC: Carolina Academic Press.

Smith, V. 1998. *Not just race, not just gender: Black feminist readings.* London: Routledge.

Western, B. 2006. *Punishment and inequality in America.* New York: Russell Sage Foundation.

Wexler, A. 1984. *Emma Goldman: An intimate life.* New York: Pantheon Books.

## Chapter 9

Bourdieu, P. 1986. The forms of capital. In *Handbook of theory and research for the sociology of education*, ed. J.G. Richardson, 241–58. Wesport, CT: Greenwood Press.

Bourdieu, P., and J.C. Passeron. 1970. *Reproduction in education, society and culture.* Thousand Oaks, CA: Sage.

Braddock, J.H. 1981. Race, athletics, and educational attainment: dispelling the myths. *Youth & Society* 12:335–350.

Braddock, J.H., D.A. Royster, L.F. Winfield, and R. Hawkins. 1991. Bouncing back: Sports and academic resilience among African American males. *Education and Urban Society* 24:113–131.

Carter, P.L. 2005. *Keepin' it real: School success beyond black and white.* New York: Oxford University Press.

Coleman, J.S. 1988. Social capital in the creation of human capital. *American Journal of Sociology* 94:95–120.

Conchas, G.Q. 2006. *The color of success: Race and high-achieving urban youth.* New York: Teachers College Press.

Dance, L.J. 2002. *Tough fronts: The impact of street culture on schooling.* New York: Routledge.

Eitle, T.M., and D.J. Eitle. 2002. Race, cultural capital, and the educational effects of participation in sports. *Sociology of Education* 75:123–146.

Ferguson, A.A. 2000. *Bad boys: Public schools in the making of black masculinity.* Ann Arbor: University of Michigan Press.

Flores-Gonzalez, N. 2002. *School kids/street kids: Identity development in Latino students.* New York: Teachers College Press.

Harris, O. 1995. Athletics and academics: Contrary or complementary activities. In *Sport, racism and ethnicity*, ed. G. Jarvie, 124–149. New York: Falmer Press.

———. 1998a. Race, sport and future orientation. In *African Americans in sport*, ed. G.A. Sailes, 241–60. New Brunswick, NJ: Transaction.

———. 1998b. The role of sport in the black community. In *African Americans in sport*, ed. G.A. Sailes, 3–13. New Brunswick, NJ: Transaction.

Lewis, A.E. 2003. *Race in the schoolyard: Negotiating the color line in classrooms and communities.* New Brunswick, N.J.: Rutgers University Press.

Lopez, N. 2003. *Hopeful girls, troubled boys: Race and gender disparity in urban education.* New York: Routledge.

Loury, G. 1977. A dynamic theory of racial income differences. In *Women, minorities, and employment discrimination*, ed. P. Wallace and A. La Mund, 153–186. Lexington, MA: Lexington Books.

May, R.A.B. 2008. *Living through the hoop: High school basketball, race and the American Dream*. New York: New York University Press.

Miller, K.E., M.J. Melnick, G.M. Barnes, M.P. Farrell, and D. Sabo. 2005. Untangling the links among athletic involvement, gender, race, and adolescent academic outcomes. *Sociology of Sport Journal* 22:178–193.

Noguera, P. 2003. *City schools and the American Dream: Reclaiming the promise of public education*. New York: Teachers College Press.

Noguera, P., and J.Y. Wing. 2006. *Unfinished business: Closing the racial achievement gap in our schools*. San Francisco: Jossey-Bass.

O'Connor, C. 1997. Dispositions toward (collective) struggle and educational resilience in the inner city: A case analysis of six African American high school students. *American Educational Research Journal* 34:593–629.

Roderick, M. 2003. What's happening to the boys? Early high school experiences and school outcomes among African American male adolescents in Chicago. *Urban Education* 38:538–607.

Rothstein, R. 2004. *Class and schools: Using social, economic, and educational reform to close the black-white achievement gap*. Washington, DC: Economic Policy Institute.

Royster, D.A. 2003. *Race and the invisible hand: How white networks exclude black men from blue-collar jobs*. Berkeley: University of California Press.

Sabo, D., M.J. Melnick, and B.E. Vanfossen. 1993. High-school athletic participation and postsecondary educational and occupational mobility—A focus on race and gender. *Sociology of Sport Journal* 10:44–56.

**Chapter 10**

Andersen, M. 2001 Restructuring for whom? Race, class, gender, and the ideology of invisibility. *Sociological Forum* 16:181–201

Baca Zinn, M., and B.T. Dill 2005. Theorizing difference from multiracial feminism. In *Gender through the prism of difference*, ed. M. Baca Zinn, P. Hondagneu-Sotelo, and M.A. Messner, 23–28. Needham Heights, MA: Allyn & Bacon.

Beck, H. 2004. The collapse of Kobe. *New York Times*, December 17.

Benedict, J. 1999. *Public heroes, private felons: Athletes and crimes against women*. Boston: Northeastern.

———. 2005. *Out of bounds: Inside the NBA's culture of rape, violence, and crime*. New York: Harper.

Browne, A. 1989. *When battered women kill*. New York, NY: The Free Press.

Brownmiller, S. 1975. *Against our will: Men, women, and rape*. New York: Bantam Books.

Brush, L. 2001. Poverty, battering, race, and welfare reform: Black–white differences in women's welfare-to-work transitions. *Journal of Poverty* 5:67–89.

Brush, L., J. Raphael, and R. Tolman. 2003. Effects of work on hitting and hurting. *Violence Against Women* 9 (10): 1213–1230.

Collins, P.H. 1994. Shifting the center: Race, class, and feminist theorizing about motherhood. In *Mothering: Ideology, experience, and agency*, ed. E. Glenn, G. Chang, and L. Forcey, 45–66. New York: Routledge.

———. 2004. *Black sexual politics: African Americans, gender, and the new racism*. New York: Routledge.

Davis, A. 1983. *Women, race, and class*. New York: Vintage Books.

Griffin, Susan. 1979. *Rape: The politics of consciousness*. New York: Harper &Row.

Guinier, L., M. Fine, and J. Balin. 1997. *Becoming gentlemen: Women, law school, and institutional change*. Boston: Beacon Press.

Hattery, A. 2008. *Intimate partner violence*. New York: Routledge.

Hattery, A., and E. Kane. 1995. Men's and women's perceptions of non-consensual sexual intercourse. *Sex Roles* 33:785–802.

Hattery, A., and E. Smith. 2007. *African American families*. Thousand Oaks, CA: Sage.

Hattery, A., and E. Smith. 2009. Race and intimate partner violence. In *Interracial relationships in the 21ˢᵗ century*, ed. E. Smith and A. Hattery. Durham, NC: Carolina Academic Press.

Hindelang, M.J. 1978. Race and involvement in common law personal crimes. *American Sociological Review* 43:93–109.

Hock, L. 2008. What's in a name? Fred Goldman's quest to acquire O.J. Simpson's right of publicity and the suit's implications for celebrities. *Pepperdine Law Review* 35:347–389.

King, D. 1988. Multiple jeopardy, multiple consciousness: The context of a black feminist ideology. *Signs* 14:42–72.

Koss, M. 1985. The hidden rape victim: Personality, attitudinal, and situational characteristics. *Psychology of Women Quarterly* 9:193–212.

Koss, M., Goodman, L.A., Browne, A., Fitzgerald L.F., Keita, G.P., and Russo, N.F. 1994. *No safe haven: Male violence against women at home, at work, and in the community*. Washington, DC.: American Psychological Association.

Lorde, A. 2007. *Sister outsider: Essays and speeches*. Trumansburg, NY: Crossing Press.

MacKinnon, C. 1991. *Toward a feminist theory of the state*. Cambridge, MA: Harvard University Press.

Markovitz, J. 2006. Anatomy of a spectacle: Race, gender, and memory in the Kobe Bryant rape case. *Sociology of Sport Journal* 23:396–418.

Messner, M.A., and W.S. Solomon. 1993. Outside the frame: Newspaper coverage of the Sugar Ray Leonard wife abuse story. *Sociology of Sport Journal* 10:119–134.

Oates, J.C. 2006. *On boxing.* New York: Harper.

Rich, A. 1980. Compulsory heterosexuality and lesbian existence. *Signs* 5:631–660.

———. 1995. *Of woman born: Motherhood as experience and institution.* New York: Norton.

Sanday, P. 2007. *Fraternity gang rape.* New York: New York University Press.

Schoen, L. 1996. Out of bounds: Professional sports leagues and domestic violence. *Harvard Law Review* 109:1048–1065.

Smith, E. 2006. Hey stud: Race, sex, and sports. *Journal of Sexuality and Culture* 10 (2): 3–32.

———. 2007. *Race, sport and the American Dream.* Durham, NC: Carolina Academic Press.

———. 2008. African American men and intimate partner violence. *Journal of African American Studies* 12:156–179.

## Chapter 11

Capraro R.L. 2000. Why college men drink: Alcohol, adventure, and the paradox of masculinity. *Journal of American College Health* 48:307–315.

Carrigan, T., B. Connell, and J. Lee. 1987. Toward a new sociology of masculinity. In *The making of masculinities: The new men's studies,* ed. H. Brod, 63–102. Winchester, MA: Allen & Unwin.

Coakley, J. 2004. *Sports in society: Issues and controversies.* 8th ed. New York: McGraw-Hill.

Connell, R.W. 1995. *Masculinities.* Berkeley: University of California Press.

Connell, R.W., and J.W. Messerschmidt. 2005. Hegemonic masculinity: Rethinking the concept. *Gender & Society* 19:829–859.

Denham, B.E. 1997. *Sports Illustrated,* "The War on Drugs," and the Anabolic Steroid Control Act of 1990: A study in agenda building and political timing. *Journal of Sport & Social Issues* 21:260–273.

———. 1999. Building the agenda and adjusting the frame: How the dramatic revelations of Lyle Alzado impacted mainstream press coverage of anabolic steroid use. *Sociology of Sport Journal* 16:1–15.

———. 2004. Toward an explication of media enjoyment: The synergy of social norms, viewing situations, and program content. *Communication Theory* 14:370–387.

———. 2008. Masculinities in hardcore bodybuilding. *Men and Masculinities* 11:234–242.

Eitzen, D.S. 2006. *Fair and foul: Beyond the myths and paradoxes of sport.* 3rd ed. Lanham, MD: Rowman & Littlefield.

Garber, G. 2005. A tormented soul. http://sports.espn.go.com/nfl/news/story?id=1972285.

Guskiewicz, K.M., M. McCrea, S.W. Marshall, R.C. Cantu, C. Randolph, W. Barr, J.A. Onate, and J.P. Kelly. 2003. Cumulative effects associated with recurrent concussion in collegiate football players. *Journal of the American Medical Association* 290:2549–2555.

Guskiewicz, K.M., S.W. Marshall, J. Bailes, M. McCrea, R.C. Cantu, C. Randolph, and B.D. Jordan. 2005. Association between recurrent concussion and late-life cognitive impairment in retired professional football players. *Neurosurgery* 57:719–726.

Hatty, S.E. 2000. *Masculinities, violence, and culture.* Thousand Oaks, CA: Sage.

Hoberman, J. 2005. *Testosterone dreams: Rejuvenation, aphrodisia, doping.* Berkeley: University of California Press.

Kimmel, M. 1996. *Manhood in America: A cultural history.* New York: Free Press.

Klein, A.M. 1993. *Little big men: Bodybuilding subculture and gender construction.* Albany: State University of New York Press.

Kolbe, R.H., and P.J. Albanese. 1996. Man to man: A content analysis of sole-male images in male audience magazines. *Journal of Advertising* 25:1–20.

Lawrence, J.S., and R. Jewett. 2002. *The myth of the American superhero.* Grand Rapids, MI: Eerdmans.

Leach, M. 1994. The politics of masculinity: An overview of contemporary theory. *Social Alternatives* 12:36–38.

Luciano, L. 2001. *Looking good: Male body image in modern America.* New York: Hill and Wang.

Messner, M. 1987. The meaning of success: The athletic experience and the development of male identity. In *The making of masculinities: The new men's studies,* ed. H. Brod, 193–212. London: Allen & Unwin.

Messner, M. A. 1992. *Power at play: Sports and the problem of masculinity.* Boston: Beacon Press.

———. 2007. The masculinity of the governator: Muscle and compassion in American politics. *Gender & Society* 21:461–480.

Messner, M.A., M. Dunbar, and D. Hunt. 2000. The televised sports manhood formula. *Journal of Sport & Social Issues* 24:380–394.

O'Neil, J. 1990. Assessing men's gender role conflict. In *Men in conflict: Problem solving strategies and interventions,* ed. D. Moore and F. Leafgren, 22–38. Alexandria, VA: American Association of Counseling and Development.

O'Neill, D. 2007. The Big Red's stars of the 1970s, like many of their contemporaries, feel tossed on the scrap heap by the National Football League. *St. Louis Post Dispatch*, October 28, D1.

Pleck, J.H. 1981. *The myth of masculinity*. Cambridge, MA: MIT Press.

Rabadi, M.H., and B.D. Jordan. 2001. The cumulative effect of repetitive concussion in sports. *Clinical Journal of Sports Medicine* 11:194–198.

Schwarz, A. 2007. For Jets, silence on concussions signals unease. *New York Times*, December 22, A1.

Trujillo, N. 1991. Hegemonic masculinity on the mound: Media representations of Nolan Ryan and American sports culture. *Critical Studies in Mass Communication* 8:290–308.

———. 2001. Machines, missiles and men: Images of the male body on ABC's Monday Night Football. In *Contemporary Issues in sociology of sport*, ed. A. Yiannakis and M.J. Melnick, 223–236. Champaign, IL: Human Kinetics.

**Chapter 12**

American Association of University Women. 1992/1995. *How schools shortchange girls*. New York: Marlow.

Bettie, J. 2003. *Women without class: Girls, race and identity*. Berkeley: University of California Press.

Bourdieu, P. 1979/1984. *Distinction: A social critique of the judgement of taste*. Cambridge MA: Harvard University Press.

Connell, R.W. 1987. *Gender and power*. Stanford: Stanford University Press.

Cooky, C. 2006. Getting girls in the game: A qualitative analysis of urban sport programs. PhD diss., University of Southern California, 2006.

Cooky, C. 2009. Girls just aren't interested in sport: The social construction of interest in girls' sport. *Sociological Perspectives* 52 (2).

Cooky, C. 2009. Do girls rule? Understanding popular culture images of "girl power!" and sport. In *Learning sport through culture: Exploring the role of sports in society* (2nd ed.), ed. S. Prettyman and B. Lampman. Lanham, MD: Rowman & Littlefield.

Denner, J., B. Meyer, and S. Bean. 2005. Young Women's Leadership Alliance: Youth–adult partnerships in an all-female after-school program. *Journal of Community Psychology* 33 (1): 87–100.

Denzin, N.K., and Y.S. Lincoln. 2003. *The landscape of qualitative research: Theories and issues*. 2nd ed. Thousand Oaks, CA: Sage.

Dworkin, S.L., and M.A. Messner. 1999. Just do . . . what? Sport, bodies and gender. In *Revisioning gender*, ed. M.M. Ferree, J. Lorber, and B.B. Hess, 341–364. Thousand Oaks, CA: Sage.

Faludi, S. 1991. *Backlash: The undeclared war against American women*. New York: Crown.

Foucault, M. 1981/1990. *The history of sexuality, vol. 1*. New York: Vintage.

Giddens, A. 1984. *The constitution of society: Outline of the theory of structuration*. Berkeley: University of California Press.

Girls in the Game. www.girlsinthegame.org.

Gramsci, A. 1971. *Selections from the Prison Notebooks*. New York: International Publishing.

Hays, S. 1994. Structure and agency and the sticky problem of culture. *Sociological Theory* 12 (1): 57–72.

Hays, S. 2004. *Flat broke with children: Women in the age of welfare reform*. New York: Oxford University Press.

Jarrett, R.L., P.J. Sullivan, and N.D. Watkins. 2005. Developing social capital through participation in organized youth programs: Qualitative insights from three programs. *Journal of Community Psychology* 33 (1): 41–55.

Lareau, A. 2003. *Unequal childhoods: Class, race and family life*. Berkeley: University of California Press.

Lubeck, S., and P. Garrett. 1990. The social construction of the "at-risk" child. *British Journal of Sociology of Education* 11 (3): 327–340.

Mahoney, J.L., and H. Stattin. 2000. Leisure activities and adolescent antisocial behavior: The role of structure and social context. *Journal of Adolescence* 23:113–127.

McHale, J.P., P.G. Vinden, L. Bush, D. Richer, D. Shaw, B. Smith. 2005. Patterns of personal and social adjustment among sport-involved and noninvolved urban middle school children. *Sociology of Sport Journal* 22 (2): 119–136.

Messner, M.A. 2002. *Taking the field: Women, men and sports*. Minneapolis: University of Minnesota Press.

Miller, K.E., M.J. Melnick, G.M. Barnes, M.P. Farrell, and D. Sabo. 2005. Untangling the links among athletic involvement, gender, race and adolescent outcomes. *Sociology of Sport Journal* 22 (2): 178–193.

Orenstein, P. 1994. *School girls: Young women, self-esteem, and the confidence gap*. New York: Anchor Books.

Pedersen, S., and E. Seidman. 2004. Team sport achievement and self-esteem: Development among urban adolescent girls. *Psychology of Women Quarterly* 28:412–422.

Pipher, M. 1994. *Reviving Ophelia: Saving the selves of adolescent girls*. New York: Ballantine.

Placier, M.L. 1993. The semantics of state policy making: The case of "at-risk." *Education, Evaluation, & Policy Analysis* 15 (4): 380–395.

Sabo, D., K. Miller, M.J. Melnick, and L. Heywood. 2004. *Her life depends on it: Sport, physical activity and the health and well-being of American girls.* East Meadow, NY: Women's Sport Foundation.

Sideman, S. 1998. *Contested knowledge: Social theory in the postmodern era.* 2nd ed. Cambridge, MA: Blackwell Publishers.

Sturken, M., and L.Cartwright. 2001. *Practices of looking: An introduction to visual culture.* New York: Oxford University Press.

Sugden, J., and A. Tomlinson. 2002. Theory and method for a critical sociology of sport. In *Power games: A critical sociology of sport,* ed. J. Sugden and A. Tomlinson, 3–22. London: Routledge.

Tracy, A.J., and Erkut, S. 2002. Gender and race patterns in the pathways from sport participation to self-esteem. *Sociological Perspectives* 45 (4): 445–466.

United States Census Bureau. 2004. Historical poverty tables. www.census.gov/hhes/www/poverty/histpov/hstpov2.html.

Videon, T.M. 2002. Who plays and who benefits: Gender, interscholastic athletics and academic outcomes. *Sociological Perspectives* 45 (4): 415–444.

West, C., and D.H. Zimmerman. 1987. Doing gender. *Gender & Society* 1 (2): 125–151.

Willis, P. 1977. *Learning to labor: How working class kids get working class jobs.* New York: Columbia University Press.

Wilson, B., P. White, and K. Fisher. 2001. Multiple identities in a marginalized culture: Female youth in an "inner-city" recreation/drop-in center. *Journal of Sport and Social Issues* 25 (3): 301–323.

Worland, G. 2003. Girls program goes far beyond fun and games. *Chicago Tribune,* September 21, 1.

## Chapter 13

Apter, M. 2006. *Reversal theory: Motivation, emotion and personality.* 2nd ed. Oxford, England: Oneworld.

Associated Press. 2008. Tiger OK with "lynch" joke. http://nbcsports.msnbc.com/id/22556443/.

Billings, A.C. 2003. Portraying Tiger Woods: Characterizations of a "black" athlete in a "white" sport. *The Howard Journal of Communications* 14:29–37.

Brown, C. 2000. A dominating Tiger Woods wins Open by 15 strokes. *New York Times,* June 19. www.nytimes.com/2000/06/19/sports/golf-a-dominating-tiger-woods-wins-open-by-15-strokes.html?scp=1&sq=&st=nyt.

Campbell, S. 2008. Great Scott? Not yet. Aussie pushes self in his quest to catch Tiger. *Houston Chronicle,* March 23. www.chron.com/CDA/archives/archive.mpl?id=2008_4536259.

Chambliss, D.F. 1989. The mundanity of excellence: An ethnographic report on stratification and Olympic swimmers. *Sociological Theory* 7:70–86.

Cole, C.L., and D.L. Andrews. 2000. America's new son: Tiger Woods and America's multiculturalism. *Cultural Studies: A Research Volume* 5:109–124.

Dailey, T. 1999. *Muhammad Ali: The greatest of all time.* New York: Penguin Books.

Davis, A. 1983. *Women, race, and class.* New York: Vintage Books.

Dawkins, M.P. 2004. Race relations and the sport of golf: The African American golf legacy. *Western Journal of Black Studies* 28:327–331.

Diaz, J. 2007. A time of turmoil turns to triumph for Tiger Woods: What really happened inside his camp. *Golf Digest,* December 17. http://sports.espn.go.com/golf/columns/story?columnist=diaz_jaime&id=3158267.

Dunning, E. 1999. *Sport matters: Sociological studies of sport, violence and civilization.* London: Routledge.

Edwards, H. 1969. *Revolt of the black athlete.* New York: Free Press.

Feinstein, J. 1999. *The majors: In pursuit of golf's holy grail.* Boston: Little, Brown.

———. 2008. Once again, Woods proves he is superior. *Washington Post,* June 17. www.washingtonpost.com/wpdyn/content/article/2008/06/17/AR2008061701039_pf.html.

Gladwell, M. 2008. *Outliers: The story of success.* Boston: Little, Brown.

Golfer says comments about Woods "misconstrued": Retailing sponsor critical of remarks. 1997. CNN.com, April 21. www.cnn.com/US/9704/21/fuzzy/.

Hack, D. 2008. Lee Elder opened the fairways for black golfers at Augusta. *Sports Illustrated,* April 1. www.golf.com/golf/tours_news/article/0,28136,1727848,00.html.

Hall, R.E. 2001. The Tiger Woods phenomenon: A note on biracial identity. *The Social Science Journal* 38:333–336.

Hattery, A., and E. Smith. 2007. *African American families.* Thousand Oaks, CA: Sage.

Johnson, R. 2007. From cub to man: Tiger reveals demanding workout regimen. ESPN.com, July 2. http://sports.espn.go.com/golf/news/story?id=2921413.

Johnston, J.H. 1970. *Race relations in Virginia and miscegenation in the South, 1776–1860.* Amherst: University of Massachusetts Press.

McLaughlin, E. 2008. Tiger OK with "lynch" remark, but Sharpton ready for battle. CNN.com, January 10. www.cnn.com/2008/US/01/10/tilghman.woods.

Mitchell, K. 2008. Woods' legacy the poorer for making the game richer. *The Observer*, April 6. http://observer.guardian.co.uk/sport/story/0,,2271377,00.html#article_continue.

Mulkay, M., and G.N. Gilbert. 1981. Putting philosophy to work: Karl Popper's influence on scientific practice. *Philosophy of the Social Sciences* 11:389–407.

Patterson, O. 1998. *Rituals of blood: Consequences of slavery in two American centuries*. Washington, DC: Civitas Counterpoint Books.

Pells, E. 2005. Lack of minority golfers irks Woods: One decade after Tiger's debut, black golfers haven't risen. *The Daily Texan*, June 16. www.dailytexanonline.com/sports/lack-of-minority-golfers-irks-woods-1.978327.

Peters, T., and N. Austin. 1989. *A passion for excellence: The leadership difference*. New York: Grand Central.

Rosaforte, T. 2007. Tour insider: Warrior, athlete & father: Is there a more complete professional than Tiger anywhere in any sport? *Golf Digest*, August 15. www.golfdigest.com/golfworld/columnists/2007/08/20070815insider?printable=true.

Rothkopf, D. 2008. *Superclass: The global power elite and the world they are making*. New York: Gardner.

Sirak, R. 2008. Golf Channel announcer suspended 2 weeks for "lynch" Tiger comment. GolfWorld.com, January 14. http://sports.espn.go.com/golf/news/story?id=3189374.

Smith, E. 2007. *Race, sport and the American dream*. Durham, NC: Carolina Academic Press.

Smith, G. 1996. The chosen one. *Sports Illustrated*, December 23. http://vault.sportsillustrated.cnn.com/vault/article/magazine/MAG1009257/index.htm.

U.S. Department of Education, National Center for Education Statistics. 2007. *The condition of education 2007* (NCES 2007–064).

Veblen, T. 1899/2008. *Theory of the leisure class*. New York: Oxford University Press.

Wilbon, M. 2005. I come to praise Tiger, not to bury him. *Washington Post*, July 19. http://pqasb.pqarchiver.com/washingtonpost/access/868952651.html?dids=868952651:868952651&FMT=ABS&FMTS=ABS:FT&fmac=&date=Jul+19%2C+2005&author=Michael+Wilbon&desc=I+Come+to+Praise+Tiger%2C+Not+Bury+Him.

## Chapter 14

Alexander, S.M. 2003. Stylish hard bodies: Branded masculinity in *Men's Health* magazine. *Sociological Perspectives* 46:535–554.

Benedict, J.R. 1998. *Athletes and acquaintance rape*. Thousand Oaks, CA: Sage.

Benedict, J., and D. Yeager. 1998. *Pros and cons: The criminals who play in the NFL*. New York: Warner Books.

Berry, B. 2007. *Beauty bias: Discrimination and social power*. Westport, CT: Praeger/Greenwood.

———. 2008a. *The power of looks: Social stratification of physical appearance*. Hampshire, England: Ashgate.

———. 2008b. Interactionism and animal aesthetics: A theory of social reflected power. *Society and Animals* 16:75–89.

Berry, B., and E. Smith. 2000. Race, sport and crime: The misrepresentation of African Americans in team sports and crime. *Sociology of Sport Journal* 17:171–197.

Blumer, H. 1969. *Symbolic interactionism: Perspectives and methods*. Englewood Cliffs, NJ: Prentice Hall.

Bordo, S. 1995. *Unbearable weight: Feminism, Western culture, and the body*. Berkeley: University of California Press.

Chang, J., ed. 2006. *Total chaos: The art and aesthetics of hip-hop*. Cambridge, MA: Basic Civitas Books.

Egan, T. 2002. For image-conscious boys, steroids are powerful lure. *New York Times*, November 22, A1, A22.

Etcoff, N. 1999. *Survival of the prettiest: The science of beauty*. New York: Anchor Books.

Goffman, E. 1959. *The presentation of self in everyday life*. New York: Doubleday.

Katz, S. 1995. The importance of being beautiful. In *Down to earth sociology* (8th ed.), ed. J.M. Henslin, 301–307. New York: Free Press.

Kolata, G., J. Longman, T. Weiner, and T. Egan. 2002. With no answers on risks, steroid users still say "yes." *New York Times*, December 2, A1, A19.

Loughlin, S. 2008. Neanderthal sex. *Fitness Rx*, January, 146–148.

Mead, G.H. 1974. *Mind, self and society*. Chicago: University of Chicago Press.

Sisario, B. 2008. Jeepers, rapper, where'd you get those arms and torsos? *New York Times*, January 15, B1 and B7.

Thomas, D. 2007. *Deluxe: How luxury lost its luster*. New York: Penguin Press.

## Chapter 15

Anderson, B. 1983. *Imagined communities: Reflections on the origins and spread of nationalism*. 2nd ed. London: Verso.

Bale, J., and J. Maguire, eds. 1994. *The global sports arena: Athletic talent migration in an interdependent world*. London: Cass.

Bourdieu, P. 1986. *Distinction: A social critique of the judgement of taste*. London: Routledge.

Braithwaite, L. 1953. Social stratification in Trinidad. *Social and Economic Studies* 2 (2 and 3): 5-175.

Burdsey, D. 2006. If I ever play football, Dad, can I play for England or India: British Asians, sport and diasporic national identities. *Sociology* 40 (1): 11–28.

Cain, P., and M. Harrison, eds. 2001. *Imperialism: Critical concepts in historical studies.* Vol. II. London: Routledge.

Carrington, B. 2007. Merely identity: Cultural identity and the politics of sport. *Sociology of Sport Journal* 24 (1): 49–66.

Dunning, E., J. Goudsblom, and S. Mennell, eds. 2000. *The civilizing process: Sociogenetic and psychogenetic investigations.* Oxford, UK: Blackwell.

Dunning, E., and S. Mennell. 1996. Preface. *The German: Power struggles and the development of habitus in the nineteenth and twentieth centuries.* New York: Columbia University Press.

Elias, N. 1978. *What is sociology?* London: Hutchinson.

———. 1987/1991. *The society of individuals.* Oxford, UK: Blackwell.

———. 1996. *The German: Power struggles and the development of habitus in the nineteenth and twentieth centuries.* New York: Columbia University Press.

———. 1939/2000. *The civilizing process.* Oxford, UK: Blackwell.

Guttmann, A. 1993. The diffusion of sports and the problem of cultural imperialism. In *The sports process: A comparative and developmental approach,* ed. E. Dunning, J. Maguire, and R. Pearton, 125–138. Champaign, IL: Human Kinetics.

Hargreaves, J. 2002. Globalisation theory, global sport, and nations and nationalism. In *Power games: A critical sociology of sport,* ed. J. Sugden and A. Tomlinson, 25–43. London: Routledge.

Held, D., and A. McGrew, eds. 2004. *The global transformations reader: An introduction to the globalization debate.* Oxford, UK: Blackwell.

Houlihan, B. 1994. Homogenization, Americanization and creolization of sport: Varieties of globalization. *Sociology of Sport Journal* 11:356–375.

———. 2003. Sport and globalisation. In *Sport and society: A student introduction,* 345–363. London: Sage.

James, C.L.R. 1963. *Beyond a boundary.* London: Hutchinson.

Kabukuru, W. 2005. Kenya: Athletes for sale? *New African,* July. BNET Business Network http://findarticles.com/p/articles/mi_qa5391/is_200507/ai_n21381001

Kidd, B. 1991. How do we find our own voices in the new "world order"? A commentary on Americanization. *Sociology of Sport Journal* 6 (3): 95–117.

Klein, A. 1991. Sport and culture as contested terrain: Americanization in the Caribbean. *Sociology of Sport Journal* 8:79–85.

Lagerstrom, U. 2000. MacDonald Bailey and the early Trinidad sprint stars. *Track Stats* 38 (2): 44–56.

Lewis, A. 1938/1977. *Labour in the West Indies: The birth of a workers movement.* London: New Beacon Books.

Linley, B. 2000. Tracking down the full career of MacDonald Bailey. *Track Stats* 38 (3): 47–55.

Maguire, J. 1999. *Global sport: Identities, societies, civilizations.* Cambridge: Polity Press.

———, ed. 2005. *Power and global sport: Zones of prestige, emulation and resistance.* London: Routledge.

Mandle, J. 1994. *Caribbean hoops: The development of West Indian basketball.* New York: Gordon and Breach.

Miller, D. 2000. Bailey stop-watch ticks on. *Daily Telegraph,* December 10. www.telegraph.co.uk/sport/othersports/athletics/2994383/Bailey-stop-watch-ticks-on.html.

Polley, M. 1998. *Moving the goalposts: A history of sport and society since 1945.* London: Routledge.

Scobie, E. 1972. *Black Britannia: A history of blacks in Britain.* Chicago: Johnson.

Smith, A. 1998. *Nationalism and modernism: A critical survey of recent theories of nations and nationalism.* London: Routledge.

Smith, A., and D. Porter, eds. 2004. *Sport and national identity in the post-war world.* London: Routledge.

Thomas, R. 1987. *The Trinidad labour riots of 1937: Perspectives 50 years later.* St. Augustine: University of the West Indies, Trinidad Campus: Extra-Mural Unit.

Tomlinson, J. 1991. *Cultural imperialism: A critical introduction.* London: Printer.

Watman, M. 1968. *The history of British athletics.* London: Hale.

Williams, E. 1942. *History of the people of Trinidad and Tobago.* New York: A & B Books Publishers.

**Epilogue**

Dunning, E., ed. 1972. *Sport: Readings from a sociological perspective.* Toronto: University of Toronto Press.

Gallagher, R. 2008. *Ernie Davis: The Elmira Express, the story of a Heisman Trophy winner.* New York: Ballantine Books.

Page, C.H. 1973. Book review of E. Dunning, ed., *Sport: Readings from a sociological perspective.. American Sociological Review* 79 (2): 474–476.

# Index

*Note:* The italicized *f*, *t*, and *n* following page numbers refer to figures, tables, and footnotes respectively.

# About the Editor

**Earl Smith, PhD,** is director of American ethnic studies and professor of sociology at Wake Forest University in Winston-Salem, North Carolina. He has more than 20 years of experience as an instructor and researcher of topics in sociology of sport, and he has gained recognition as a Rubin Distinguished Professor. He focuses on the intersection of sociological, psychological, and economic theories and empirical research in sport.

In 2008, Smith was awarded the North American Society for the Sociology of Sport (NASSS) Book Award. He has also served as president of NASSS. In 2008-2009, the department of anthropology and sociology at Colgate University in Hamilton, New York, presented Smith with the Arnold A. Sio Distinguished Professor of Community and Diversity Award.

A former competitive runner, Smith now walks to stay fit and enjoys bird watching and spending time outdoors. He resides in Winston-Salem, North Carolina.

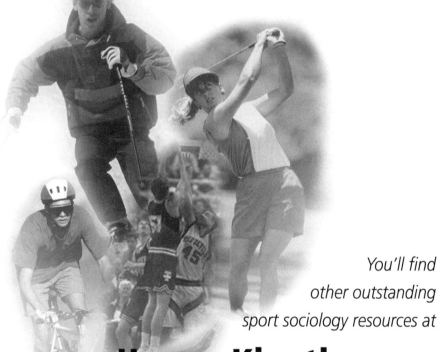